RVer's Best Guide to the Oregon Coast

By Peggy & Mark Day

Your guide to the best campgrounds and activities from Astoria to Brookings

Dedication

To Peggy Bilida, the greatest mother in the world and a constant source of inspiration and love

Acknowledgments

This book would still be in the computer had it not been for a woman who we respect and admire for her travel writing and extraordinary photographic skills. More than that, she has been a friend, sister, and one of the best examples of a person who really lives by the golden rule. Donna Ikenberry gave the encouragement and support that was so helpful in making the transition from idea to actual writing and photography. We will be forever grateful and feel blessed to call her our friend.

All inquiries should be addressed to:

Frank Amato Publications, Inc.
P.O. Box 82112, Portland, Oregon 97282

Book Design: Alan Reid, Layout: Kathy Johnson
Photos: Peggy Day

Title page photo: View south from Ecola Point toward Crescent Beach.

Printed in Canada
1 3 5 7 9 10 8 6 4 2

ISBN: 1-57188-070-4
UPC : 0-66066-00297-6

"No work is more important than teaching the children that the God-given beauty of Oregon is their heritage."

Quote by Jessie M. Honeyman on the "Needle" at Jessie M. Honeyman State Park

Table of Contents

RVer's Best Guide to the Oregon Coast

Chapter 1. Introduction

Chapter 2. Maps

Chapter 3. Road Information

Chapter 4. Map Grid A1: Astoria to Seaside

Chapter 5. Map Grid A2: Cannon Beach to Pacific City

Chapter 6. Map Grid A3: Neskowin to South Beach (includes Lincoln City and Newport)

Chapter 7. Map Grid A4: Waldport to Florence

Disclaimer

This book has been created to provide the best information that RVers need to have a successful travel experience. Every effort has been made to ensure that this guide is as complete and accurate as possible. The information however, is current only up to the printing date. The publisher and authors make no claims regarding the safety of any activities discussed in the book. Campgrounds can go from best to worst with a simple change of management. Roads can become impassable with a single winter storm. In all cases, use common sense and ask questions if in doubt. Please use your own judgment regarding the safety and suitability of any and all coastal recreational activities and locations. When in doubt, first consult with local experts (chambers of commerce or road information hotlines) regarding the safety of planned activities. The purpose of this guide is to suggest to the reader opportunities for camping or recreation. The authors or the publisher shall have neither liability nor responsibility to any person or entity with respect to any loss or damage caused, or alleged to be caused, directly or indirectly by the information contained in this book.

Chapter 1
How to Use This Guide

Cool breezes, rugged cliffs, wonderful sunsets, all of this and more along 362 miles of spectacular coastline with public access nearly the whole way. The Oregon coastline is varied; there are mountains running right into the sea as well as wide flat sandy beaches that let you walk for miles and miles. It has been described as the most beautiful coastline in the US. The story of how it was saved for the public to enjoy forever is a tribute to the forward thinking and support of some of our most famous governors.

"In the administration of this God-given trust, a broad protective policy should be declared and maintained. No local selfish interest should be permitted, through politics or otherwise, to destroy or even impair this great birthright of our people."

Oswald West, 1949
Former Oregon Governor
1911-1915

How Our Oregon Coast Was Saved For the Public Forever

1913; our beaches become a public highway

With this statement Oswald West lobbied for his idea where he advised the legislature that all Oregon beaches should be designated as a public highway because there was no other route along the coast. This was a very crafty idea. The legislature liked it and amended the existing 1899 legislation which covered only 30 miles of the north coast to include the entire tideland on the ocean shores from the Columbia River to California as a public highway. Years later Oswald was known to say, "I pointed out that thus we would come into miles and miles of highway without cost to the taxpayer. The Legislature and the public took the bait—hook, line and sinker."

1966; citizens complain that their access is being denied

In 1966, a motel at Cannon Beach blocked off a section of the sand with logs to give their guests a private place at the shore. This propelled into legislation the clarification of how far up the beach the public was allowed free access. In 1967, the Beach Bill which was signed into law by Governor Tom McCall was praised by him as "One of the most far-reaching measure of its kind enacted by any legislative body in the nation." This bill protected 16 feet above the sea level markers already established by the U.S. Coast and Geodetic Survey. Estuaries were given even more protection. In simple terms, the beach has public access allowed for the most part along the dry sands up to the vegetation line.

This is why our coast is so unspoiled today and you, the visitor, can walk and enjoy it from one end of our beautiful state to the other.

Keeping Our Coast Beautiful

When you visit the coast and see how little litter we have, it is because of the annual beach cleanup that the organization SOLV (Stop Oregon Litter and Vandalism) coordinates each year. By far, the largest amount of litter collected is cigarette butts. In 1996 this amounted to about 100,000 butts. The beach cleanups were started 14 years ago by Oregon Dept. of Fish & Wildlife, and this type of program has spread all over the U.S. as well as overseas. For more information on how you can help, call: (503) 844-9571 or (800) 322-3326 to join in the spring and fall cleanup drives of our beaches.

Please treat the coast and all environments as if they were your own home. Use the containers that are widely available for trash and the ashtrays in your car for cigarettes. Many of the areas on the coast are wildlife refuges, such as tidepools, so practice the wilderness ethic and, "Take only pictures, leave only footprints." Better yet, always carry a spare bag with you and pick up litter whenever you see it. Involve children in this practice to ensure they will carry on the tradition of loving our coast. We believe that Oregon has the most beautiful coast in the U.S. Please do all you can to help keep Oregon beautiful so we all can enjoy camping and exploring it.

Using Camping Guides

The Oregon Coast is a huge, long playground where the RVer will find hundreds of campsites to choose from, great restaurants to sample, museums and gift shops to explore, countless hiking opportunities, and challenging golf courses to play. Deciding where on the Oregon Coast to camp and what to do can be an awesome task. Well, this book is for you—we've done the hard work for you.

We have struggled for years by juggling three or more different camping books to get all the information we need about campgrounds and the things to do in the surrounding areas. Sometimes, when we called using the phone numbers listed in those guides, or expected a special place, the information we depended on was wrong. Nothing can ruin a trip like disappointment. This book is designed to show you where those campgrounds, activities and services are that can make a successful trip a breeze. This book is for people who want accurate information about the best campgrounds and the activities that can be enjoyed in the surrounding areas. It is not meant to be an encyclopedia of campgrounds on the Oregon Coast, just the ones we feel are the best. We want to show you where the really great campgrounds are. If you want the best information so you can decide ahead of time or on the spur of the moment, here it is.

We all have different levels of desired comfort when we camp. This book will recommend the "best" whether it be a public campground for peace and solitude or an RV resort complete with pools and saunas. That way you can choose what type of setting you would like for your RV trip.

We guarantee to have visited each and every campground listed but many things can change after our visit. Call or check with the local public agency or private campground before you go to find out if there will be any problems in visiting or if there are any road access problems you should be aware of. Ask these questions specifically and do not assume that this information will be volunteered. If you are confused, call a different number to double-check.

Camping Evolves

When we were much younger, we looked with disdain on people who had to have some sort of hard shell around them when they camped. Then later we began camping in the back of a pickup truck with a canopy on it and found it had some distinct advantages. Add another five years and we had bought a camper for the truck which had cupboards that could be permanently packed. What a treat! Now that my husband and I are getting close to retirement, we have a 29-foot fifth-wheel. We've sure come a long way from the days of tent camping. The increase in the number of larger RVs on the roads and in the parks proves that more convenient camping is on the rise. Also, there are more retirees than ever and they are living longer to enjoy the RVing lifestyle.

It's good that we all appreciate from whence we came and where we might be going. Some travel books are targeted to a single style of camping. This book tries to take a more flexible view of RVing and present excellent options for any choice from rustic to the resort type of RV camper.

We like to base camp. Base camping utilizes a central campground for periods of a week or more. By base camping in the center of an area rich with activities, you can spend more time sightseeing and less time driving and setting up.

Camping is only half the fun. What do you do once you're there? Are you an avid all-day hiker or just a walk-around-the-block person. Do you want to go to a good restaurant for breakfast or shop for a gift for Aunt Mary? It's so much fun to sit down before or after arriving at a site and have a list of exciting things to do to pick from. The kids love it and it enhances the anticipation of a great time. It's even better if the list is sorted by major types of activities. That way you don't have to read a whole chapter just to pick out what you would like to do. We've included that for you.

RVers will especially appreciate this book for the detail provided on access roads, length of sites, and rig size limitations. If you're still not sure, you can call the phone number provided for confirmation about your size of RV. Semi or full-time RVers will appreciate the attention to the everyday needs they face like laundry, propane, diesel, post offices, and dump stations.

If you have thumbed through the book trying to decide whether to buy, you may have noticed that we have included only the "best" campgrounds. Other guides that list all campgrounds attempt to give you this information with a rating system. We have found it applied inconsistently, especially the environmental ratings. Each and every campground has been visited by us and inspected to assure you would be comfortable staying there.

So, hit the road. With this book you will have some of the smoothest traveling and camping ever. Happy trails!

How To Use This Guide

• Getting there

All roads described in this guide are the major highways to take an RV over the coast range. If you see a road on a map that you would like that is not in the book, call the Oregon Department of Transportation to verify that your rig will be able to use the road safely.

• Based on the Oregon campground map

This guide uses the grid system from the "Oregon Campground Guide Map". It shows most of the public agency campgrounds in Oregon but does not list city, county or private campgrounds. We list both the best private and public campgrounds in each grid area so you will have a much better selection. We use that map together with an "Official Highway Map of Oregon" when traveling.

• Choosing a campground—to reserve or not?

We don't usually reserve campsites but that's because we have the luxury of traveling midweek. If you plan to visit the Oregon Coast on the weekend during the summer season, a reservation is a must. Some popular parks such as Fort Stevens State Park near Astoria, are booked solid from Memorial Day to Labor Day every weekend. During the week you can usually get a spot no matter what time of the year it is. Oregon started a new reservation system in 1996 so call ahead and make your reservation.

• Choosing activities

Deciding how to spend your leisure time is a personal choice. This book gives you many choices and arranges them so you can find the type of activity that you like to do quickly and easily. This helps maximize your time and makes planning much easier.

• Fishing

There are three brochures that are very helpful for people who like to do marine fishing on the coast. They are the North Coast, Central Coast, and South Coast guides "Marine Fishing in Oregon". The brochures have maps and locations describing the type of facilities available for marine fishing on the coast. Obtain these brochures from Oregon Dept. of Fish and Wildlife, Marine Region Office, 2040 SE Marine Science Dr., Newport, OR 97365, (541) 867-4741.

• Locating RV services

You hope you won't have to use these, but if the sewer hose gets a hole in it, it's helpful to know where you can get another one fast. If you're not mechanically inclined and you need a tire changed on your rig, a mobile RV service just might come in handy.

• Volunteer camp hosting

Many organizations offer a free campsite and utilities in return for a commitment of working a few hours per week. In Oregon there are many public and private agencies that advertise for these positions. Look for the listing of volunteer opportunities at the end of each campground list by map grid.

Explaining Some of the Categories

Best Campgrounds

Some campground guides use ratings which we found to be inconsistent. Our "best" campgrounds may be more subjective but in all cases we visited each campground, measured the sites, drove the interior roads and asked ourselves the question, "Would we feel comfortable staying here?". We also checked access to the campground, maneuvering in and out of the sites, beauty of the environment, proximity to things to do and whether the campground was well-maintained. If the campground passed those tests and allowed a 30-foot or longer rig to camp easily and they fit our camping categories, we included them in the book. Some decisions were hard to make as there was more than one campground that measured up. In those cases, you may find alternate suggestions.

The public campgrounds are separated from private campgrounds because some RVers prefer one over the other. In case you think we omitted your favorite campground, use the mail-in form in the back so we can research it and include it for the next update.

Campground Fees

The daily fees in the book represent the summer (highest) rates for the park in 1996. Opportunities for saving money can be offered over the daily fees, such as the 7th night free. You may want to take this savings into account when making your travel plans. Oregon State Parks have especially attractive rates during what is called "Discovery Season" (normally October to April). Some parks must charge a local tax, with other parks it is already included in the daily rate. In any case, always ask if the campground offers discounts and if a local tax will be applied to the posted fee. Campsite fees often change yearly at both public and private parks.

Day-Use Fees

Many state parks on the coast charge day-use fees. If you are camping in one, the day-use fee is included with your daily campsite fee. An annual day-use park permit can be purchased at any state park that gives you access to all state parks.

Pets

Pets are allowed in any of the campgrounds listed in this book. Some of the parks charge an extra fee for pets and some limit the number of pets per camper. These are the customary rules for pets in most public and private parks:

- Pets must be on a 6-foot leash at all times
- Owners must remove their pet's waste in the campsite and any other park areas
- Pets may not be left unattended (owners cannot leave the pet alone tied outside or in the trailer)
- Owners who have pets that disturb other campers safety, comfort, and peace will be asked to leave

Many private parks are getting very strict about pet rules and do not offer refunds to campers who are asked to leave.

Abbreviations used in this book

Certain abbreviations are used throughout this book and the following legend will help you understand them. They are easy to memorize once you get used to reading them.

Partial hookups:
Water and electricity only

Full hookups:
Water, electricity, sewer

GS:
Good Sam discount

AAA:
AAA discount

Dump:
Waste disposal station

Amp:
(amperage; the type of electrical plug to use at the pedestal)

Pull-thrus:
Pull in and then pull straight out

Restaurants:
$ = Inexpensive
$$ = Moderate
$$$ = Expensive

Activities on the Coast

Biking

Our criteria for this category was that RVers would like relatively short, level routes. The routes suggested are mostly short trips with the maximum being about 30 miles round-trip. You can still get the benefit of the exercise and views by just taking the trips up to your own skill level. For us, an 18-mile bike trip is a full day's outing.

Bookstores

We have some full-time RV friends who are constantly looking for used bookstores to get new paperbacks and sell their old ones. Space is a real premium in an RV so we have included both new and used bookstores. Be sure to check out the libraries as they often have free one-on-one paperback exchanges. Besides, it's a great place to hang out on a rainy day on the coast and if you have kids, there is usually a separate children's section—some with storytimes.

Ecotourism

These activities allow the RVer to learn more about the flora, fauna, history, and culture of the area they are visiting. Some of the activities are self-guided and can be done on your own.

Exercise Routes or Leisure Walks

We try to get our daily exercise and it's helpful to have a place away from the traffic that is relatively flat where we can walk. The same terrain could be used for an easy stroll. We've included these for you.

View north from Otter Point at Gold Beach.

Hiking

You won't find any backpacking routes in this book. We look for easy .5- to 8-mile hikes—some easy and handicap accessible. There is usually a great reward at the end like a waterfall or old-growth trees. We enjoyed these hikes and hope you do too.

Restaurants

We ate out a lot and these are the best restaurants that we found or were recommended highly by the locals. If we missed yours, send us an update on the form in the back of the book.

RV Services

Diesel

We listed only the stations that had easy in and out access for RVs with no overhead obstructions. These stations have good access for any RV whether you need gasoline or diesel.

Dump Stations

These are the waste dump stations provided by a local town, state park, or rest stop. The dump stations listed do not charge a fee unless noted.

RV Parts & Services

The businesses listed were personally interviewed and inspected by us. We also asked the managers of various local campgrounds who they would recommend if one of their guests had a problem.

Shopping/Groceries

Most of the selections in this category were chosen for convenience (one-stop

View south from Ecola Point toward Crescent Beach.

shopping) or because they accept credit cards. Many of our full-time RV friends use their credit cards extensively, even for groceries, to keep from having to carry cash.

Post Offices

These were listed in case you want to have your mail forwarded to a local area where you are staying. The zip codes are listed so you can have your mail sent to you in care of General Delivery, Town, OR, Zip Code. You can just walk up to the counter and ask if there is any mail under your name.

How to plan your RV trip using this guide

- Pick a grid that you want to visit from the map
- Decide on the best route across the Oregon Coast range for that grid
- Call about road conditions
- Select a campground that meets your preferences
- Call about campground reservations
- Use the "Road Information" chapter to get to the campground safely and relaxed
- Get your RV set up in the campground
- Use this book to locate activities you want to do
- Visit the local Chamber of Commerce
- Pick up a list of the seasonal activities in the area
- Ask if all the restaurants are still open
- Get out your calendar and plan your activities

Relax and enjoy the beautiful Oregon Coast!

Chapter 2

Map Section

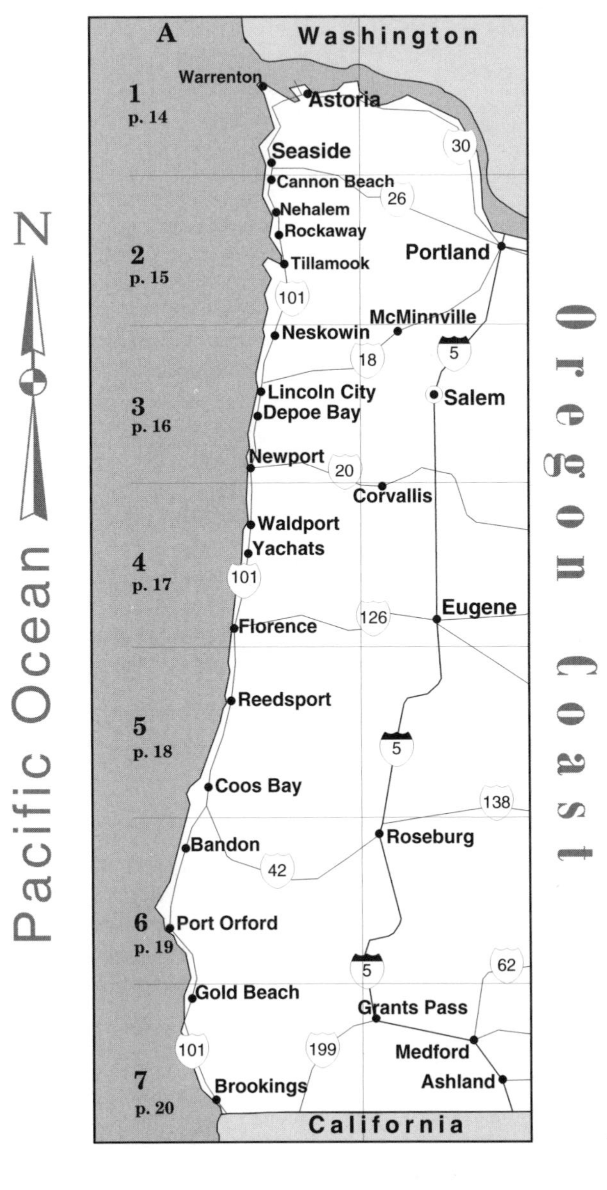

Grid A1: Astoria/Hammond/Seaside

Campgrounds

1. Astoria/Warrenton/Seaside KOA, (800) KOA-8506, p. 35
2. Ft. Stevens State Park, Warrenton, (503) 861-1671, (800) 452-5687, p. 34
3. Kampers West Kampground, Hammond, (503) 861-1814 (800) 880-5267, p. 36
4. Circle Creek RV Pk, Seaside, (503) 738-6070, p. 36

Diesel

- Hammond: Corkys 4 Way Stop, 1180 Pacific Drive, (503) 861-2088
- Astoria: Youngs Bay Texaco, 490 W. Marine Drive, (503) 325-9274
- Astoria: Val's Shell, 452 W. Marine Drive, (503) 325-8131
- Astoria: Carmichael Chevron, 510 Marine Dr., (503) 325-0605
- Seaside: Trucke's 1 Stop, 1921 Hwy. 101, (503) 738-8863

RV Parts and Service

- Warrenton: Skipanon Marine & RV Supply, 69 NE Heron, (503) 861-3626
- Seaside: HWI Coast Center Hardware, 1217 Hwy. 101, (503) 738-5491

Dump Stations

- Astoria: 33rd St. & Hwy. 30
- Warrenton: Fort Stevens State Park
- Seaside: Hwy. 101 & Broadway

Grid A2: Cannon Beach/Manzanita/Tillamook Area

Campgrounds

1. RV Resort at Cannon Beach, (503) 436-2231, (800) 847-2231, p. 54
2. Nehalem Bay State Park, Nehalem, (503) 368-5943, (800) 452-5687, p. 54
3. Barview Jetty County Park, Garibaldi, (503) 322-3522, p.55
4. Tillamook Bay City RV Park, Tillamook, (503) 377-2124, p.55
5. Cape Lookout State Park, Netarts, (503) 842-4981, (800) 452-5687, p. 55
6. Bay Shore RV Park, Netarts, (503) 842-7774, p. 55
7. Whalen Island County Park, Sand Lake, (503) 322-3477, p. 56

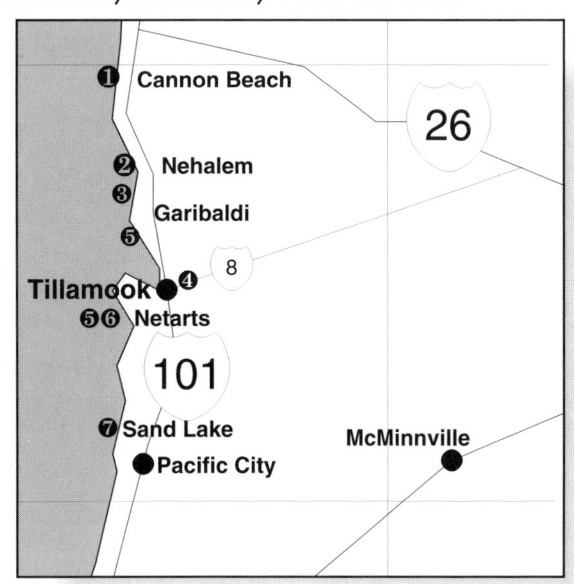

Diesel

- Cannon Beach: RV Resort at Cannon Beach, Hwy. 101 & Elk Creek Rd., (503) 436-2231
- Nehalem: Bayside Gardens Texaco, 36453 Hwy. 101 N., (503) 368-5150
- Garibaldi: Sheldon Texaco, 701 Garibaldi Ave., (503) 322-3770
- Tillamook: Tillamook Texaco, 15 Main St., OR 97141, (503) 842-5555
- Beaver: Beaver Texaco, 24485 S. Hwy. 101, (503) 398-2828

RV Parts and Service

- Cannon Beach: Nearest is Skipanon in Warrenton
- Nehalem/Manzanita: See Warrenton RV services or Tillamook RV services
- Tillamook: Tillamook RV Repair & Sales, Inc., 2150 Hadley Road, (503) 842-7702 or 1-800-235-7702

Dump Stations

- Cannon Beach: RV Resort at Cannon Beach
- Nehalem: Nehalem Bay State Park
- Nehalem: at Tideland Road
- Garibaldi: Barview Jetty County Park
- Netarts: Cape Lookout State Park
- Sand Lake: Whalen Island Park

Grid A3: Neskowin to South Beach

Campgrounds

1. Devil's Lake State Park, Lincoln City, (541) 994-2002, (800) 452-5687, p. 75
2. Lincoln City KOA, (541) 994-2961, (800) KOA-2791, p. 76
3. Devil's Lake RV Park, Lincoln City, (541) 994-3400, p. 76
4. Holiday RV Park, Depoe Bay, (541) 765-2302, (800) 452-2104, p. 76
5. Beverly Beach State Park, Newport, (541) 265-9278, (800) 452-5687, p. 76
6. South Beach State Park, South Beach, (541) 867-4715, (800) 452-5687, p. 77
7. Agate Beach RV Park, Newport, (541) 265-7670, p. 77
8. Newport Marina RV Park #1, Newport, (541) 867-3321, p. 77
9. Pacific Shores RV Resort, Newport, (541) 265-3750, (800) 333-1583, p. 77

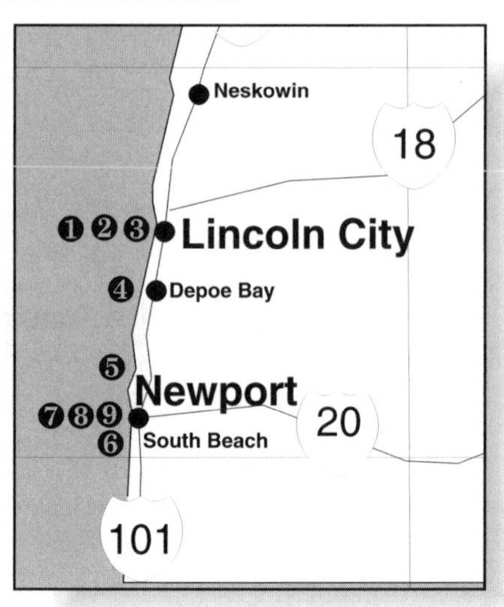

Diesel

- Lincoln City; Shell, Garrison Fuel, 1410 SE. Hwy. 101, (503) 994-2661
- Lincoln City; Chevron Car Wash & Food Mart, 2320 NE. Hwy. 101, (503) 994-8448
- Newport: Ron's BP Inc., 1517 N. Coast Hwy., (541) 265-5803

RV Parts and Service

- Lincoln City: Quality RV Service of Oregon, Inc., (541) 994-5514
- Lincoln City: A to Z RV Services & Supplies, 660 SE Hwy. 101, (541) 994-7447
- South Beach: Marine & RV Service Inc., 4354 S. Hwy. 101, (541) 867-3704
- Newport: Pacific Shores RV Resort, 6225 Hwy. 101, (541) 265-3750 (supplies)
- Newport: Wal-Mart has an excellent selection of parts and supplies.

Dump Stations

- Lincoln City: 660 SE Hwy. 101
- Newport: Beverly Beach State Park
- Newport: Marina RV Park
- Newport: 555 SW Hwy. 101
- South Beach: South Beach State Park

Grid A4: Waldport/Yachats/Florence

Campgrounds

1. Alsea Bay RV Park, Waldport, (541) 563-2250, p. 95
2. Beachside State Park, Waldport, (541) 563-3220, (800) 452-5687, p. 96
3. Cape Perpetua CG/Siuslaw NF, Yachats, (541) 563-3211, p. 96
4. Sea Perch RV Park, Yachats, (541) 547-3505, p. 97
5. Rock Creek CG Siuslaw NF, Yachats, (541) 563-3211, p. 97
6. Carl G. Washburne State Park, Florence, (541) 997-3851, p. 97
7. Alder Dune CG-USFS Siuslaw NF, Florence, (541) 268-4473, p. 98
8. Sutton Campground-Siuslaw NF, Florence, (541) 268-4473, p. 98
9. Heceta Beach RV Park, Florence, (541) 997-7664, p. 98
10. B & E Wayside RV & Mobile CG, Florence, (541) 997-6451, p. 98

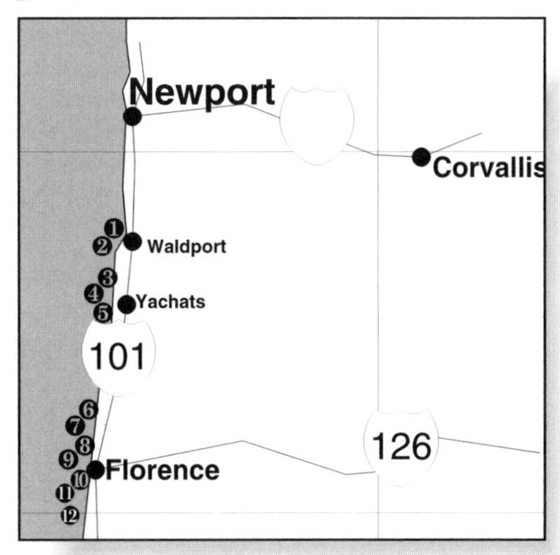

11. Harbor Vista Park (Lane County Park), Florence, (541) 997-5987, p. 99
12. Jessie M. Honeyman State Park, Florence, (541) 997-3641, (800) 452-5687, p. 99

Diesel

- Yachats: Yachats Texaco, 935 N Hwy. 101, (541) 547-3882
- Florence: Bob Miles Texaco, 813 Hwy. 101N, (541) 997-9737
- Florence: Florence Chevron Foodmart, 1839 Hwy. 101, (541) 997-3351

RV Parts and Service

- Florence RV & Automotive Specialists, 4390 Hwy. 101 (541) 997-8287

Dump Stations

- Waldport: Beachside State Park
- Florence: Carl G. Washburne State Park
- Florence: Heceta Beach RV Park
- Florence: Harbor Vista Park
- Florence: Jessie M. Honeyman State Park

Grid A5: Dunes City to Coos Bay Area

Campgrounds

1. Lagoon CG,Siuslaw NF, Florence, (541) 271-3611, p. 113
2. Carter Lake CG,Siuslaw NF, Florence, (541) 271-3611, p. 113
3. Coho RV Park, Reedsport, (541) 271-5411, p. 113
4. Surfwood Campground, Reedsport, (541) 271-4020, p. 114
5. Umpqua Lighthouse State Park, Winchester Bay, (541) 271-4118, (800) 452-5687, p. 114
6. Windy Cove Douglas County Park A & B, Winchester Bay, Park A, (541) 271-4138, Park B (541) 271-5634, p. 115
7. William M. Tugman State Park, Reedsport, (541) 759-3604, (800) 452-5687, p. 115
8. North Eel Creek/Siuslaw NF, Reedsport, (541) 271-3611, p. 115
9. Osprey Point RV Resort, Lakeside, (541) 759-2801, p. 116
10. Bastendorff Beach County Park, Charleston, (541) 888-5353, p. 116
11. Charleston Marina RV Park, Charleston, (541) 888-9512, p. 116
12. Oceanside RV Park, Charleston, (541) 888-2598, (800) 570-2598), p. 116

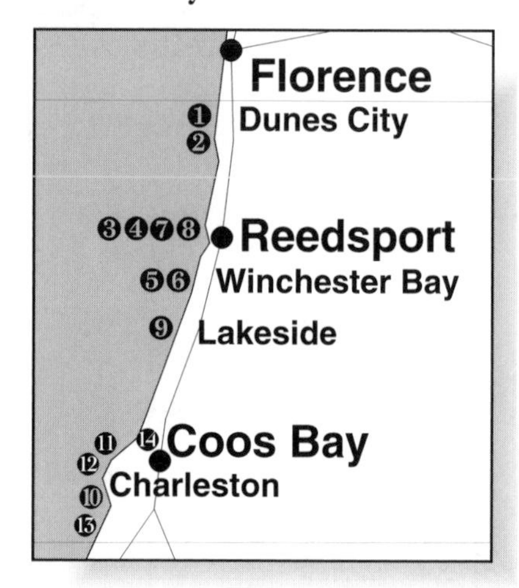

13. Sunset Bay State Park, Charleston, (541) 888-4902, (800) 452-5687, p. 117
14. Lucky Loggers RV Park, Coos Bay, (541) 267-6003, (800) 267-6426, p. 117

RV Parts and Service

- Reedsport: Smith River Trailers Sales, Inc., 909 Winchester Ave., (541) 271-3107
- Coos Bay: Bert's RV Supplies & Service, 810 S. Broadway, (541) 269-1338
- Coos Bay: Gib's RVs, sales, service, parts, 1845 Ocean Blvd., (800) 824-4388

Diesel

- Reedsport: Henson Texaco, 2118 Winchester Ave. (Hwy. 101), (541) 271-4912
- North Bend: Shell, Marion & Virginia Ave., bypass Hwy 101 to Cape Arago
- North Bend: Texaco 1700 Sherman, (Hwy. 101), (541)756-5731
- Coos Bay: Bassett Hyland Chevron, 1059 Evans Blvd., (541) 269-5682
- Coos Bay: Davis Oil Texaco, 1670 Ocean Blvd., (541) 888-3465

Dump Stations

- Reedsport: Coho RV Park
- Winchester Bay: Salmon Harbor Marina
- Lakeside: Tugman State Park
- Coos Bay City: at Front St.
- Charleston: Bastendorff Beach County Park
- Charleston Marina RV Park
- Charleston: Oceanside RV Park
- Charleston: Sunset Bay State Park

Grid A6: Bandon to Port Orford area

Campgrounds

1. Bullards Beach State Park, Bandon, (541) 347-3501, (800) 452-5687, p. 134
2. Bandon-Port Orford KOA, Langlois, (541) 348-2358, (800) 562-3298, p. 134
3. Boise-Cope Curry County Park/at Floras Lake, (541) 247-7074, p. 134
4. Cape Blanco State Park, Port Orford, (541) 332-6774, (800) 452-5687, p. 136
5. Elk River Campground, Port Orford, (541) 332-2255, p. 136
6. Port Orford RV Trailer Village, Port Orford, (541) 332-1041, p. 136

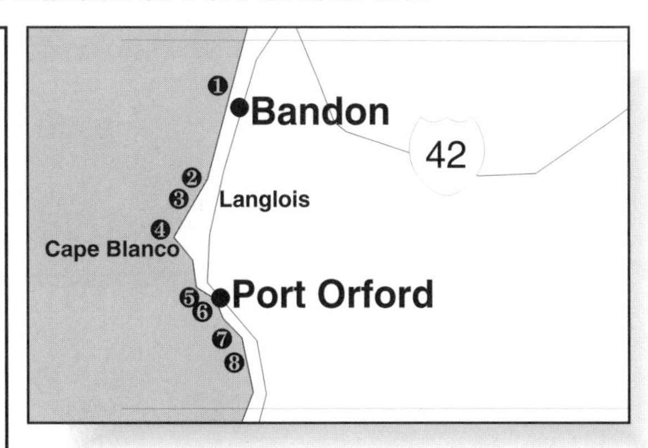

7. Humbug Mountain State Park, Port Orford, (541) 332-6774, (800) 452-5687, p. 136
8. Arizona Beach, Port Orford, (541) 332-6491, p. 137

Diesel

- Bandon: Bandon Texaco, 465 2nd St.
- Port Orford: Chevron, 12th St. & Hwy. 101

RV Parts and Service

- Port Orford: Budwyn's Custom Shop, 92765 Silver Butte Rd., (541) 332-1895

Dump Stations

- Bandon: Bullards Beach State Park
- Port Orford: Cape Blanco State Park
- Port Orford: Humbug Mountain State Park

Grid A7: Ophir to Brookings area

Campgrounds

1. Four Seasons RV Resort, Gold Beach, (541) 247-4503, (800) 248-4503, p. 148
2. Honey Bear Campground, Ophir, (541) 247-2765, (800) 822-4444, p. 148
3. Indian Creek Recreation Park, Gold Beach, (541) 247-7704, p. 148
4. Ireland's Ocean View RV Park, Gold Beach, (541) 247-0148, p. 149
5. Kimball Creek Bend RV Resort, Gold Beach, (541) 247-7580, p. 149
6. Oceanside RV Park, Gold Beach, (541) 247-2301, p. 149
7. Quosatana CG/Siskiyou NF, Gold Beach, (541) 247-6651, p. 150
8. Curry County Fairgrounds, Gold Beach, (541) 247-4541, p. 150
9. Harris Beach State Park, Brookings, (541) 469-2021, (800) 452-5687, p. 150

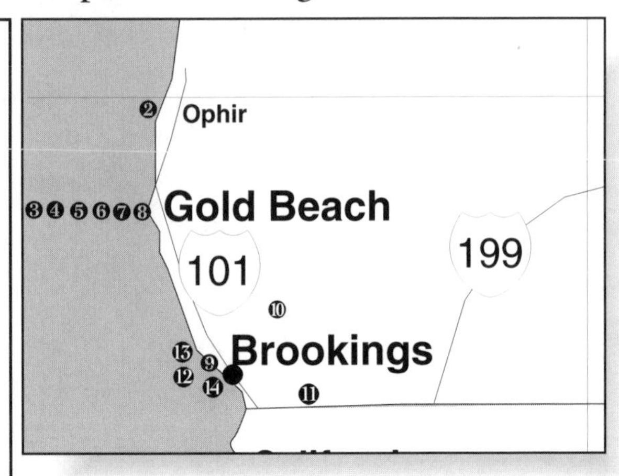

10. Loeb State Park, Brookings, (541) 469-2021, p. 150
11. Winchuck/Siskiyou NF, Brookings, (541) 469-2196, p. 150
12. Harbor Beachfront RV Park, Brookings, (541) 469-5867, (800) 441-0856, p. 151
13. Whaleshead Beach Resort, Brookings, (541) 469-7446, (800) 943-4325, p. 152
14. Riverside Campground, Brookings, (541) 469-4799, p. 151

Diesel

- Gold Beach: Howard's Excel Services, Shell, 1025 S. Ellensburg (Hwy 101), (541) 247-6010
- Brookings: Harbor Shell & Foodmart, 16021 Hwy. 101, (541) 469-4113

RV Parts and Service

- Gold Beach: Roque River RV, 94144 Wedderburn Loop, (541) 247-5004 or (800) 249-5004
- Brookings: Don's RV Repair (99070 W. Freeman Lane, (541) 469-6476)

Dump Stations

- Gold Beach at 5th & Hwy. 101
- Brookings Rest Area, 2 miles north on Hwy. 101
- Brookings: Harris Beach State Park

Chapter 3

Road Information

Introduction

This chapter will provide the driver with the information necessary to anticipate driving conditions in advance. It is not our intent to list every steep grade and every sharp curve, only those we believe the driver needs to be aware of. In general, only grades exceeding 5% and one mile in length are included and curves requiring a speed less than 40 mph.

The coast highway has many waysides and day-use parks that provide a perfect rest area, as well as special views. We have listed those that we believe are the best and the most accessible for an RV. Be aware that travel on Hwy. 101 can be slow in certain areas. You will not average 55 mph as you might expect on a freeway. For the coast, an average of about 40 mph is probably closer to reality.

Hwy. 101 runs north and south with the Pacific Ocean to the west and the coast mountain range to the east. The ascents and descents that do occur are from crossing the basalt capes that provide some of the scenic beauty of this highway. Unless you entered Oregon on Hwy. 101 from California or Washington you will have to select a route over the Coast range. This range of mountains has no high summits and should pose little problem for the RV driver. We have personally driven all the roads but Mother Nature has been known to change our road conditions. We suggest before starting your trip that you call the Oregon Dept. of Transportation Road Condition Report Hotline (541) 889-3999 to get the most current condition of the roads for your route.

Yaquina Bay Bridge from Yaquina Bay State Park.

Watching the birds from the observation deck over Wolf Bay wetlands near Astoria.

Mileposts

This chapter will enable the navigator to read to the driver via milepost numbers what will be coming up on the road. The whole family can join in helping the driver by looking for milepost numbers or signs indicating a noted wayside may be coming up.

Road conditions are reported to the closest milepost number even though the actual grade change begins between mileposts. All directions for routes to the coast presume the driver is heading for the coast (traveling west). All directions for the coast highway are reported going from north to south. If your direction is the opposite read the road directions in reverse.

Take a break

Rest areas, day-use parks, and waysides that are RV friendly and provide a relaxing atmosphere are listed in this section. It is our belief that traveling should be enjoyable and that means many stops to enjoy Mother Nature and reduce the tension of driving. Take your time and enjoy the incredible scenery along the coast.

Grade Percents

The grade percents used in this book are from Oregon state highway databases. Where the databases were accurate to two decimal places for every change in grade, we thought this too much detail for the reader. The percents used are rounded to full numbers in most cases.

The effect of a change of 1% in grade will differ by RV due to the variability of engines, drive trains, and weight just to name a few. As an example, we pull a 29-foot fifth-wheel weighing 8,500 pounds with a 3/4 ton truck that has a turbo diesel engine, automatic transmission, 4.10 rear axle. A 5% grade is insignificant to us. A 6% grade will cause us to drop down a gear within a quarter of a mile. Use this book and monitor the grade percent's impact to your RV. Quickly, you will learn which grade percents are important to you.

Section 1: Getting to the Coast

Hwy. 30, Portland to Astoria

This road parallels the Columbia River providing beautiful scenery for all but the driver. There are three hills worth noting on this road.

At **milepost 46** you will enter the town of Rainier with the speed limit dropping down to 40 mph then 30 mph. There are short, steep declines to the stop lights so watch your speed in this community.

Just past the Longview bridge and **milepost 48** is a one-and-one-half-mile 7% ascent. There are two turnouts for views of Mt. St. Helens; at **milepost 49** and near the summit at **milepost 50.**

At **milepost 55** is a one-mile climb of continuous 6% grade with a three-mile descent of 5% grade starting at **milepost 58**.

At **milepost 73** is a two-mile ascent starting at 5% with the last mile being a 7% grade. The descent is a rolling four miles with three short 5% grades interspersed between 1% to 4% grades.

Catching an updraft on the winds atop Tillamook Head.

Take a break

There is a rest area 22 miles before reaching Astoria at **milepost 75**.

Starting at **milepost 89** to the Astoria city limits you will encounter 30 to 35 mph curves.

City of Astoria:

The major concern for the driver is navigating through the town of Astoria with its narrow lanes. Hwy. 30 makes a couple of turns within the town and the navigator needs to be on their toes. Don't even think of taking your RV up the hilly streets of Astoria, especially toward the Astoria Column. The roads are steep and the crossroads make steep angles that will cause your back end to drag. We saw bikes on the back of an RV get banged pretty hard on the pavement.

Hwy. 26, Portland to Hwy. 101:

You will encounter four summits in the coast range. We were able to pull our 29-foot 5th-wheel without getting below 45 mph on the ascents and hardly used the brakes on the descents. The first is the longest pull with the last being the steepest.

Milepost 46 is a five-mile ascent starting at 3.5% grade then it varies in grade with a 6% grade between **milepost 45** and **44**. The descent on the west side is two miles of 5% grade starting at **milepost 40**.

The second summit is at **milepost 35**. It has a steady four-mile 5% grade ascent and no descent.

Indian long boat overlooking Youngs Bay near the Astoria Column on Coxcomb Hill.

Take a break

A rest stop is 31 miles from Seaside at **milepost 28**.

The third summit is at **milepost 28** with a one-mile 6% grade ascent and a four-mile 5% grade descent starting at **milepost 26**.

The last summit is at **milepost 16** starting the two-mile-plus ascent with a steep 6% grade and never getting below a 5% grade. The descent is also over 2 miles and varies between 4% and 6% grade. The descent starts past **milepost 14**.

Hwy. 6, Portland to Tillamook:

There are two summits to cross for those taking this road to Tillamook. The road has 35 and 40 mph curves across the coast range but is easily navigable by an RVer.

Milepost 45 begins a one-mile 5% ascent to a fairly level summit then a one-half-mile

6% descent starting at **milepost 44**.

Milepost 43 is the beginning of a ten-mile ascent starting with 1% to 3% grades for seven miles then three miles of 5% grade.

Milepost 33 starts a five-mile rolling descent. The first descent is a 5% grade for one mile followed by one half mile of 2% grade, one mile of 5% grade, two miles of lesser grades, and completing the descent with one half mile of 5% grade.

Hwy. 18 Portland to Lincoln City

Hwy. 18 is a major arterial from Portland to the central coast. The road is well maintained, has wide swinging curves, and one summit of 760 feet. This road has had a dramatic increase in traffic and traffic accidents. It is heavily patrolled, drive safely and within the speed limit.

Milepost 18 starts a one-mile ascent at 4% grade that quickly reaches 6% grade. There is no descent.

Milepost 15 starts a less than one mile 5% grade ascent to the summit. The descent is one half mile at 5% grade.

Hwy. 22 Salem to Hwy. 18

For those travelers coming north on I-5, Hwy. 22 offers an intersection to Hwy. 18. This road has one summit to cross.

Milepost 9 starts a three-mile ascent starting with gentle grades with the last mile being a 6% grade climb. The descent is one mile with grades fluctuating between 6% and 7%.

Hwy. 20 Corvallis to Newport

A very winding road sometimes following the Yaquina River. It has several short and steep ascents and descents many of them with sharp curves.

Milepost 48 is a one-mile ascent starting at 3% grade for the first half mile and then increasing to 6% for the remaining distance.

Milepost 40 is a one-and-one-half-mile ascent starting with less than 3% grade for one mile then increasing to a 6% grade for the last half mile. The descent starts immediately at a steady 6% grade for one mile ending at **milepost 37**.

Milepost 31 is a two mile 6% grade descent as you start dropping out of the coast range.

Milepost 12 is a one-and-one-half mile ascent starting at 2% grade and ending with a half mile 6% grade. The descent is less than one mile of 6% grade.

Milepost 4 begins a one-and-one-half mile gentle climb that includes a one half mile 6% grade.

Hwy. 34 Corvallis to Waldport

This road follows the Alsea River and is even more winding than Hwy. 20. It has a 1,231-foot summit to cross ten miles out of Philomath.

Milepost 52 begins the long four-mile ascent as the road winds toward the summit. It begins at 5% grade for one mile increasing to 7% grade for one half mile before a 2% grade breather for two miles. It ends with a 7% grade for the last one half mile.

Milepost 48 is the start of the three-mile descent with one half mile of 7% grade then dropping to grades of 5% or less for the remaining two and one half miles.

Hwy. 126 Eugene to Florence

There is one summit in the coast range with five miles of grade and a small summit twenty miles out of Eugene.

Milepost 37 begins the three-fourths-mile 6% grade ascent over Cougar Pass. The

Strolling the "prom" at Seaside.

descent begins at **milepost 36** and is a full one mile in length with grades between 5% and 7%.

Milepost 25 is the start of a steady 6% climb for five miles with the summit a tunnel. The descent starts immediately at over 6% grade for one mile then drops to below 3% grade for the remaining four miles. On the descent you will encounter 40 mph curves.

Hwy. 38 Curtin to Reedsport

Hwy. 38 follows the beautiful Umpqua River. It is one of our favorite drives, although winding in some places where you will encounter 25 to 35 mph curves. There is one climb as you leave the valley into the coast range with no descents worth mentioning.

Milepost 38 starts a less-than-one-mile ascent; the first half mile is 5% grade then 7% grade to the summit.

Hwy. 42 Roseburg to Coos Bay

For a large portion of this seventy-seven-mile arterial the meandering is along the middle fork of the Coquille River. You can expect many curves, down to 20 mph, as you enjoy the beauty of this scenic drive.

Milepost 60 you will see the incline for the ascent over a 1,472-foot summit. The total ascent will be two and one half miles starting with one mile of 5% grade, a half mile of 6% grade, a short breather of 2% grade and completing with less than a mile of 5% grade.

Milepost 57 is the summit and the descent starts immediately with a short 5% grade leveling off for a half mile then a one-and-one-half-mile 5% grade to the bottom.

Milepost 50 precedes another descent of nearly one mile of 6% grade, a leveling for half a mile. Then another 6% grade for less than one half mile.

Hwy. 42S Coquille to Bandon

This eighteen-mile road for those wishing to go south offers no grades or curves to report. It meanders with few sharp curves as it follows the Coquille River.

Section 2: Traveling Hwy. 101, Astoria to Brookings

Map Grid A1: Hwy. 101, Astoria to Seaside

Between Seaside and the Hwy. 26 junction is a short stretch of road with multiple 35 mph curves. The speed limits posted on the curves are accurate.

Map Grid A2: Hwy. 101 Cannon Beach to Tillamook

Cannon Beach

At Cannon Beach, past **milepost 26**, there is a half-mile 5% grade ascent with the one mile of 6% grade descent starting past **milepost 27**.

On the descent there are two curves and congestion from the Cannon Beach onramps. Keep your speed under control in this stretch.

Cannon Beach has three exits. From Exit 1 to Exit 3 there is a loop going through the town offering access to parking lots and views of Haystack Rock. The road is navigable for an RV but we do not recommend it for large RVs. Parking on the main downtown street for RVs is extremely limited, the road is narrow with 15 mph curves and the congestion of vehicles and pedestrians is heavy. There is a parking lot with pull-thru RV spaces at the end of 2nd street near the visitors center.

There are two mountains, Cape Falcon and Neahkahnie Mountain, with 5% grades that should not stress the vehicle or the driver. The main focus of this drive will be watching for bikers and maintaining the curve speeds.

Milepost 30: For the next three miles the road has multiple 35 mph curves that in the summer can cause traffic congestion.

Milepost 35: The ascent for Cape Falcon starts just before the tunnel at about one half mile past **milepost 35**. The ascent continues at a steady 5% grade for one and one half miles. The descent starts at **milepost 37** for two miles of continuous 5% grade.

Milepost 39: The ascent for Neahkahnie Mountain begins with a slight climb then increases to a 5.5% grade for 2 miles.

Take a break

Before reaching the summit at **milepost 41** is a view area turnoff offering fantastic views of the beaches and the rock work the CCC (Civilian Conservation Corp.) performed to build Hwy. 101. The turnoff is large enough to handle all RVs.

Manzanita

Milepost 41: The descent is two and one half miles starting with a slight decline then increasing to 5.5% grade for a mile, almost level for half a mile, then ending with a 5.5% descent at the Manzanita junction. Watch for 30 mph curves through the city limits of Manzanita.

Nehalem

Milepost 45: Just before entering Nehalem is a short one-third-mile climb of 7.5% to

Newport's waterfront is a great place to stroll.

9% grade and a one-third-mile 9% grade descent into Nehalem. The speed limit reduces to 30 mph in the middle of the descent which will require braking.

Take a break

There is a great place for a break at **milepost 49**. Watch for the brown Manhattan Beach Wayside sign and turn right at the sign. Cross the tracks and immediately turn left driving down a lane to the wayside. There are six pull-thrus for RVs. This wayside is a great stopping place with picnic tables, restrooms, and access to the beach.

From Tillamook

Three Capes Scenic Loop: This beautiful drive is best done in the tow vehicle. The road itself is navigable but stressful to the driver. The major restriction is a lack of parking for large rigs at the scenic view waysides and towns. The Three Capes scenic loop, Pacific City to Tillamook, is 33 miles of narrow winding road. The Three Capes; Cape Kiwanda, Cape Lookout, Cape Meares creates short but steep ascents and descents up to 9% grade. The towns of Oceanside and Cape Meares have no turnaround for RVs over 20 feet.

There are direct roads from Hwy. 101 in Tillamook to Netarts and Sand Lakes. These are the best routes to the campgrounds in this locale.

Take a break

There is a rest area at **milepost 70**. This rest area is a single road in and out with a turnaround past the rest rooms. Parking for an RV is limited to unmarked parallel parking by the restrooms.

Hemlock

From the little town of Hemlock, **milepost 76**, Hwy. 101 begins fourteen miles of winding road with 20, 30, and 35 mph curves. Although the speed limit is 55 mph, we never got over 45 mph on the two test trips.

Take a break

At **milepost 93** there is a viewpoint large enough for RVs with entrances at both ends of the parking area. This can be used as a place to pull over and relax, enjoying the views of the Pacific Ocean.

Map Grid A3: Hwy. 101 Neskowin to South Beach

Take a break

Neskowin Wayside is an excellent place to take a break. Not only is there the parking area with restrooms but a short walk places you on the beach with scenic views. The parking area of the wayside is all straight-in parking. An alternative is to turn off Hwy. 101 at the wayside but take the road left past the wayside towards the grocery store. A turnaround area with space for parking will be on your left.

Cascade Head

Milepost 99 starts a one-and-one-half-mile 6% grade ascent to Cascade Head. The descent starts at 7% grade for one half mile followed by one and one half miles of 6% grade. The descent includes 45 mph curves. If you prefer to bypass these steep grades, Old Hwy. 101 is the road to the left at **milepost 99**. It is a narrow but fairly level road with one single lane bridge. At the fork in the road you can choose to exit at either Otis on Hwy. 18 or return to Hwy. 101 at **milepost 104**. This alternative will add 5 miles to your trip. We saw motor homes using this route when we drove this scenic loop in our tow vehicle.

Take a break

The stretch of road between Lincoln City and Newport has many state park waysides that offer fantastic views and an opportunity to rest. The ones listed are RV accessible and worth the time to pull over and take a break.

Fogarty Creek State Park, **milepost 125**, has ample space for RVs with pull-through parking. Large picnic area protected from the wind on the east side of Hwy. 101. A beautiful little beach is accessible on a short paved walkway.

Boiler Bay State Park, **milepost 126**, has some parallel parking. Whales may be seen year-round from this park. Stop and use your binoculars. You may be lucky.

Agate Beach, **milepost 138**, ample pull-through spaces for RVs. Rest rooms and beach access. After turning off the highway, the navigator should watch for the brown state park sign to turn left for entrance to the parking area. Agate beach got its name for the many agates found after storms. Sand has now washed in covering the gravel bars making it more difficult to find them. Try your luck.

Cape Foulweather

Milepost 130 starts the ascent over Cape Foulweather at a constant 6% grade for one mile. The descent is a 5% grade for 2 miles. The descent has several 45 mph curves.
Note: Devil's Punch Bowl and Otter Crest Trail are not RV accessible.

Map Grid A4: Hwy. 101 Waldport to Florence

Take a break

Ona Beach State Park, **milepost 149**, is an excellent spot to take a break. Large parking area with easy access for RVs. This day-use park is several acres in size with a large grassy and treed area with many hidden trails for kids and pets. The picnic tables are spread apart and many placed with views of the estuary of Beaver Creek. A bridge takes the visitor across Beaver Creek estuary to the beach and a lovely cove.

Driftwood Beach State Park, **milepost 153**, is an eight-acre day-use park with RV parallel parking. Limited picnic facilities. The view of the ocean is from a sand bluff.

Milepost 157, Patterson Memorial State Park is accessible for RVs providing ample parking, picnic facilities, and access to the beach.

Yachats

Milepost 164 as you leave Yachats southbound and cross the Yachats River bridge you will encounter 25 mph and 30 mph turns.

Cape Perpetua Visitors Center

Milepost 167, RV parking is in the upper level, but is limited to about 8 pull-thrus. Plan to spend several hours in this area for learning about and exploring the coast. All the exciting opportunities for this unique area are detailed in the "Activities" section.

Take a break

Milepost 176, Carl G. Washburne State Park day-use is on the ocean side of Hwy. 101. The best parking for RVs is in the dump station outer area. (Keep an aisle open for those using the station).

Heceta Head

Milepost 177 begins the ascent over Heceta Head. It is a short one third mile at 6% grade with the descent also at 6% grade. Immediately into the descent you will encounter a 25 mph curve followed by a 30 mph curve.

Milepost 178 immediately starts the next two-mile ascent of 2% to 5% grades through 25 mph curves. The two-mile descent begins at **milepost 180** at 5% grade but quickly drops to 2% grade with sweeping 40 mph curves.

Take a break

Milepost 178, Heceta Head Lighthouse (Devil's Elbow State Park) has no RV parking in their asphalt parking area. At the bottom of the entrance road, just before the turn into their parking area, swing out onto the gravel and park underneath the Hwy. 101 bridge. You will have a little longer walk but will get to enjoy this up close view and tour of the Heceta Lighthouse. The viewpoints on Hwy. 101 south of this entrance are large enough for RVs and have fantastic panoramic views of the lighthouse and vicinity.

Take a break

Milepost 185, Sutton Recreation day-use Area (drive to the end of the road) has pull-through parking for RVs. An asphalt walk leads to the Holman Vista, an overlook of the Sutton Creek estuary. A great place for a road break.

Map Grid A5: Hwy. 101 Dunes City to Charleston

Take a break

Milepost 200 is the Oregon Dunes Overlook, one of the few places where miles of dunes are visible without hiking into them. Ample pull-thru parking for RVs is available. There are great trails out into the dunes from this overlook. Also picnic tables and restrooms. Don't miss this stop.

Milepost 204 begins a one-mile 5% grade. The descent of three miles starts at 3% grade, a leveling to slight incline, a second 3% grade and ends with one mile of 6% grade. There are 40 and 45 mph curves on both the ascent and the descent.

Winchester Bay

Milepost 216, leaving Winchester Bay, begins a one-mile 6% grade ascent. The descent does not start for 3 miles and is a one-half-mile 5% grade ending at **milepost 221**.

Mingus Park at Coos Bay has a lovely Japanese garden and lake.

Map Grid A6: Hwy. 101 Bandon to Port Orford

Many of the waysides on this stretch of road are not RV friendly and are not recommended other than the ones listed below.
Milepost 247 begins a one-and-one-half-mile climb starting with a one-mile 6% grade and completing with a one-half-mile 4% grade.
Milepost 254: The descent is also one and one half miles long with a 5% grade for the first half mile and a 7% grade for the last mile. Fortunately, there are no sharp curves on this descent. This descent is followed immediately by a short one-mile ascent of less than 5%.

Take a break

Milepost 259 is Bullards Beach State Park with the Coquille Lighthouse at the day-use area. There is ample parking and beautiful views of marshes, the Coquille River, North Jetty, and the ocean.

Bandon

Milepost 261, or is it 269?? at the intersection of Hwy. 101 and Hwy. 42S the mileposts take an eight-mile jump. The southbound driver is at **milepost 261** while the northbound driver is at **milepost 269**. The original highway ran on what is now Hwy. 42S and was eight-miles longer than the current highway.

Milepost 270 (11th street), this is the north access to Beach Loop Drive. It is not recommended for RVs.

South Access to Cape Arago

Milepost 253: If you are northbound you will see the state's brown sign pointing you to a shortcut to Charleston and state parks. The faint of heart will continue to Coos Bay turning left on Commercial Street. For the brave at heart this winding, narrow 12-mile road will save you 15 miles but little time. The road changes names and is known as Seven Devils Road and Beaver Hill Road. It winds along the ridge top with rolling ascents for four miles, rolling plateau for seven miles, and a descent for one mile of which the last quarter mile is close to 10% grade. The short steep grades may reach 10%

Whalen Island Park is a jewel of a campground on the estuary of Sandlake.

with 15, 20, and 25 mph curves. Expect to average 25 mph for these twelve miles. We took our 29-foot 5th-wheel on this road and had no problems.

Port Orford

Take a break

Battle Rock day-use area at the south end of Port Orford provides a good place to take a break with the visitor's center, access to the beach, restrooms all combined with ample parking.

Humbug Mountain

At **milepost 304** you start the climb over Humbug Mountain. There are several pull-outs large enough for big RVs and offering ocean views.

Milepost 304 starts the gradual one-mile ascent of Humbug Mountain. The descent is two miles with the first mile gradual and then increasing to 6% grade for the last mile. At the completion of the descent you will immediately hit 30 mph curves for one and one half miles as the road winds through a canyon.

Milepost 311 starts the next one-mile ascent which is two 5% grades separated by a quarter mile level section. Watch the descent of straight 6% grade for one mile with 30 mph curves.

Milepost 313 is an ascent starting at 6% for a little over half a mile then completing the mile with gradual grades.

Map Grid A7: Hwy. 101 Ophir to California Border

Take a break

Milepost 319 is a state rest area. This is a small rest stop with limited parking space, a couple of picnic tables, and the restrooms. There are separate in and out roads for easy access.

Geisel Monument and **Otter Point waysides** are definitely not for RVs.

Cape Sebastian

Milepost 331 is the start of the climb over Cape Sebastian. The total ascent is two and one half miles. The first mile is a 5% grade with a brief 3% grade break in the middle. The last mile and a half is 6% grade. The descent starts with one half mile of less than 1% grade then becomes a 6% grade for one half mile completing the descent past **milepost 336**.

Take a break

Milepost 336: For the next mile there will be pull-outs with beautiful views. You will be able to see from the road whether they are large enough for your RV.

Meyers Beach at **milepost 337** is especially nice with Meyers Creek emptying into the ocean.

Cape Ferrelo

Milepost 340 is the beginning of four short climbs as you progress toward Cape Ferrelo. The first is a one-mile ascent and one-mile descent both with light grades at their beginnings and 6% grades for their last half miles. The summit is at **milepost 341**.

Milepost 342: You immediately start the next climb of one mile at 6% grade while the descent is less than a mile of 5% grade.

Milepost 344 is the start of a gradual climb for four miles to past **milepost 348** and the descent is only one half mile of 6% grade.

Take a break

Milepost 344: You are entering Samuel H. Boardman State Park, a long stretch of coastline. For the next ten miles you will see wayside signs. Those that require turning onto a road are mostly not RV accessible. The viewpoints as pull-outs on the road are RV accessible with trails, usually steep, to the beach. You will be able to gauge from the road which viewpoints you wish to turn off on. Listed are our recommendations.

Milepost 345, Arch Rock Point Picnic Area, is a loop parking lot with parallel parking, restrooms, picnic tables.

Milepost 346: Thunder Rock Cove and Natural Bridge viewpoint. Park at the Natural Bridges Cove wayside. A short walk on the asphalt trail gives a spectacular view of the natural bridges. On the north end of the wayside a short walk on the coast trail provides a view of Thunder Rock Cove.

Milepost 350 is the last ascent which is less than a mile of 6% grade. The descent starts immediately and is also less than a mile of 5% grade.

Take a break

Milepost 352.6: Lone Ranch Picnic Area. Excellent place for a break. RV accessible even though there is limited parking. Picnic tables right at the beach, restrooms, lots of beach to explore.

Milepost 356 has a rest area on the east side. The truck and RV pull-thrus are at the upper level. During the summer months a visitor's center is open. A dump station is available at this rest area.

Milepost 356 across Hwy. 101 from the rest area is Harris Beach State Park with a nice day-use area on the beach. There are a limited number of parallel parking spaces at the day-use area and additional spaces up the road by the campground turn off.

Welcome to California

Map Grid A1: Astoria to Seaside

Introduction

The northern Oregon Coast has some of the longest stretches of wide, flat, sandy beaches in Oregon. Most of it is totally accessible as the dunes are relatively low and there are so many access roads that let you get to the mighty Pacific Ocean within minutes. There are bustling tourist towns like Cannon Beach and small sleepy charming burgs like Gearhart. Astoria offers much in history and architectural charm with its older Victorian homes. On the northern coast, you can have solitude or be entertained with many activities. This part of the Oregon Coast also gets more visitors in the summer because of its proximity to the Portland metro area. But don't let that discourage you. Keep reading and you'll find just what you are looking for during your travels on the northern coast.

Astoria's average rainfall is about 63 inches per year and the temperatures range from 41° to 65°.

Section 1: Best Campgrounds

Astoria to Seaside

Best public campground for base camping

Astoria: Fort Stevens State Park, (503) 861-1671 or reservation (800) 452-5687, p. 34

Best private campgrounds for base camping

Astoria: Astoria/Warrenton/Seaside KOA (800) KOA-8506, p. 35

Alternative: Kampers West Kampground, Warrenton, (503) 861-1814 or (800) 880-5267, p. 36

Seaside: Circle Creek RV Park & Campground, open March 15 to Nov. 1, (503) 738-6070, p. 36

Campground Descriptions

Fort Stevens State Park, open all year, Ridge Rd., Hammond, OR 97121 (503) 861-1671 or reservation (800) 452-5687

Location: Off Hwy. 101, 10 miles west of Astoria near Hammond on the Pacific coast. Elevation: Sea level

From Astoria, take the Hwy. 101 bridge across Youngs Bay toward Warrenton. Turn right at the Hammond turnoff, follow the signs, and drive 4 miles to the park.

Description of area: Fort Stevens is located on a peninsula at the mouth of the Columbia River but it has thick forests with large Sitka spruce and Douglas firs. The park also provides access to the Pacific Ocean and the Columbia River with beautiful

Examining the rusting schooner, Peter Iredale, *that went aground at Fort Stevens State Park in 1906.*

views of the mountains of the Northwest. The South Jetty in the park is a favorite spot for surf fishermen. Fort Stevens is the largest public campground for sites (594) in Oregon but don't let that discourage you. Many of the sites have lots of forest cover between them. If you expect to camp on a weekend between Memorial Day and Labor Day, reservations should be made months ahead.

At Fort Stevens State Park, the kids will love the activities as there are 8.5 miles of paved bike paths throughout the lovely woods, wetlands, and near the beach. The park has fishing, biking, hiking trails, historical batteries to explore and walking on the beach. Coffenbury Lake (freshwater) offers a great swim area for the kids as well as fishing platforms for catching trout and perch. This is a great place to stay for a week in the off season.

252 tent sites, 129 partial hookups, 213 sites with full hookups for RVs of any length. The loops of H, I, and J have the densest woods with more cover between the sites. Unfortunately, these sites are generally closed after Labor Day. There are many pull-thrus for large RVs. All interior roads and sites are asphalt and easily accessible. Restrooms, showers, dump, firewood can be purchased, playgrounds, camp hosts, supplies/propane/PO available in Hammond 2 miles away, recycling, fishing, swimming, hiking, phones, group camp, amphitheater, nature programs, handicap access. Open all year. Rates $17.00-$20.00, with lower off-season rates.

Alternate site: There is a Kampground of America (KOA) directly across from the entrance to Ft. Stevens. This private campground also has Kamping Kabins. This park gives you the opportunity to ride your bike across the street and enjoy all the activities at Fort Stevens. There is a day-use fee charged at Coffenbury Lake in the state park all year but not for bicyclists.

Best Private Campground: Astoria area

Astoria/Warrenton/Seaside KOA, open all year, 1100 NW Ridge Road, Hammond, OR 97121, (800) KOA-8506.

Location: Off Hwy. 101, 10 miles west of Astoria near Hammond. Elevation: sea level. From Astoria, take the Hwy. 101 bridge across Youngs Bay toward Warrenton. Turn

You can enjoy the sweeping grassy areas at this campground near Seaside.

right at the Hammond turnoff, follow the signs, and drive 4 miles to the park.

Description of area: This private park is right across the road from the entrance to Fort Stevens State Park. The KOA is well done with some trees, play equipment for the kids, large swimming pool, and recreation room with big screen TV and games. The biggest advantage though is the close proximity to Fort Stevens State Park. You can ride your bike across the street and take advantage of the 8.5 miles of bike trails or just walk to the beach. Ask for their special KOA discounts from October to April. Open all year.

300 sites for rigs up to 55 feet in pull-thrus and 30 feet for back-ins. The back loop is gravel. Full and partial hookups with 30 amp service, restrooms, showers, phone, cable TV, laundry, groceries, RV supplies, propane, heated pool, spa, horsehoes, game room, playground, rec field. Daily rates: $20.95 to $29.95. Ask about their lower weekly, monthly or off-season rates.

Alternate: Kampers West Kampground, open all year, 1140 NW Warrenton Dr., #324, Warrenton, OR 97146, (503) 861-1814 or (800) 880-5267.

250 sites, full and partial hookups, (30/50 amp), cable TV, dump, laundry, restrooms, showers, 4 pay phones, convenience store, propane, stream bass fishing, fish-cleaning station, and a great playground for the kids. Pull-thrus and back-in sites up to 50'. They also give the Good Sam 10% discount. Rates from $15.00-$20.00. Ask about weekly, monthly, and seasonal rates. This park is surrounded by natural wooded habitat where an occasional deer can be spotted.

Best Private Campground: Seaside area

Circle Creek RV Park & Campground, open March 15-Nov. 1, HCR 63, Box 210, Seaside, OR 97138 (503) 738-6070

Note: Best centrally located base camp for exploring north to Astoria, south to Cannon Beach

Location: From Seaside travel 1 mile south on Hwy. 101 to the entrance and turn right.

Description of area: This lush green park is set just off Hwy. 101 but nestled in a lovely pastoral setting of green lawns with treed hills all around. Sites and roads are paved and spaced wide apart with some pine trees between sites. The best sites for quiet are in the back next to the little creek—sites 10-13. A bonus for this park is that they give the Good Sam discount of 10% on daily rates or you can opt for the 7th day free. With the park being only one mile south of Seaside it offers the traveler the opportunity to relax in a quiet, green setting while camping and still spend some time touring bustling Seaside. Actually, Astoria is not that far either. We enjoy base camping here because you are close to Astoria, Seaside and Cannon Beach but you are well away from the crowds. You have all the conveniences needed and the management takes excellent care of the park. Watch the surrounding meadows for the elk which frequent this area.

44 paved sites, 5 pull-thrus (across grass), back-ins up to 60 feet, full or partial hookups (30 amp), cable TV, restrooms, showers, dump, phone, laundry. Daily rate: $19.00 full hookups, $17.00 partial hookups; ask about the lower weekly and monthly rates off season. There are also lots of tent sites in the large grassy meadow.

Volunteer/Camp Host Opportunities

Fort Stevens State Park, (503) 861-1671

Gnat Creek Fish Hatchery, 18 miles east of Astoria off Hwy. 30, Rt. 2, Box 2198, Clatskanie, OR 97016 (503) 455-2234.

Big Creek Fish Hatchery, 15 miles east of Astoria off Hwy. 30, Rt. 4, Box 594, Astoria, OR 97103 (503) 458-6512

Section 2: Activities in Astoria Area

Astoria/Warrenton area

Astoria was founded in 1811 by John Jacob Astor's fur traders and is the oldest settlement west of the Mississippi. Lewis and Clark spent the winter near here at the end of their long journey west in 1805. Astoria is for explorers and its museums and memorials give you a real flavor for those times in the 1800s. For history buffs, Astoria is the place. There are many artfully preserved Victorian homes to be seen, some as bed and breakfasts. Astoria has a charm quite unmatched by any other city on the Oregon coast.

Don't Miss

- Astoria Maritime Museum
- Ft. Clatsop National Memorial
- Fort Stevens Museum and abandoned military fort

Highly Recommended

- Astoria Column
- 8.5 miles of biking trails at Fort Stevens State Park
- Captain George Flavel House

Auto Tours

Youngs River Falls Loop, 28 miles, (see Clatsop County Visitors Guide at Astoria Chamber of Commerce). This loop goes through the pastoral setting of family farms along the Youngs River. Youngs River Falls is the furthest point of the loop.

Walluski Loop, 18 miles, (see Clatsop County Visitors Guide at Astoria Chamber of Commerce)

Biking

Fort Stevens State Park has over 8 miles of easy, paved paths and a number of unmarked bark trails that take you through the forests and wetlands to the ocean and to the end of the peninsula. This could be a whole day's outing with the kids if you stop and play at the many side paths to the ocean.

Walluski Loop, 18 miles, (see Clatsop County Visitors Guide at Astoria Chamber of Commerce)

Bookstores

Godfather's Books & Espresso Bar, 1108 Commercial, Astoria, (503) 325-8143. A great place to relax, browse for books, and get a cup of espresso at the same time.
Books Etc, 1015 Commercial, Astoria (503) 325-8143. New and used paperbacks.

Family Activities with Children

The Children's Museum, 475 11th St./Exchange St., Astoria, (503) 325-8669. There is an admission charge. You can get a 50% off coupon at the Astoria Chamber of Commerce or at the museum. A nice large space for children to play. They also have crafts sessions for children 2 years to 12 years old.

Cullaby Lake and Carnahan County Park, 7 miles south of Astoria off Hwy. 101, is a great place for a picnic, swimming, boating, and fishing for trout, bass and bluegill. There is lots of play equipment for the children in two separate areas. Try the road that goes past the bathroom for another secluded area. This is the site of hydroplane races during the Astoria Regatta Celebration each summer. Don't miss seeing the turn of the century, hand-built, Finnish house located next to the camp host site.

Fort Stevens State Park has great fishing platforms at Coffenbury Lake. The lake is stocked with a few steelhead and trout. There is a day-use charge at the lake all year. Don't forget the bike trails; paved, easy, and very scenic. There is also swimming and a two-mile hike around the lake. Paddle boats can be rented during the summer months.

Annual Events

Astoria/Warrenton Chamber of Commerce,
111 W. Marine Dr., (503) 325-6311, for detailed maps and infomation

January
Jazzy Blues

February
N. Coast Symphonic Band

March
Spring Craft Fair

April
50s Cruise In
Crab & Seafood Festival

May
Stock Car Races
Maritime Week
Columbia River Bicentennial Celebration

June
Rose Festival Fleet arrives
Scandinavian Midsummer Festival

July
Old-Fashioned Fourth of July
Fort Stevens Celebration
Play: "Shanghaied In Astoria"

August
Clatsop County Fair
Astoria Regatta
Play: "Shanghaied In Astoria"

September
Fort Stevens Civil War Re-enactment
Astoria Arts Celebration

October
Great Columbia Crossing 8-mile Scenic Run

December
Santa Lucia Festival of Lights
Victorian Christmas Dinner
Lower Columbia Christmas Boat Parade
Nutcracker Ballet

Fishing for steelhead and trout on Coffenbury Lake at Fort Stevens State Park.

Fort Stevens military batteries provide ample space for children to run, climb, and explore the concrete gun batteries. Built to protect the Columbia River during the Civil War as an earthen fort, it was converted to concrete for WWII. It is the only fort in the USA fired on during WWII.

Fort Clatsop is a great place in the summer for the kids to see reenactments of life as it was when Lewis and Clark wintered here on their journey west. The players dress in period costumes and give you a sense of "being there" during those times in the 1800s.

Tapiola Park and Pool, June-August, Denver Street and Marine Dr., Astoria, (503) 325-0769. Call for fees and summer hours. There is a large heated swimming pool and a small wading pool. The park also has picnic tables and play equipment—a great family stop for a few hours.

Astoria Riverfront Cruise, Tiki Charters 352 Industry, next to Red Lion Inn, Astoria (503) 325-7818. See Astoria from the water on a 60- to 90-minute riverfront cruise. These cruises are narrated year-round. Admission fee is charged.

Ecotourism

***What is Ecotourism?** - A responsible travel experience that contributes to the understanding of an area's natural and cultural environment.*

Charter ecotours or river cruises are a great way to explore the Columbia River Estuary. Get out on the water and see the marine environment and wildlife close-up by boat. Tours can range from 2-8 hours excursions at prices starting from $15.00 to $60.00 per person. For more information regarding charter ecotours or river cruises, contact the Astoria-Warrenton Area Chamber of commerce or refer to their "Ecocharters" brochure.

Self-guided Ecotour, the Astoria Chamber of Commerce has a great Ecotours brochure that will take you on various auto tours on your own to explore the marine environment around Astoria. Also ask for the brochure "Columbia River Estuary Driving Tour of the Natural and Cultural Resources".

Exercise or Leisure Walking

Obtain a walking map of the historic homes in the downtown Astoria area from the Astoria Chamber of Commerce. Historic homes like the 1885 Queen Anne-style Flavel

House are a feast for the eyes. Astoria has some of the most beautiful period homes in the area.

Take a walk along Astoria's working waterfront. Start at 12th Street (parking lot on 11th Street) and use the Rail walkway to view marine life and the bustling fishing industry's waterfront. End up at the 6th St. pier and observatory platform that looks out over the Columbia River. Stop at Ricciardi's for espresso or lunch.

Fishing/Clamming

Clamming is allowed anywhere along the beaches. The season is open September 1 to July 15. Best digging is at extremely low tide.

Fort Stevens State Park, fishing, South Jetty off the rocks, popular redtail surfperch spot.

Astoria Boat Basin, (503) 325-8279, boat launch, boat moorage, rental boats, charter office, fish-cleaning station, restrooms.

Deck at waterfront and Sixth St., sturgeon, salmon.

Hammond Boat Basin, (503) 861-1461. boat ramp, charter office, bait and tackle.

Handicap Restrooms

Warrenton Boat Basin, (503) 861-2110, boat launch, moorage, charter office, bait and tackle, fish-cleaning station, restrooms.

Galleries/Arts

The Astoria Chamber of Commerce can provide a map showing two dozen art galleries, bookstores and antique shops many of them within easy walking distance of each other. One that we especially like is:

Ricciardi Gallery, 108 10th Street (503) 325-5450, more than 2000 square feet of oils, acrylics, watercolors, fabric art, wooden boxes, fine pottery, reproductions. Relax with an espresso or soup and bread on site.

Golf

There are no public golf courses in the Astoria area. See "Golf: Seaside/Gearhart."

Hiking/Waterfalls

Youngs River Falls. This falls drops 65 feet over mossy canyon walls. 100 years ago this was the site of a pulp mill; and now it's a small county park with a short trail down to a picnic site. This is an uncrowded place to get away for a picnic. Drive 10 miles southeast from Astoria on S.R. 202. At Olney, turn south on the paved road marked Youngs River Falls. Stay to the right and continue for 4 miles to the unmarked parking area and take the short trail to the base of the falls.

Fort Stevens State Park has two self-guided walking tours of the fort that take about one hour each to complete. There is also a nature trail through forested wildlife habitat. Ask for a trail map when entering the park. There are miles of trails and a nice two-mile trail around Coffenbury Lake. Make sure to take the short hike out on the beach to the shipwreck Peter Iredale.

The Oregon Coast Trail starts at the South Jetty (end of Jetty Rd., Fort Stevens) and continues to the California border. Special maps of the trail are available at the Astoria Chamber of Commerce for those who may want to hike all or just segments of this beautiful coastal trail.

Short Hikes Around Astoria

Cathedral Tree Trail, 1 mile round trip, can be accessed at 28th and Irving in Astoria.

The beautiful rose gardens at the Fort Stevens Military Museum.

A wide and graveled but sometimes steep forest path leads to the giant Sitka spruce called Cathedral Tree (300 years old, 200 feet tall, 8-foot diameter). A delightful green old growth forest with special charm and lots of benches for resting on the way up. If you're feeling energetic, continue on the clearly marked trail (1 1/2 mile) up to the Astoria Column.

Astoria Waterfront starting from the Maritime Museum, take a long walk in either direction along the railroad right-of-way. Watch all the boats and maritime activities as well as the sea birds and sea lions.

Local History/Museums/Lighthouses

Columbia River Maritime Museum & Maritime Park in downtown Astoria, 1792 Marine Dr., (503) 325-2323, invites you to explore the vessels that plied the Pacific Northwest rivers and waterways. This is a museum for all ages as many different types of watercraft fill the main hall, some so big you can jump in. There is a great view of the Columbia River from the observation deck. The lightship *Columbia*, docked adjacent to the museum, is available for touring. There is an admission charge for the museum.

Fort Clatsop National Memorial, (Rt. 3, Box 604FC, (503) 861-2471). Ft. Clatsop is a replica of the Lewis and Clark winter outpost of 1805-1806 named after the Clatsop Indians. This was a hard and wet winter that tested the explorers survival skills. The fort was built after the Corps of Discovery finished their long journey west to explore and record what they saw for President Thomas Jefferson. During the summer months (Memorial Day-Labor Day) from 9 a.m. to 5:30 p.m. daily, there are many outdoor demonstrations of life during those times. Music, dance, and chores provide an authentic look at life during the early 1800's. Follow the signs from US101 south of Astoria.

Fort Stevens Historical area, Hammond, (503) 861-2000. This civil-war vintage outpost is located 10 miles west of Astoria with a museum, rose garden, and lots of cement gun batteries to explore.

The Historic Flavel House, 441 8th street, (503) 325-2563, is a period example of the cities best Queen Anne architecture. Built in 1885 by Captain George Flavel, the Flavel House is a monument to the luxurious style and architecture of the Victorian era.

Rusted poles show the end of the schooner, Peter Iredale, *that went aground in 1906. Bow in background.*

It is very close to the Heritage Museum, 1618 Exchange Street, (503) 325-2203, whose exhibits depict natural history, geology, Native American artifacts, early immigrants and settlers of the region, and important nautical events.

Uppertown Firefighters Museum, 30th & Marine Dr., (503) 325-2203. On display are hand-pulled, horse-drawn and motorized vehicles, fire fighting equipment and memorabilia.

Washington State Lighthouses

Lighthouse at Cape Disappointment is perched on a 287-foot cliff and was built in 1856 to guard the mouth of the Columbia. It is still in use today at the treacherous joining of the Columbia River and the Pacific Ocean. From Astoria, take the bridge across to Washington and follow Hwy. 101 north 11 miles to Illwaco. In the center of town go straight on Loop 100, following the signs for Ft. Canby for 3 miles. At the crossroads for the boat launch, go straight half-mile to the Interpretive Center. The Interpretive Center has walk-through exhibits of photographs, artifacts, and journal entries from the Lewis and Clark expedition. Admission is free. The Center's hours are 10 a.m.-5 p.m. daily. There are also 2 easy trails; one to the lighthouse (1.2 miles round trip) and a Coastal Forest Trail (1.4 mile loop).

The North Head Lighthouse was built in 1898 just north of Cape Disappointment. It stands 174 feet above sea level. It was automated in 1961 and there are tours of the lighthouse in the summer. At the lighthouse, there are also easy hiking trails from .6-3.4 miles long. From Astoria, take the bridge across to Washington and follow Hwy. 101 north 11 miles to Illwaco. In the center of town turn toward Ft. Canby on Loop 100. Travel 2 miles and turn right on North Head Lighthouse Road. There is a gravel parking lot on the left.

Photo Opportunities

- Astoria Waterfront, especially at the foot of 6th Street
- Peter Iredale wreck at Ft. Stevens State Park
- Astoria Column has a panoramic view at the top with Youngs Bay and river basin below
- Sunsets at any place along the coast
- Twilight Creek Eagle Sanctuary, 8 miles east of Astoria on Hwy. 30

Restaurants/Espresso

$=Inexpensive • $$=Moderate • $$$=Expensive

Shilo Inn at Warrenton, $$, 1609 E. Harbor Dr., Warrenton (503) 861-2245. Great food, dinner offerings include lite meals for those watching their calories. They will also split dinners. From Astoria, take US101 across the Youngs Bay bridge toward Seaside, turn right just as you cross the bridge.

Columbian Cafe, $, 1114 Marine Dr., Astoria (503) 325-2233. A small, funky, mostly vegetarian cafe that has the best soup and bread around. The menu is eclectic; ask what the chef's special is for the day and be sure your palate can take the heat. Call for days and hours. Cash and checks only.

Ricciardi Gallery, $, 108 10th Street, Astoria, (503) 325-5450, Espresso, pastries, homemade soup and bread.

Ricciardi's Cannery Cafe, $$, #1 Sixth Street, Astoria, (503) 325-8642. Open daily, Sunday brunch, take-out. Our favorite! A wonderfully light and airy cafe right by the observation deck at the foot of 6th Street. The windows all around let you see the splendor of the mighty Columbia River with Washington State as a backdrop. Food is excellent with many interesting choices to pick from. Great place to relax, eat, and watch the river. The restaurant is the second business for owner Corinne Ricciardi. She started the fine art gallery and espresso cafe at 108th 10th St., just four blocks to the east in 1989. A lovely place at any time of day.

Pig 'N Pancake, $, 146 W. Bond, Astoria, (503) 325-3144. Open early for breakfast with extensive menu choices.

Rosemary Baking Co., $, #10 Sixth St., Astoria, (503) 325-0580. Distinctive breads, sandwiches, soup, and pastries. The smell in this tiny cafe is intoxicating. Watch Lorna make her scrumptious fresh bread.

Special Local Places

Visit the 125-foot **Astoria Column** with a pictorial frieze depicting events that shaped the Northwest on 600-foot-high Coxcomb Hill. You can climb to the top up the spiral staircase.

This column was a joint project of the Great Northern Railroad and the descen-

Enjoying the 125-foot tower on Astoria's Coxcomb Hill.

dants of John Jacob Astor to commemorate a 1926 cross-country rail excursion. The viewing platform is a straight-up climb of 164 steps on a circular staircase. Be sure you are up to it and take your time if you get out of breath. The view from the top on a clear day will dazzle you as you gaze out at Youngs Bay and the coastline to the south. You can almost see the big ships in the 1800s coming in to port. To get an authentic glimpse of what they looked like be sure to stop at the Columbia Maritime Museum in downtown Astoria. A visit to the Astoria Column is free. Drive to the top of 16th Street and follow the signs.

Wildlife Viewing

Twilight Creek Eagle Sanctuary, 8 miles east of Astoria (off Hwy. 30 on Burnside Rd.). This protected bald eagle habitat area has a platform affording views over the marshes of Wolf Bay Wetlands. You can see over 40 eagles feed and roost in season. There is one pair of eagles named the "Twilight Eagles" that stay all year. This is a very peaceful setting to watch the birds from the observation deck.

Astoria Working Waterfront, end of Sixth Street. You will find the river viewing platform where harbor seals, California sea lions and different bird species can be seen.

At the Astoria Chamber of Commerce, ask for the "Columbia River Estuary Driving Tour of the Natural & Cultural Resources".

Ft. Stevens State Park, whale watching, (December-January, March-April).

Section 3: Activities in Seaside/Gearhart Area

Seaside was Oregon's first seashore resort and it is still one of the coast's most popular destinations. Families especially enjoy the many shops and arcades on Broadway, as well as the Town Center Carousel and the bumper cars. Seaside's Broadway Street can be quite busy in the summer but after Labor Day the pace is much slower and more relaxed.

Gearhart is like a small northern neighbor of Seaside but has its own lodging, restaurants, and two golf courses. It traces its beginnings back to 1890 when it became a popular beach getaway for affluent Portlanders. It's a lot smaller and slower-paced than Seaside with miles of uncrowded beaches perfect for kite flying and pleasant hikes.

Don't Miss

• Broadway, Seaside's main street and several lateral streets have been converted for pedestrian traffic. Stroll along and savor the aroma of fresh-made candy and foods. Choose from a wide assortment of shops, restaurants, and services. Enjoy amusement rides, window shopping, and arcades. Seaside pedestrian traffic is heavy in the summer months. Find a spot to park (the mall on Hwy. 101 or 1st and Columbia), wear your

Annual Events in Seaside

Check with Seaside Chamber of Commerce,
7 N. Roosevelt (Hwy. 101), (800) 444-6740, for specific dates

January
Barbershop Quartet

February
Seaside...and all that Jazz

April
Seaside...And 'Awl That Country'

June
TRLBY Kite Festival

July
Miss Oregon Pageant

August
Budweiser Beach Volleyball Tournament
Dahlia Parade

September
Golf Tournament

October
Oregon Dixieland Jubilee

November
Christmas Gift Fair

December
Yuletide At Seaside

comfy walking shoes and enjoy the town on foot.

• The promenade ("the prom") offers two miles of paved walkway past Seaside homes and resorts on one side and gorgeous dunes on the other. In 1908, a wooden promenade was built along the ocean front. In 1920, it was reconstructed, this time with concrete. It incorporated the "turnaround" for automobiles which is the official end of the Lewis and Clark Trail. Use the "prom" for a leisurely stroll or for your daily exercise circuit. Broadway intersects the promenade at its mid-point. There is limited parking at the north end of the promenade; 12th Street. 5 RV pull-thru spaces 30 feet in length, 7 pull-thru spaces 20 feet in length.

Highly Recommended

• Pacific Way Bakery and Cafe, Cottage and Pacific Way, Gearhart, (503) 738-0245. Pastries or breakfast, lunch, or dinner.

Biking

On the Prom, you can rent bicycles at the Prom Bike Shop, 622 12th street, (503) 738-8251. Their equipment includes 3-wheel cycles, trainers, tandems, all terrain bicycles, child carriers and bicycle trailers which are enclosed and can carry up to 150 pounds of precious children.

Around town on a surrey, Seaside Surrey Rental, 332 S. Columbia, (503) 738-0242. Try a 4-wheel surrey with either two pedals or four and the whole family can ride the town together.

Bookstores

Charlie's Turnaround Books, 111 Broadway, (503) 738-3211. New books.

Buck's Book Barn, 1023 Broadway; east side of Hwy. 101. Wide selection of used books.

Family Activities with Children

Play on the beach at Seaside and enjoy the swingsets and volleyball nets provided. In the summer at the turnaround, you will see many beautiful kites being flown. A world record was recently set for the most kites on 2 strings—104. There is also a kite flying festival in Seaside, ask at the Visitors Center for dates.

Seaside Aquarium, 200 N. Promenade, Seaside, (503) 738-6211, had a new baby seal born in June 1996. You can buy food and feed the seals. Look for the discount coupon in the "Seaside Information Guide" from the Chamber of Commerce. There is an admission charge.

The Million Dollar Walk as the locals call it, Broadway Street, downtown Seaside. The variety of restaurants, fast-food, arcades, video games, candy and gift shops, and souvenir shops could relieve you of quite a few dollars if you spent much time here. The kids love it however, and can spend all day. You may have a hard time getting them back to the ocean once they've seen "Broadway".

Broadway Park, 1140 Broadway; east side of Hwy. 101, on the banks of the Neawanna Creek where you will find covered picnic sites, restrooms, basketball hoops, tennis courts, and a horseshoe pit with horseshoes. There are two separate playground areas with lots of different play equipment and also an exercise unit with stations for adults. Kids could easily spend the afternoon here and the adults could picnic. The interpretive signs along the creek explain the ecosystem and how it evolved to where it is today. Limited RV parking in asphalt lot with no pull-thrus.

Seaside Youth Center, 1140 Broadway, (503) 738-3311 or (503) 738-3192, next to Broadway Park. Come to the other side of Broadway (east of Hwy. 101) and find a nice place away from the crowds. There is a swimming pool and a drop-in center for youth with pool tables, bumper pool, ping pong, TV, electronic games, computer access and

Sunset on the Promenade at Seaside.

programmed activities with a skateboard barn in the back. Preschool, arts & crafts, and health and fitness programs are also offered.

Exercise or Leisure Walking Routes

The Prom at Seaside, a 2-mile-long cement walk that's perfect for morning exercise of up to 4 miles round-trip or just strolling and enjoying the charming beach cottages and ocean. Be sure to stop and look at the replica of the Lewis and Clark Salt Works (marked by a sign on the prom). At the north end, the prom has a large parking lot with pull-thru parking for RVs. There are two bathrooms along the prom.

Stroll along the **Necanicum River**, start at Quatat Marine Park near Broadway in downtown Seaside and walk along the sidewalk next to the river to 12th street and back again. This is a lovely river with some ducks to be seen along the way. You will pass the Seaside Museum and could park in their lot, see the museum, and then take a walk along the river.

Fishing/Clamming

Surf fishing is popular at "**The Cove**" on Sunset Blvd.

Necanicum River in Seaside, 12th Ave. bridge, steelhead and salmon can be caught (in season).

Razor clams can be dug during minus tides on the wide flat beaches.

Galleries/Arts

Seaside Guild of Artists in Heritage Square on Broadway, downtown Seaside, displays works of local artists.

Golfing

There are three public golf courses to choose from; one 18-hole course and two 9-hole courses.

The Highlands Golf Club, 1 Highland Road, Gearhart, OR 97138, (503) 738-5248. Take Del Ray Beach Access Road 5 miles north of Seaside. This is an attractive 9 hole, par 30 golf course tucked naturally into the trees and rolling dunes. It consists of six par 3 and three par 4 holes.

Gearhart Golf Links, North Marion Street, Gearhart, OR 97138, (503) 738-3538. In Gearhart at the signal light turn toward the beach then right on Marion Street. This is a popular 18 hole, par 72 golf course with all the amenities. It is considered to be the oldest golf course in Oregon established in 1892.

Seaside Golf Course, 451 Avenue U, Seaside, OR 97138 (503) 738-5261. Take Avenue U on the south end of Seaside. This is a 9 hole, par 35 golf course along the Necanicum River. It consists of three par 3, four par 4, two par 5 holes.

Hiking

Seaside offers miles of flat beach excellent for hiking. Head north toward the mouth of the Necanicum River where the estuary offers glimpses of sea birds, herons and other wildlife such as elk, otter, and beaver.

Tillamook Head Recreation Trail, 6 miles one way to Ecola State Park. On January 8, 1806, William Clark and members of the Lewis and Clark expedition traveled a perilous trail across Tillamook Head. You can to but the going is a little easier now. The trail over Tillamook head is part of the Oregon Coast Trail system, passing by stands of old growth Sitka spruce and containing several viewpoints. The Tillamook Lighthouse can be seen from Lookout Point. A word of caution however, wear good hiking boots as the trail can be wet and slippery—even in August.

Getting there from Hwy. 101, turn west on Avenue U, drive to Edgewood Street and turn left. It will turn into Sunset Blvd. Pass "The Cove" and watch the many surfers catching the waves. There are picnic tables at the cove. Continue on Sunset Blvd. past some spectacular homes to the top where there is a parking area at the trailhead. It is marked 6 miles to Indian Beach at Ecola State Park but some views of the ocean can be had by only hiking 4.5 miles (elevation gain=880 feet) to the top of Tillamook Head and returning back down to the trailhead instead of going to Ecola State Park. This way you won't have to go all the way down and back up again.

Sunset Beach to Gearhart; 6 miles one way, drive 5 miles north of Gearhart on Hwy. 101 and turn left at the sign for Sunset Beach. Drive past the golf course until you reach the ocean in about 1 mile. There is limited parking. Walk south on the smooth, wide beach toward Tillamook Head, the hill jutting out into the ocean up ahead. At 6 miles the hike ends at the mouth of the Necanicum River. Turn around and return to Sunset Beach.

Local History/Museums/Lighthouse

The Seaside Museum and Historical Society, 570 Necanicum Drive, (503) 738-7065, is a small museum with information about the indians and Lewis and Clark.

The Butterfield Cottage is right next door and admission to the museum gets you a tour of this house. It is reported to be the first cottage built in Seaside by the Butterfields in 1893, jewelers from Portland who used it as a summer home. In those days, Mom and the kids spent the summers at the beach and the "Daddy trains" would bring the breadwinners to visit their families on Fridays and return them to their jobs in Portland on Sunday. It was moved from its original site to be next to the museum and has many examples of the furnishings and clothing of the time.

Tillamook Rock Lighthouse was built in 1880 on a 3/4-acre island one mile offshore of Tillamook Head. This retired lighthouse now serves as a federal wildlife refuge for nesting sea birds and can be viewed from Ecola State Park near Cannon Beach or at the viewpoint along the Tillamook Head Trail.

This lovely little covered bridge near Yachats was built in 1938 and is one of the shortest in the state.

Photo Opportunities

- The Prom, the boardwalk along the ocean at Seaside
- Tillamook Head, at the top
- The Cove on Sunset Blvd.

Restaurants/Espresso

Pacific Way Bakery and Cafe, $$, Cottage and Pacific Way, Gearhart, (503) 738-0245. Open 7 a.m.-7 p.m. all year Thurs.-Mon. for breakfast, lunch, dinner. Smoke-free. The only restaurant in downtown Gearhart, it has the best pastries and breads on the Northern Oregon Coast. Dreyers ice cream and espresso also. Lisa Allen bakes all the pastries and breads using her own recipes since 1988. Be forewarned though, her pastries sell out by 11 a.m. in the summer.

For a really elegant and sumptuous meal, this is the best restaurant around. Walking up to the restaurant you are swept along by the heady smells of herbs and fresh food cooking. Inside you will find a pleasant nostalgic decor with great service and food. They also have the most innovative pizza menu—how about Thai chicken pizza, marinated chicken, green onions, sweet peppers, cilantro, and spicy peanut sauce. Don't forget to try the tempting sweets like Belgian chocolate truffle torte or cappuccino cheesecake.

The Stand, $, 220 Avenue U, Seaside, (503) 738-6592. Open Mon-Sat for lunch and dinner. A small cafe with great, inexpensive Mexican food. The custom veggie burritos are especially tasty and huge. You can request black beans instead of pintos.

Dooger's Seafood & Grill, $$, 505 Broadway, Seaside, (503) 738-8108. Open for lunch and dinner. Good friendly service, with great seafood. Smoke-free. It's so good there may be a line outside on summer weekends.

Pig 'N Pancake, $, 323 Broadway, 738-7243. Open early. The place to go for breakfast in Seaside.

Valerie's, $, an espresso bar at the Inn at the Shore, 2275 S. Prom/Ave. U, Seaside, (503) 738-8430. This is a cozy spot with a little patio right next to the beginning of the promenade in a quiet part of Seaside. You can sit and enjoy the ocean and relax. They are open daily at 7 a.m. and have seagull food, chips, pastries, juices, herb teas, soda, espresso, and a book lending library.

Wildlife Viewing

Estuary Park at the mouth of the Necanicum River (Holiday Dr. across from the high school) has a viewing platform and steps that take you down to the river. Keep your eyes open for great blue heron, elk, beaver, or otters.

Section 4: RV Parts & Services from Astoria to Seaside

Diesel

Astoria: Corky's 4 Way Stop, 1180 Pacific Drive, Hammond, (503) 861-2088. This is the closest location from Fort Stevens Campground located at the 4 way stop north of the campground entrance, intersection of Pacific Dr. and Lake Dr. Access to the pumps and propane is good with no overhead structures.

Astoria: Youngs Bay Texaco, 490 W. Marine Drive, Astoria, (503) 325-9274. This station is on the north side of the street in Astoria west of the Astoria bridge to Washington. It has the widest in and out access of the listed stations. It also has a car wash large enough to handle RV rigs.

Astoria: Val's Shell, 452 W. Marine Drive, Astoria, (503) 325-8131. This station is on the north side of the street in Astoria west of the Astoria bridge to Washington. They have both propane and diesel with good access.

Astoria: Carmichael Chevron, 510 Marine Dr., Astoria, (503) 325-0605. This station is located in the heart of Astoria at the intersection of 6th and Hwy. 30. Access in and out for a large rig is adequate.

Seaside: Trucke's 1 Stop, 1921 Hwy. 101, 738-8863. No overhead obstructions. Access adequate.

Dump Station

Astoria: A free dump station is provided by the town of Astoria. It is located exactly at **milepost 97** on Hwy. 30, east side of town next to the Sentry grocery store. The entrance is at 33rd street. The dump location is between the road and the side of the grocery store. Turn off the road at the west end of the grocery store, then make an immediate right to the dump. The best way to exit is to turn left and loop around the Sentry parking lot exiting back onto Hwy. 30 from the east lane of the parking lot.

Seaside: Free dump located behind the visitors center, Hwy. 101 & Broadway. Do not turn into the visitor's center entrance. Turn in at the dump sign located north of the visitors center on Hwy. 101. Wide entrance and RV pull-through parking is available as well as the city provided dump station.

Library

Astoria Library, 450 10th St., (503) 325-7323. Open Tues.-Sat. A very nice library with two stories of cataloged books. A large selection of periodicals is available with comfy chairs for reading on the main level.

Seaside Library, 60 N. Roosevelt (Hwy. 101) & 1st Street, (503) 738-6742. Open 6 days a week, closed Mondays. You can read local and Portland newspapers, periodicals, books. Visitor membership available $5 for one month. Books, audio books, current movie videos are available to check out.

Laundry

Astoria: Clean Services Coin Laundry, 823 W. Marina Dr., (503) 325-2027, open 7 days, attendant

Seaside: Holladay Coin Laundry, 57 N. Holladay Dr., (503) 738-3458, self-serve, free TV, large washers

Medical

Astoria: Columbia Memorial Hospital, 211 Exchange, (503) 325-4321. 24-hour emergency care

Seaside: Providence Seaside Hospital, 725 S. Wahanna Rd., (503) 738-8463. 24-hour emergency care

Propane

Astoria/Warrenton/Seaside KOA, 1100 NW Ridge Road, Hammond, OR 97121, (503) 861-2606

Astoria: Val's Shell, 452 W. Marine Drive, Astoria, (503) 325-8131

Hammond: Corkys 4 Way Stop, 1180 Pacific Drive, Hammond, (503) 861-2088.

Seaside: Suburban Propane, junction Hwy. 101 & Hwy. 26, (503) 738-6206, (800) 404-6206. Parts and repair. Take frontage road at Cannon Beach Lumber just north of the junction. Open M-F, 8-5. Lots of space for parking and turn around.

Seaside: Del's Chevron, 1215 S. Holladay; intersection Holladay and Hwy. 101, (503) 738-3651.

RV Parts & Service

Astoria: Skipanon Marine & RV Supply, 69 NE Heron, Warrenton, (503) 861-3626. They are the full-service parts and RV services for the north coast. They carry a large supply of all types of RV parts.

Seaside: RV Supplies & Parts, HWI Coast Center Hardware, 1217 Hwy. 101, (503) 738-5491, on the south end of Seaside carries a good stock of RV parts and supplies.

Shopping/Groceries

Astoria: Youngs Bay Plaza (At Warrenton across the Youngs Bay Bridge) Fred Meyer One-Stop Shopping, Costco, Lamont's, Shilo Inn Restaurant

Seaside: Shopping Mall at Broadway & Hwy. 101 has Safeway (accepts credit cards, open 7 days, 6 a.m.-midnight, deli, bakery, videos, ATM, McDonald's, Lazerquick

USPO

Astoria Post Office: 748 Commercial St., 97103 (503) 325-2141
Seaside Post Office: 300 Avenue A, 97138 (503) 738-5462

Chapter 5

Cannon Beach to Pacific City

Map Grid A2: Cannon Beach to Pacific City

Introduction

This stretch of the coast begins with the shops and galleries of sophisticated Cannon Beach and ends with the lush, green dairy farming fields of Tillamook and Sandlake. Quite a contrast. Cannon Beach is an artsy, small beach town packed with galleries and shops to browse. The town is very well kept with colorful flowers blooming everywhere in season. It is a strolling town with lots of benches for resting along Hemlock Street as you spend your day and your money. Long known as an artists colony, this special town is known for its blend of sophistication. Cannon Beach got its name when a cannon from a Navy survey schooner, *USS Shark*, washed ashore in 1846 and was salvaged.

The big scenic attraction here is Haystack Rock and the wide sandy beaches to be walked. Haystack Rock, a protected marine garden, is a photographer's delight against the sunsets. At low tide, there are approximately nine miles of walkable beach, from Ecola Park on the north to Falcon Cove to the south. The climate in Cannon Beach is mild year-round, with normally over 300 frost-free days. Normal rainfall is about 76 inches per year. Average temperature in Jauary is 36°-49°, July 51°-67°.

South of Cannon Beach is Tillamook County where you will find 22,000 people and 40,000 cows. That should tell you that the atmosphere there is much more laid back than Cannon Beach. A word of warning—the campgrounds can get very busy when the salmon or steelhead are running. September and February seem to be the busiest. Be sure to get your reservations in early for campgrounds in this grid.

Expect an outdoor recreation wonderland in this area. You will see rugged coastal headlands, and enjoy beachcombing along the placid beaches, or you might even catch a Chinook salmon in Tillamook or Nehalem Bay. You can take a short hike to the highest waterfall in the coast range, or a leisurely auto tour along the Three Capes Scenic Route. Enjoy this diverse area.

Section 1: Best Campgrounds from Cannon Beach to Tillamook Area

Best Public Campgrounds

Best public campground with full or partial hookups

Cape Lookout State Park, open all year, Netarts Bay, (503) 842-4981, reservations (800) 452-5687, p. 55

Alternate: Nehalem Bay State Park, open all year, Nehalem, (503) 368-5943, reservations (800) 452-5687, p. 54

Seagull resting at Indian Beach day-use area in Ecola State Park.

Best public campground for solitude and scenic beauty

Cape Lookout State Park, open all year, Netarts, (503) 842-4981, reservations (800) 452-5687, p. 55

Alternate: Whalen Island County Park (Tillamook County), open all year, Sand Lake, (503) 322-3477, p. 56

Best public campground for base camping

Barview Jetty County Park, Garibaldi, open all year, (503) 322-3522, p. 55

Best public campground for families with children

Nehalem Bay State Park, open all year, Nehalem, (503) 368-5943, reservations (800) 452-5687, p. 54

Best Private Campgrounds

Best private campground with luxurious facilities

RV Resort at Cannon Beach, open all year, Cannon Beach, (503) 436-2231, or (800) 847-2231, p. 54

Best private campground with Good Sam discount

Tillamook Bay City RV Park, open all year, Tillamook, (503) 377-2124, p. 55

Best private campground for solitude and scenic beauty

Bay Shore RV Park, open all year, Netarts, (503) 842-7774, p. 55

Beach strollers admire the famous Haystack Rock at Cannon Beach.

Best private campground for base camping

Bay Shore RV Park, open all year, Netarts, (503) 842-7774, p. 55

Campgrounds Descriptions

Cannon Beach

RV Resort at Cannon Beach, P.O. Box 219, Cannon Beach, (503) 436-2231 or (800) 847-2231). Open all year, Good Sam discount, AAA

Location: At Cannon Beach, east of Hwy. 101, near Pacific Ocean. Southbound on Hwy. 101. take second Cannon Beach exit (East)

Description: One of the nicest landscaped and best facilities in a private park with lots of shade. RV Resort at Cannon Beach—gorgeous but spendy. This private park is right behind the downtown area of Cannon Beach. The park has lots of trees, play equipment for the kids, large swimming pool, spa, and recreation room with big screen TV and games. The biggest advantage to this park is the close proximity to Cannon Beach. You can walk to the downtown area or the beach from the park or take the free Cannon Beach shuttle van which stops at the park daily every hour.

There are 100 sites with full hookups, (30/50 amp), 11 pull-thrus, 11 acres, max. length 60', $33.00 summer, $22.00 winter, lower weekly, monthly rates off season, dump, cable TV, restrooms, showers, security, phone, laundry, groceries, propane, indoor heated pool & spa, rec hall, game room, activities, playground, rec field, convenience store and gift shop, gasoline, diesel.

Nehalem

Nehalem Bay State Park, 8300 3rd St., Manzanita, (503) 368-5943, reservations (800) 452-5687). Open all year

Location: South of Manzanita off Hwy. 101, on Nehalem Bay Spit. Take Hwy. 101 south of Manzanita to the Bayshore Junction (Texaco on the corner) and follow the signs to the park.

Description: On the Pacific Ocean just on the other side of a sheltering dune, sites are on a flat, grassy plain with plenty of beach pines for privacy. Great place for bike riding and hiking. Lots of wide, flat sandy beaches for the kids to play on. Short trails up and over the dunes to the beach, bike trails, beachcombing, good crabbing, clamming or fishing on the bay.

284 partial hookups sites, (30 amp), 890 acres, gray water cones, dump, max. length 50', $19.00 daily rate with lower off-season rates, restrooms, showers, camp host, phone, horse camping, summer planned activities, playground.

Garibaldi

Barview Jetty County Park, Cedar St., Garibaldi, (503) 322-3522. Open all year

Location: On the jetty at Tillamook Bay at Barview. One mile south of Rockaway Beach, turn right at Cedar St. and follow signs.

Description: Nice spacious open park near the ocean with good facilities and restaurants nearby.

285 sites on a large grassy area right next to the jetty. 60 sites with full hookups, (30/50 amps), 13 pull-thrus, max. length 45', $18.00 night for full hookup, $14.00 no hookups, restrooms w/showers, dump, phone, restaurant across street. Handicap accessible.

Tillamook

Tillamook Bay City RV Park, on the east side of Hwy. 101, **milepost 61.5**, (503) 377-2124. Open all year

Location: Three miles north of Tillamook on the east side of Hwy. 101

Description: 46 sites in a well taken care of park. This is a good stopover as it is right on Hwy. 101, but you may want to consider road noise in your decision.

30 full-hookup sites, (30/50 amp), 16 tent sites, 15 pull-thrus, max. length 60', daily rate $18.50 for full hookups, lower weekly rate, GS, restrooms, showers, cable TV, phone, laundry

Netarts

Cape Lookout State Park, 13000 Whiskey Creek Rd., Netarts, (503) 842-4981, reservations (800) 452-5687. Open all year

Location: On Netarts Bay Spit, a 5-mile-long breakwater for the bay. From Hwy. 101 at Tillamook, take the Netarts Highway. (Three Capes Tour) and follow the signs for Cape Lookout State Park.

Description: One of our all-time favorite parks on the coast. It must be everyone else's too because reservations are almost mandatory during the summer for weekend camping. Camp sites are either right on the ocean with no cover or in tall dense woods of Douglas fir and Sitka spruce. Located on the Netarts sand spit at the base of the cape, there's plenty to do here both for hiking enthusiasts or those who prefer just strolling along the ocean. Great facilities and great views. What more could you want?

250 sites, 1,946 acres, 50 full hookups, (30 amp), max. length 50', $16.00-$20.00 daily rate with lower off-season rates, restrooms, showers, dump, camp host, phone, planned activities in summer, playground, hiking trails.

Bay Shore RV Park & Marina, P.O. Box 218, Netarts, (503) 842-7774. Open all year

Location: On the Three Capes Scenic Drive in a quiet area on Netarts Bay with a great view. From Hwy. 101 in Tillamook, travel west 5.8 miles on Netarts Hwy. to Bilyeu Ave., turn left and go 1 mile past the junction for Cape Lookout.

Description: Located near the sleepy town of Netarts, Bay Shore RV Park is in a nice quiet fishing area right on Netarts Bay. You can watch the fishermen go out on one of the most pristine bays in Oregon or rent a boat and try your luck. If you stay here be sure to take the short 3-mile drive to Oceanside for lunch, dinner, or dessert at Roseanna's. Good food with a dynamite view of the ocean.

53 full hookups (30 amp), 6 pull-thrus, max. length 45', daily rate $18.50, 7th night free, restrooms w/showers, cable TV, phone, restaurant nearby, propane, laundry, boat rentals, boat ramp, dock, marina, rentals, crabbing, clamming, fishing, crab cooker.

Sand Lake

Whalen Island Park, Tillamook County, (503) 322-3477. Open all year

Location: On the Sand Lake Estuary among pastoral farming fields. From Tillamook, drive 7 miles south on Hwy. 101 take the Sand Lake exit, pass the store and go 2 miles ahead, turn right at brown tent camping sign. Eight acres surrounded on three sides by the Sand Lake Estuary 4.5 miles north of Cape Kiwanda on the Three Capes Scenic Loop.

Description: This park is out of the way and a little hard to find but for scenic beauty, it's worth it. It's not fancy (no hookups) but the setting is lovely and peaceful. Campsites are anywhere you can pull off on the grass. Located in a quiet farming area right on the edge of Sand Lake. (The ATVers are on the other side of the lake). Because the park is located in a sleepy rural area, this is a nice place to get away from it all. This would be a great place for fishing, canoeing or birdwatching. Shore birds and bald eagles are a common sight.

40 open grassy sites with tables, some shaded, no hookups, max. length 45', dump, camp host, daily rate: $10.00, restrooms, water. Approximately five of the sites could accommodate larger RVs but will require some leveling.

Volunteer/Camp Host Opportunities

State Parks

Nehalem Bay State Park, (503) 368-5943
Cape Lookout State Park, (503) 842-4981
Tillamook County Parks, Park Host Program, (503) 322-3477
Nehalem Fish Hatchery, Nehalem, (503) 368-6828
Trask Fish Hatchery, Tillamook, (503) 842-4090

Section 2: Activities in Cannon Beach area

Be prepared to shop, browse galleries and eat in Cannon Beach. If enjoying nature is your preference, go to nearby Ecola State Park to provide contrast to the bustle of Hemlock St. Relax by walking along the beach to view Haystack Rock and at low tide view the many sea creatures in the protected tidepools. Cannon Beach has it all—the tourist trip and nature lover's walks.

Don't Miss

- Ecola State Park and hike to Indian Beach
- Haystack Rock and the tide pools

Highly Recommended

- Stroll along the galleries and shops in Cannon Beach

Biking

Mike's Bike Shop, 248 N. Spruce St., (503) 436-1266. Rent 3-wheelers or mountain bikes.

Manzanita Fun Merchants, 1140 S. Hemlock, (503) 436-1880, features 3-wheel tricycles for rent which are for use on the sand. They also have mountain. bikes and strollers, complementary trailers for toddlers, hours vary with the tide. Call first.

There is a nice wide, flat bike path along both sides of S. Hemlock St. in Tolovana that has light traffic.

Bookstores

Cannon Beach Book Company, 132 N. Hemlock, (503) 436-1301, is a large bookstore with an extensive collection of books and a nice browsing atmosphere.

Ecola Square Books, 123 S. Hemlock, upstairs, Ecola Square, (503) 436-0805, children's books and a very good selection of Northwest regional guides.

Exercise Routes or Leisure Walking

Along the beach north or south from Tolovana Beach Wayside Park
North or south from Haystack Rock at Cannon Beach

Family Activities with Children

Tolovana Beach Wayside, at the south end of Hemlock St. in Tolovana, is a great place for beach access, picnic tables, benches, children's playground, and public restrooms, handicap access. There are great views of Haystack Rock and the Needles. Easy access in and out for RVs.

Cannon Beach City Park is located at 2nd & Spruce by the Chamber of Commerce. It has picnic tables, playground, tennis courts, basketball, rollerblade and skateboard areas, softball and soccer fields available for public use. This is also the location for Sunday afternoon concerts in the summer. The best RV parking is at the east end of 2nd Street.

Arcadia Park is south of town on Hwy. 101. It is a state beach access wayside with parking, rest rooms, picnic tables, and a short trail to a scenic beach in a beautiful little cove. It's a great place for children to explore the tidepools and beachcomb. The small turnaround is not recommended for large RVs.

Hug Point, south of Arcadia Park, is named for the action people take when walking the beach path (hugging the cliff). Low tide is your only time to make it around safely. Parking and restrooms available. You can explore tidal caves, hike to a small waterfall, and view what's left of the old roadbed. Not recommended for RVs—no turnaround in parking area.

Les Shirley Park, downtown Cannon Beach, end of 5th street has interpretive signs explaining the estuary. A pretty park where the kids will like to play in shallow Elk Creek. It is tucked away in a more quiet corner of Cannon Beach.

Annual Events

Check with Cannon Beach Chamber of Commerce
207 N. Spruce St., (503) 436-2623, for specific dates

April
Puffin Kite Festival

June
Sand Castle Contest

July
Sunday Concerts in the Park) July 4-Labor Day)

November
Stormy Weather Festival

December
Lamplighting Ceremony
Christmas Train Ride
Coaster Theater, Dickens Festival

Exploring the caves and sandstone stacks on Hug Point near Cannon Beach where you have to "hug" the rock to pass around it.

Fishing

Try **Elk Creek** upstream for trout by hiking up the creek on the east side of Hwy. 101.
Necanicum River near Seaside

Galleries/Arts

White Bird, 251 N. Hemlock, (503) 436-2681, has a variety of arts & crafts
Haystack Gallery, 183 N. Hemlock, (503) 436-2547, features prints and photography
Jeffrey Hull Watercolors, 178 N. Hemlock, (503) 436-2600, has a collection of delicately brushed landscapes
The Oregon Gallery, 223 N. Hemlock (503) 436-0817, features stunning scenic photography by Ron Keebler, as well as many gift items.
Coaster Theater, 108 N. Hemlock, (503) 436-1242, has a variety of good summer plays and year-round entertainment

Hiking/Waterfalls

Ecola State Park. We do not recommend that RVs be driven up to Ecola State Park. The road sustained much damage in the February 1996 storms and many parts of the road are one lane only and very rough. Located north of Cannon Beach, the park offers some of the most spectacular views of the Oregon Coast. There are breathtaking high views of Cannon Beach's Haystack Rock with row upon row of coast range mountains fading into the background.
Indian Beach Trail takes you up to catch a look at the Tillamook Rock Lighthouse and an old army bunker. The trail is marked 2 miles long but don't let that scare you as there are great views just 1/2 mile up. This is a good graveled trail with a few slippery spots. Wear your hiking boots. This is the south end of the Tillamook Head Recreation Trail that starts in Seaside.

Hike for miles along the wide, flat sandy beaches from Elk Creek to Tolovana Wayside and beyond.

Oswald West State Park, south of Hug Point and named after one of our governors, has three hiking trails through lovely old growth. Picnic tables, primitive campsites

(walk-in) and public restrooms are available. A short hike takes you to Short Sands Beach, a beautiful and secluded cove.
Hug Point, south of Arcadia Park. Walk north and you will pass by a cliff where Pigeon Guillemots may be seen in April. The second cove north has a small waterfall and large caves for exploring. The next cliff is Hug Point where a road was blasted in the rock in the early 1900s just wide enough for a Model T to drive through so they wouldn't get stuck in the sand.

Local History/Museums

"Historical House", Sunset & Spruce St., (503) 436-9301, is open to the public where visitors may view artifacts, old photos, and audiovisuals of long-time area residents.

Photo Opportunities

- Ecola State Park, from Indian Beach trail, and day-use area
- Haystack Rock, morning or sunset
- Hug Point State Park, the caves and waterfall
- Tolovana Beach Wayside, Tolovana
- Wildlife viewing platform at the east end of 2nd Street.

Restaurants/Espresso/Bakery

Note: Some restaurants close on Tuesday or Wednesday in Cannon Beach.

Brady's Cannon Beach Bakery, $, 144 N. Hemlock, (503) 436-2592, bake their treats in one of the few remaining brick hearth ovens on the West Coast. This is the place for mouth-watering desserts or bread. Open daily, closed Tuesday.
Doogers Seafood & Grill, $$, 1371 S. Hemlock, (503) 436-2225, is always a great place for seafood and chowder
Morris' Fireside Restaurant, $$, 257 N. Hemlock, (503) 436-2917, in a hand-hewn log building, open daily from 8 a.m. to 8 p.m. A good choice for breakfast, lunch or a great seafood dinner. They have an extensive breakfast menu and servings are large. The one place in Cannon Beach you can count on to be open every single day.
Midtown Cafe, $, 1235 S. Hemlock, (503) 436-1016, is famous for their burritos as well as soups and salads. Excellent homemade light fare. The best breakfast place. Breakfast and lunch Wed.-Sat., 7 a.m.-3 p.m.
Lazy Susan Cafe, $, 126 N. Hemlock, (503) 436-2816. Try breakfast for omelets, waffles with fresh fruit and good home-fries. Wonderful smells and cozy atmosphere. Charming place—best for breakfast.
The Homegrown Cafe, $, 3301 S. Hemlock, (503) 436-1803, is a smoke-free, vegetarian restaurant. Opened in January 19, 96 by Rebecca O'Day (from New Mexico), it has a real homey atmosphere with a lovely outdoor deck. Rebecca is an excellent cook and, along with her daughter, presents food that is picture perfect. Open for breakfast, lunch, or dinner. Checks and cash only.
Fultano's Pizza, $, 200 N. Hemlock, (503) 436-9717, has a 30 item salad bar, pizza, calzone, subs, and pasta, take out. Open daily.
Heather's Cafe, $, 271 N. Hemlock, (503) 436-9356, a tiny cafe tucked in a nice quiet setting at the north end of Cannon Beach is a grand place for dinner on the veranda or just a rich espresso. Good salads and homemade soups. Try their Sopa De Lime soup. "Top-drawer eats", says the *Oregonian.* Closed Wed. and Thurs. Checks and cash only.
Pig N' Pancake, $, open in 1997, S. Hemlock St. Always a good place for a huge selection of breakfast fare.
Espresso, The Local Scoop, $, 156 S. Hemlock, (503) 436-9551. A light, airy, smoke-free place for ice cream, soups, sandwiches, burgers and lite fare menu. Eat indoors or on their outdoor deck. Open daily from 7 a.m.

Playing in the surf at Indian Beach, Ecola State Park.

Special Local Attractions

There is a free shuttle that runs daily every 30 minutes that goes north and south from Cannon Beach to Tolovana and stops at many different points. The shuttle is an all year environmentally friendly van which runs on natural gas and meets ADA specifications. It also includes a bike rack. Park your RV at the end of 2nd St. and take the bus. Sunday concerts in the Cannon Beach City Park occur from the 4th of July through Labor Day sponsored by the Cannon Beach Arts Association.

Wildlife Viewing

Haystack Rock is one of 1400 sites in the Oregon Islands Wildlife Refuge. Puffins, pelagic cormorants, pigeon guillemots and the western gull all nest there. Puffins arrive in April and stay until early August. Walk north toward Chapman Point and you may see brown pelicans flying along the shore looking for fish. At the Ecola Creek Estuary, herons, waterfowl and dippers are birds you may see. Go further toward Chapman Point and you may see (in season) the largest single colony of common murres in the world.
Cannon Beach's innovative sewage ponds use natural processes to filter water after primary treatment. Here, you may find green backed herons, pileated woodpeckers, and in season, wood ducks, mallard, northern shovelers, ring-necked ducks, buffleheads, mergansers among others. Don Thompson Wastewater Treatment System, east end of 2nd St., wildlife viewing platform.
Ecola State Park is a good place to bring your binoculars to get a closer look at the sea lion and bird rookeries on the off-shore rocks. At the right time of year, you just might be lucky enough to sight migrating gray whales.

Ecola Point and Haystack Rock are great places for tidepooling. This is a marine garden refuge. Please leave all critters in the tidepools.

Section 3: Activities in Nehalem, Manzanita, and Wheeler

Manzanita, Nehalem, and Wheeler are three small towns in close proximity, each with their own distinctive qualities. Manzanita is situated south of Neahkahnie Mountain off Hwy. 101 with seven miles of beautiful beach. Indian legend has it that a Spanish galleon went aground here long before the white man settled the area. The ships crew brought their treasure from the grounded ship and buried it at the bottom of the 1,631-foot Neahkahnie Mountain—the mountain that the Indians called the "Home of the Gods". Manzanita is a quiet up-scale residential community featuring fine restaurants.

Nehalem, perhaps a Salish Indian name for "where people live", is on the Nehalem River—famous for its salmon fishing. Hwy. 101 is its main street with three blocks of shops. Wheeler is two miles south on the Nehalem Bay where fishing, crabbing, and clamming abound.

Don't Miss

•See **Nehalem Bay** and the **Nehalem River** from the river. Rent a boat, canoe or kayak and take the easy route—high tide up river. Enjoy seeing waterfowl up close, sea lions in the bay, salmon (in season). On the river you will be floating through private farm land and woods enjoying the beauty unseen from the road.

Highly Recommended

•Stroll the **beach of Manzanita**. Hike the seven miles of beautiful beach, or take a blanket and doze in the sun. When your stomach calls, choose one of several excellent eateries to satisfy your appetite.

Biking

Nehalem Bay State Park has 1.5 miles of improved bike paths as well as many interior roads that are suitable for bike riding. A great place to take the family for an afternoon of biking.

Pedal the Beach: Rent a three-wheeler from **Fun Merchants**, 186 Laneda Ave.,

Annual Events

Check with the Nehalem Bay Chamber of Commerce, 35850 8th Street, (503) 368-5100, for specific dates.

February
Duck Daze Festival

April
Easter Egg Hunt & Bunny Hop
Easter Bonnet Parade

May
Saturday Market & Spring Festival

June
Saturday Market & Summer Solstice Celebration

July
Annual 4th of July Parade
Nehalem Crafts Fair
Salmon Derby, Sat. Market & Street Fair

August
Nehalem Art Festival
Art & Antique Festival

September
Blackberry Festival

October
Octoberfest

November
Saturday Market & Turkey Shoot
Home for the Holiday Christmas Fair

December
Christmas Fair

Manzanita, (503) 368-6606, and ride the beach from Neahkahnie Mountain to Nehalem Bay.

Tideland Road: Catch Tideland Road, at the boat ramp on Hwy. 101 south of Nehalem. Ride your bike to the co-op grocery store on Hwy. 53 for ice cream. Return back on Tideland Road. 4 miles round-trip.

Foley Creek/Miami River Loop: For a 30-mile bike ride or auto tour loop, take Hwy. 101 to Garibaldi then turn onto the Miami River loop road winding back north to Mohler. The road ends in a T intersection (Hwy. 53). Turn left and follow Hwy. 53 south back to Hwy. 101.

Nehalem Bay State Park to Manzanita; Bike Carmel Street: Carmel St. in Manzanita connects with Laneda Ave. and parallels the ocean beaches to the south. This is a quiet residential street passing the golf course with the city park one block away. Ride this road from Nehalem Bay State Park campground into downtown Manzanita.

Bookstores

Pacific Coast Books & Coffee, 60 Laneda Ave., Manzanita, (503) 368-2665, new and unique paperback books. A great place to drink an espresso and browse through a book on their deck.

Joanne's Bookshelf, 387 Laneda Ave., Manzanita, (503) 368-6311, used paperback books only.

Family Activities with Children

Short Sands Beach

Picnic at **Short Sand Beach** north of Manzanita. Explore the hidden cove, the shallow caves and tide pools at low tide. This beach is accessible only by foot, keeping the crowds small. It is a beautiful 1/2-mile walk through rain forest, giant salal and ferns. Drive to the larger parking area for Oswald West State Park campground and park east of Hwy. 101. Take the path under the highway to the beach.

Manzanita City Park

Take a break at **Manzanita's city park**; basketball, tennis, horseshoes, playground, covered picnic tables, volleyball, restrooms. From Laneda Ave. take 3rd Street south to the park on Pacific Ave. A quiet gem of a park tucked away from the main street bustle.

Fishing/Clamming

Nehalem Bay is a popular destination for Oregonians with cravings for seafood. Clams can be dug throughout the bay and mud flats at low tide. Crabbing is done from a boat (rentals available) all year with fall being the best season. Make sure you read and understand the regulations for limits and gender.

Bay fishing is good for perch and flounder. Salmon and steelhead can be caught in the bay and Nehalem River from August through November.

The following locations provide services for fishing, clamming, or boating:

Wheeler Marina, 278 Marine Dr., Wheeler, OR 97147, (503) 368-5780. On Nehalem Bay, Jim and Margie Neilson operate a full-service marina. Rent boats and canoes, purchase licenses, rent fishing gear, crabbing gear, clamming gear, crab cooking, full line of bait.

For the stream angler, take Hwy. 53 north until you reach the Nehalem Fish Hatchery (between **milepost** 7 and **8**). Turn in and park following the signs. Well-worn trails will lead you to the the fishing spots on the stream below the hatchery. You will find lots of company here in the salmon and steelhead seasons. While there, don't miss the water cascades over the cliff on the opposite side of the river.

The beautiful Nehalem River has fishermen hoping to catch a salmon.

Exercise Route or Leisure Walking

Nehalem Bay State Park, walk the 1.5-mile bike path through the dunes or take any of the several bridle paths throughout Nehalem Bay State Park. Alternate with leisurely walks along the beach. Beachcomb for treasures washed onshore: driftwood, agates.

Golfing

Manzanita Golf Course, Lake View Dr., Manzanita, (503) 368-5744, 9 hole, par 32, five par 4 holes and four par 3 holes. Reservations recommended. Driving green, putting range, all the amenities including renting of golf clubs.

Hiking

Neahkahnie Mountain Trail is a complete loop (4.5 miles) through coastal rain forest. Completing the loop requires walking Hwy. 101 for .5 mile. To and from the peak of Neahkahnie hikers see views of the ocean as well as meadows of coastal grasses and flowers. Keep your eyes open for elk grazing on the slopes. Drive 10 miles south of Cannon Beach to a shoulder parking area one mile beyond Oswald West State Park campground.

It is a 1,200-foot elevation gain from the north to the peak in three miles and an 890-foot elevation gain from the south in 1.5 miles. The south hike is the easiest way up for those not wishing to do a loop. The south ascent starts .5 miles further at **milepost 41.5**. Watch for a hikers sign. Turn east on a rocky gravel road for .5 miles to the trailhead.

Oswald West State Park: Hikers may choose one of three trails from this trailhead.

Cape Falcon Trail: Oswald West State Park north parking lot east of Hwy. 101, south of **milepost 39**. Trailhead is at the north end of the parking lot going under Hwy. 101 in a culvert. It is a five-mile round-trip to the tip of Cape Falcon. A moderate hike, elevation gain of 300 feet. Carry binoculars for whale watching. A trip through coastal forest to a treeless wind-swept cape. At the cape, take the spur trail headed west through a tunnel of salal to reach the top of Cape Falcon and majestic views.

View of the wetlands from the waterfowl viewing deck in Cannon Beach.

An alternative 1.2-mile round-trip hike is to take the Cape Falcon trail but turn and descend to Short Sand beach for beachcombing and then return.

Nehalem Bay State Park trails: There are multiple improved trails from the parking lot or from the campground to the beach, all interconnecting, that a family with young children may choose. Stop at the entrance booth and ask for a map showing the various trails in the park.

Photo Opportunities

- Multiple turnouts on Hwy. 101 north of Neahkahnie Mountain provide awesome beach and ocean views
- Nehalem River from Nehalem and the bridge

Restaurants/Espresso

Hill House Deli, $$, 12870 Hwy. 101, Nehalem, OR 97131, (503) 368-7933. Your first impression may be that this is strictly a coffee house. Look again. Once inside, you'll discover a wonderfully varied menu in a light and cozy cafe, sofas in the library, and seating on a garden patio. There are healthy choices of sandwiches and soups for lunch. Dinner is served only on Wednesday nights along with live music that ranges from classical to jazz. The small parking lot is limited to small vehicles only. RVs may park a block down in the graveled area at the bottom of the hill. We highly recommend a stop at Hill House as you tour Nehalem.

Manzanita Beach Fireside Cafe, $, 114 Laneda Ave., Manzanita, (503) 368-1001, a small 12 table cafe specializing in American home cooking. This cafe features a child's menu and dinner specials every day of the week. It is probably the best choice for a family with children.

Queen Bess Tea Room, $$$, 411 Laneda Ave., Manzanita, (503) 368-4225. Expensive, yes, but worth if for that special occasion. A bit of Olde England, and locally recognized as the finest in dining. You must make reservations for high tea in the afternoon.

Blue Sky Cafe, $$, 154 Laneda, Manzanita, (503) 368-5712. A small smoke-free cafe with some of the most unusual (and good) global dishes. Try some of their fresh fish dishes. Dinner 5:30. Open daily in summer. No credit cards.
Cassandra's Pizza, 60 Laneda, Manzanita, (503) 368-5593. Wonderful pizzas and pasta specials.

Special Local Attractions

Nehalem Bay Winery, 34965 Hwy. 53, Nehalem, (503) 368-wine, one mile off Hwy. 101 on Hwy. 53 between Nehalem and Wheeler. Housed in a European-style cross-timbered building is their tasting room (they do not actually make wine here). The winery has a pig roast BBQ several weekends during the summer which includes theatrical performances. Call for dates and times.

Wildlife Viewing

Kayak the Nehalem Bay. Rent a kayak from Annie's Kayaks in Wheeler, 487 Hwy. 101, (503) 368-6055.
Try **Nehalem Bay State Park south jetty** for spotting waterfowl, harbor seals, Roosevelt elk.

Section 4: Activities in Tillamook Area

(includes north to Rockaway Beach and Three Capes Scenic Route, south to Pacific City)

In this grid, you are in the heart of Tillamook County, one of the most fertile and productive dairy areas around. There are four bays in this area—Tillamook, Netarts, Nehalem, and Nestucca. Fishing here for salmon is very popular with boats bobbing like corks everywhere in season, especially near Tillamook Bay because of the easy access.

The Three Capes Scenic Loop can be driven or biked and shows off the Oregon Coast at its best with broad beaches and mighty headlands. You will have left the sophisticated setting of places like Cannon Beach and entered a world that is more laid back and geared toward exploring nature. Tillamook County's brochure says "Welcome to the slow lane" and it's true, life is delightfully slower here.

Tillamook came from the early Indians tribal name (Killamooks meaning "people of the land of many waters"). Indeed it is, with seventy miles of coastline, four bays, and seven rivers. It is the center of Tillamook County's thriving dairy industry. But Tillamook is also a major recreation center offering boating, fishing, clamming, hiking, hang gliding, canoeing and of course all the cheese or ice cream you can eat at the Tillamook Cheese Factory. Temperature norms range from 32°-48° in January and 49°-75° in July. Annual precipitation is 73 inches.

Garibaldi is overshadowed by the Port of Garibaldi, a working waterfront with fish canneries, fish markets, seafood cafes, and no tourist attractions. Captain Robert Gray used the bay for safe harbor in 1792. Some believe that was the first American landing on the Oregon Coast.

Pacific City is home to the other Haystack Rock on the coast. This is also where you can see the dory fleet launch their boats directly into the surf from the sandy beach—a tradition that dates back to the 1920s. Cape Kiwanda overlooks the site of the dory launch and is popular with hang gliders.

Don't Miss

- Three Capes Scenic Loop
- Tillamook County Pioneer Museum

Highly Recommended

- Tillamook Cheese Factory
- Cape Meares Lighthouse and views

Bike/Auto Tours

(See Nehalem for Miami River Road loop, Nehalem to Garibaldi.)

Nestucca River Road. Beaver is the town which serves as the entry to the Nestucca River Road., and the Upper Nestucca Recreation Area which includes campgrounds, trails, and great fishing. The mostly paved road follows the river and is a great scenic drive for an afternoon. Stop at one of the campgrounds and have a picnic or wade in the river.

Three Capes Scenic Route, is not to be missed so plan a whole day to be able to really stop, get out of your vehicle and enjoy the beauty at all points along the way. Enjoy a scenic drive over Cape Kiwanda, Cape Lookout and Cape Meares. This route offers some ot the most spectacular views of Tillamook County's coastline.

Bookstores

Rainy Day Books, 2015 2nd, Tillamook, (503) 842-7766. Both new and used books are available in this spacious store.

Ecotourism

Coastal Mountain Tours, 8505 Pike Rd., Tillamook, (503) 842-1231, takes you on a scenic, historical, and informative tour of the Tillamook Forest. Tours begin at Tillamook Shilo Inn daily, morning and afternoon in a Chevrolet Suburban 4x4. Refreshments served. Admission charged.

Farm Tours, (503) 815-1300, is a farmer-guided tour that "explores" one of our local

Annual Events

Check with Tillamook Chamber of Commerce
3705 Hwy. 101 N., (503) 842-7525, for specific dates

January
Beachcombing and whale watching

February
Sweet Adelines Concert

March
Pacific Northwest Crab Races

April
Home & Garden Show
Easter Egg Hunts

May
Quilter's Show
Kite Festival

June
June Dairy Parade and Rodeo

July
Tillamook Bayberry Faire
Days Festival, Garibaldi

August
Tillamook County Fair
Blue Grass at the Beach
Arts & Crafts Fair, Rockaway Beach

September
Tillamook Motocross Racing
YMCA Auction & Ball, Tillamook
Fish Fry, Garibaldi
Sandcastle Contest, Garibaldi

October
Haunted Cave, Fairgrounds
Fishing Contest

December
Tillamook Christmas Celebration
Whale watching
Rockaway Beach, Old-Fashioned Christmas & Decoration Contest
Christmas Tree Express, Garibaldi

The sculptured sandstone cliffs at Cape Kiwanda are a favorite resting spot for seabirds.

independent dairy farms. Tours leave the Tillamook Cheese Factory daily at 3:00 p.m. between June 17 and August 31. Each tour lasts about an hour and a half. Admission charged and includes free ice cream cone.

Family Activities with Children

Cape Lookout State Park: See campgrounds for this area.

Cape Meares State Park: Cape Meares is 10 miles west of Tillamook and the far north end of the beautiful Three Capes Scenic Drive. It is a day-use area with picknicking spots, a lighthouse with tours, the Octupus Tree, trails, and views to knock your socks off. A photographer's paradise. Cape Meares Lighthouse was constructed in 1890 and guided ships for 73 years. It stands on a headland named after John Meares, an early seafaring explorer. There are many educational interpretive signs explaining the bird colonies that make their homes on Three Arch Rocks to the south. This is a very restful place to spend a few hours strolling the lush grounds enjoying the wide vista views of the ocean.

Fun Run Express, Garibaldi, (800) 685-1719 or (503) 355-8667, will begin operations again in 1997. Ride the train in a 28-mile round-trip of coastal beauty featuring views of Tillamook Bay and the Pacific Ocean. Final destination will be inside the one remaining WWII blimp hangar and admission to view many WWII airplanes and the history of the old Naval Air Station. The blimp hangar is the largest wooden span structure left in the world. Admission fee is charged. Call for schedule.

Lillian Goodspeed Park, 3rd. and Delmonte St., Tillamook, OR. This park has a large grassy area shaded by trees for picnics as well as a basketball court, tennis court, playground, and restrooms.

Fishing/Clamming

Jetty Fishery, 27550 Hwy. 101 N., Rockaway Beach, (503) 368-5746, 3 miles north of Rockaway Beach, bait, tackle, fishing licenses, and tags, boat rental, crab ring rental and bait, clam digging gear rental, dock crabbing, fish-cleaning station, crab boilers.

View of Netarts Bay Spit from Cape Lookout.

Garibaldi Marina, 302 Mooring Basin Road, Garibaldi, (503) 322-3312, is a good source of information as well as the place for rentals needed for a day of fishing, crabbing, or clamming.

The **Trask**, **Wilson**, and **Tillamook** rivers are famous for fishing, especially salmon in season.

Tillamook Tidewater Access, a favorite bank-fishing spot along the Tillamook River is located 2 miles west of Tillamook on the road to Netarts. This new facility is barrier-free and has bank angling in the tidal waters of the Tillamook River. Both spring and fall chinook along with white sturgeon, sea-run cutthroat trout and winter steelhead can be caught at this spot. There is a 140-foot-long wooden walkway elevated above the wetlands leading to a 15 X 60-foot angling pier and resting benches. For more infomation, call (503) 842-2741.

Golfing

Alderbrook Golf Course, 7300 Alderbrook Rd., Tillamook, OR 97141, (503) 842-6413. A par 69, eighteen-hole golf course. Alderbrook Road is at **milepost 61.5** on Hwy. 101. Turn east past Bay City RV Park and within blocks you will see the course on your left. This 5,692-yard course is beautifully laid out emphasizing vista views of the coastal range. It can be a heavily used course and reservations are highly recommended.

Bay Breeze Golf, 2325 Latimer Road, Tillamook, OR 97141, (503) 842-1166. This is a cute nine-hole, 1,061-yard, par 3 course in the town of Tillamook on Hwy. 101 N. The course includes an excellent driving range and putting green. Clubs are available for rent.

Hiking/Waterfalls

Cape Meares has a great section of the Oregon Coast trail as well as a paved walk down to the Cape Meares Lighthouse which is open to the public. Be sure to take your binoculars and look for sea lions and seals on the rocks below. Octopus tree: Follow a seacliff path from the Cape Mears lighthouse to the Octopus tree, a mixed-up Sitka spruce that branched into six separate trunks.

Cape Lookout has a great trail out to the end of the cape (a super whale watching location). It is an easy 5-mile round-trip hike from the campground. The trail passes through some beautiful coastal forests before it opens into a vista of the ocean. On a clear day, you can see north to Cape Foulweather. There is also a .25-mile self-guided nature trail that begins near the campground registration booth.

Munson Creek Falls is the highest waterfall in the coast range at 266 feet. This is a waterfall worth seeing. Take Hwy. 101 south from Tillamook for seven miles and look for the small brown sign pointing west for Munson Creek Falls County Park. Follow the signs 1.6 miles to the parking area and trailhead. The lower trail is easy and goes through a lush forest to the base of the falls. To get a more excellent view, hike the upper trail for .5 mile where you will see the Triple Horsetail Falls. (In 1996, this trail was blocked by tree limbs).

Hebo Lake Loop Trail is an easy, short trail that circles a tiny gem of a lake on Mt. Hebo just east of the town of Hebo. The trail is barrier-free and has many platforms for anyone to fish for stocked trout. Take Hwy. 22 east .12 miles from the junction with Hwy. 101 in Hebo to Forest Service Road 14. Travel 14.5 miles to Hebo Lake Campground.

Sandlake has lots of dunes to explore and you can watch the many ATVs zooming over the Sahara of the Oregon Coast.

Local History/Museums/Lighthouses

Tillamook County Pioneer Museum, 2106 Second Street, Tillamook, OR, (503) 842-4553. This plain museum, founded in 1935, is easily passed up if the visitor does not look inside. Walk up to the entrance and open the door and you will immediately be struck by the extensive displays. Give yourself two hours to view the three levels of over 35,000 artifacts. While viewing the museum we heard pre-teens declaring "awesome" and seniors saying "unbelievable". You will be doing the same as you move room to room viewing wildlife displays, pioneer home life displays, early vehicles, and much more. Hours 8:00 to 5:00, Mon.-Sat., 12:00 to 5:00 on Sunday. One of our favorite museums on the coast. Donations accepted.

Naval Air Station Museum, 6030 Hangar Road, Tillamook, OR 97141 (503) 842-1130. Visit the world's largest wooden free-span structure housing operational World War II aircraft. The structure was built to house eight K-series blimps used to patrol the West Coast during the war. Displays highlight the blimps' accomplishments during the war. Admission is charged to the museum.

Photo Opportunities

- Anywhere along the Three Capes Scenic Route

Restaurants/Espresso

Rockaway Beach

The Beach Pancake House, $$, 202 Hwy. 101 N., Rockaway Beach, (503) 355-2411, for breakfast, of course.

Oceanside

Roseanna's, $$, 1490 Pacific St., Oceanside (503) 842-7351, is a diner's surprise in the tiny town of Oceanside. It is a nice place to watch the ocean from almost every table as you sample some great desserts. Has a good menu selection. They have a nice outdoor deck. Open daily all year.

Pacific City

Grateful Bread Bakery, $$, 34805 Brooten Rd., Pacific City (503) 965-7337. The light from the large windows gives this place plenty of sunshine and a great view of the

Visitor admires Octopus Tree, the large Sitka spruce at Cape Meares that has been contorted by winds.

Nestucca River and Haystack Rock. Along with the wonderful atmosphere, the menu will delight and surprise you. The omelets are served all day and are hearty and innovative. Who would have expected it in this little town? There are almost too many exciting choices to choose from. Don't forget the bakery on premises. You might decide to eat here but take home a home-baked item also—the spinach/garlic bread was heaven. Open daily for breakfast, lunch, or dinner. We highly recommend this place.

Riverhouse, $$, 34450 Brooten Rd., Pacific City, (503) 965-6722, has casual dining overlooking the Nestucca River. A cozy place with Friday and Saturday night concerts featuring jazz, blues, classical, and country. Open daily for lunch or dinner.

Tillamook

Shilo Inn Restaurant, $$, 2535 N. Main St. (Hwy. 101), (503) 842-5510. Serves breakfast, lunch, dinner. Good basic menu selections. Ask about their lite meals.

Special Local Attractions

Tillamook Cheese Factory, Tillamook County Creamery Association, 4175 Hwy. 101 N., (503) 842-4481, has a self-guided tour of the cheese-making process. Outside is a replica of the *Morning Star*, a wooden ship built by early butter and cheesemakers to ship their products to far-away ports. Lots of great RV parking.

Blue Heron Cheese Co., 2001 Blue Heron/Hwy. 101, (503) 842-8281, offers a variety of cheeses with lots of samples and a wine-tasting room for Northwest wines. There is also a nice picnic area and a petting zoo for the kids. Large RVs not recommended for turning around in the parking lot.

Bear Creek Artichokes, 11 1/2 miles south of Tillamook on Hwy. 101, (503) 398-5411, has fresh-grown fruits, veggies, and herbs for sale. Stroll around their perrenial gardens and admire a real working vegetable farm.

Three Capes Scenic Drive, a 22-mile strectch of some of the most beautiful coastline in Oregon, starts just west of Tillamook and continues to Cape Kiwanda. Don't miss it.

Many RVers like to stay at Cape Lookout State Park because it puts them in the middle of all this beauty and allows explorations north or south along the drive.
At **Oceanside**, drive to the top of Maxwell Mountain Road to watch the gray whales (spring or winter) or look for hang gliders about to take off from the cliffs.

Wildlife Viewing

Three Arches Rocks Wildlife Refuge is a national wildlife refuge located off Oceanside and home to hundreds of sea lions and seals. Thousands of sea birds can be seen nesting on the face of these rocks during the spring and summer.
At **Oceanside Wayside Park** in Oceanside. These rocks are home to many species of birds and other wildlife. Take your binoculars to see hundreds of thousands of nesting seabirds as well as a herd of sea lions and seals.
Cape Meares National Wildlife Refuge encompasses many types of coastal plants and wildlife, including offshore nesting colonies of seabirds. It is also a great whale watching site.
Trask River Hatchery, 15020 Chance Road, Tillamook, (503) 842-4090, follow the hatchery signs from Hwy. 101 south of town. Tucked into the hills east of Tillamook is the Trask River Hatchery. The hatchery has no amenities and limited parking. Absolutely no RVs of any length can drive to the hatchery. In August and November, salmon adults return to spawn. Visitors may see hatchery personnel taking the eggs and/or watch the salmon spawn in Gold Creek above the hatchery. If you are visiting in those months it would be worth a call to the hatchery to determine if a trip is worthwhile.

Section 5: RV Parts & Services from Cannon Beach to Pacific City

Diesel

Cannon Beach: RV Resort at Cannon Beach, Hwy. 101 & Elk Creek Rd., (503) 436-2231
Nehalem: Bayside Gardens Texaco, 36453 Hwy. 101 N., (503) 368-5150
Garibaldi: Sheldon Texaco, 701 Garibaldi Ave., Garibaldi, (503) 322-3770. The diesel pump is not by the gas pumps in front of the station. It is on the side street side of station making for an easy in and out.
Tillamook: Tillamook Texaco, 15 Main St., Tillamook, OR 97141, (503) 842-5555. This station is at the turn of Hwy. 101 downtown Tillamook. Propane is at the north end of their lot.
Beaver: Beaver Texaco, 24485 S. Hwy. 101, Beaver, (503) 398-2828. On the turn in Beaver with easy access.

Dump Station

Cannon Beach: Nearest dump station is in Seaside, 10 miles north or the RV Resort Campground
Nehalem: Nehalem Bay State Park campground
Nehalem: Tideland Road, Hwy. 101 south of Nehalem at boat ramp. Follow signs looping underneath Hwy. 101 for .5 miles. Road is rough but the entrance and exit to the dump station are excellent. $3.00 fee
Tillamook: None

Library

Cannon Beach: Hemlock Street & 2nd Stree, open Tues., Thurs., Sat.
Manzanita Branch Library, 571 Laneda Ave., Manzanita, (503) 368-6665. Open Mon. 1-8, Tue.-Fri. 1-5, Sat. 9-1
Tillamook County Library, 210 Ivy St., Tillamook, OR 97141, (503) 842-7702,

Yaquina Head Lighthouse from the BLM park near Newport.

open Mon.-Thurs., 9-9, Fri.-Sat. 9-5:30. Paperbacks can be checked out without a membership. Temporary 90 day membership available by paying a refundable $25 fee.

Medical Services

Cannon Beach: Nearest hospital is 10 miles north in Seaside
Nehalem/Manzanita: Nearest hospital is in Seaside or Tillamook
Tillamook County General Hospital, 1000 Third St., (503) 842-4444. 24-hour emergency care

Propane

Cannon Beach: RV Resort at Cannon Beach, Hwy. 101 & Elk Creek Rd., (503) 436-2231
Nehalem: Bayside Gardens Texaco, 36453 Hwy. 101 N., (503) 368-5150
Tillamook: Ferrellgas, 2900 3rd Street, Tillamook, OR 97141, (503) 842-2641. Propane may be purchased at this distributor as well as tanks repaired. There is ample access for entrance by an RV but backing a trailer or 5th wheel would be difficult.

Tillamook: Tillamook Texaco, 15 Main St., Tillamook, OR 97141, (503) 842-5555. This station is at the turn of Hwy. 101, downtown Tillamook.
Garibaldi: Sheldon Texaco, 701 Garibaldi Ave., Garibaldi, OR, (503) 322-3770. On Hwy. 101—the only Texaco station in town.
Beaver Texaco, 24485 S. Hwy. 101, Beaver, (503) 398-2828. On the turn in Beaver with easy access.

RV Parts & Service

Cannon Beach: Nearest is Skipanon in Warrenton
Nehalem/Manzanita: See Warrenton RV services or Tillamook RV services
Tillamook: Tillamook RV Repair & Sales, Inc., 2150 Hadley Road, Tillamook, OR 97141, (503) 842-7702 or (800) 235-7702. A full-service facility except for chassis repair. Ample room for parking and if repairs take more than one day you can stay in the rig. They do not have hookups but will supply electricity. They have a full line of supplies in their parts store. The Jacob's have run and operated the store for over ten years. If towing is required, call them and they will connect you with the tow company who has the right equipment.

Shopping/Groceries

Cannon Beach: Osburn's Grocery Store/Deli, 240 N. Hemlock. Groceries, organic produce, soup, sandwiches. Eat on the porch. Wonderful old building.
Cannon Beach: Mariners Market, 139 N. Hemlock, (503) 436-2442. Takes credit cards, has ATM, health food, drugs, deli, videos, good selection.
Nehalem/Manzanita: There are no major grocery chains or malls in these small towns. Small local grocery stores are in both towns. Offering the best selection of groceries and wines is Manzanita Grocery & Deli, 193 Laneda Ave., Manzanita, OR 97130, (503) 368-5362.
Tillamook: Fred Meyer One-Stop shopping, on Hwy. 101 just south of the Tillamook Cheese Factory
Tillamook: Safeway, on Hwy. 101 just south of the Tillamook Cheese Factory

USPO

Cannon Beach: 155 N. Hemlock St. 97110, (503) 436-2822
Nehalem: 12810 H St., 97131, Hwy. 101 north of blinking light, (503) 368-6109
Manzanita: 370 Laneda Ave., 97130, (503) 368-6110
Garibaldi: 6th & Acacia, 97118, (503) 322-3675
Tillamook: 2200 1st St., 97141, (503) 842-4711

101

Chapter 6

Neskowin to South Beach

Map Grid A3: Neskowin to South Beach

Introduction

If you like to shop or try your luck at gaming, Lincoln City is your choice. If you want peace and solitude for your beach walks, Neskowin is your best bet. If you want to see beautiful sea cliffs and whales cavorting off shore, try Depoe Bay. Depoe Bay claims to have the world's smallest harbor. The bay is on the inland side with a small outlet to the ocean over which a landmark arch bridge has been built. Depoe Bay is well known for its fishing charters and whale watching. Whales may be seen any time during the year the best opportunity being December to May. Don't miss the spouting horns at the waysides north of Depoe Bay. On stormy days these rock formations can send the plumes of water over the walkway and across the highway surprising visitors with an extra shower for the day.

This section of the coast offers something for everyone. It will also try your driving patience. The Lincoln City stretch of Hwy. 101 is unbearably slow and because of the extra attractions that have recently opened in Lincoln City, it is getting worse. You must go through Lincoln City when traveling Hwy. 101 so expect 7 miles of motel-lined congestion. If you are just passing through, you can avoid some of it by taking E. Devil's Lake Road around part of the town. The best you can do is just go slow or park it for a while and partake of some of the more relaxing activities here such as strolling along the long seven mile stretch of beautiful beaches.

Lincoln City enjoys an average summer temperature of a windy 60-70° on the beach, and 80-90° inland. Average winter daytime temperatures run in the 50s and in the 30s at night. Annual precipitation averages 72 inches per year. It is blessed with northwest winds in the summer and southwest winds in the winter—great for kite flying. Windsurfing in the ocean is also popular here.

Lincoln City is situated 11 feet above sea level with the Pacific Ocean on the west and the 680-acre freshwater Devil's Lake on the east. It has 7 1/2 miles of beach to roam with the Salmon River to the north and the Siletz River to the south.

Section 1: Best Campgrounds in Lincoln City/Newport Bay/South Beach

Best Public Campgrounds

Best public campground for scenic beauty

Lincoln City: Devil's Lake State Park, open all year, (541) 994-2002, reservations (800) 452-5687, p. 75

Newport: Beverly Beach State Park, open all year, (541) 265-9278, reservations (800) 452-5687, p. 76

Best public campground for full hookups and base camping

Lincoln City: Devil's Lake State Park, open all year, (541) 994-2002, reservations (800) 452-5687, p. 75

Newport: Beverly Beach State Park, open all year, (541) 265-9278, reservations (800) 452-5687, p. 76

Best public campground for families with children

Lincoln City: Devil's Lake State Park, open all year, (541) 994-2002, reservations (800) 452-5687, p. 75

Newport: Beverly Beach State Park, open all year, (541) 265-9278, reservations (800) 452-5687, p. 76

Alternative: South Beach State Park, open all year, (541) 867-4715, reservations (800) 452-5687, p. 77

Best Private Campgrounds

Best private campground with luxurious facilities

Depoe Bay: Holiday RV Park, open all year, (541) 765-2302 or (800) 452-2104, p. 76

Newport: Pacific Shores RV Resort, open all year, (541) 265-3750, or (800) 333-1583, p. 77

Best private campground for scenic beauty

Lincoln City: Lincoln City KOA, open all year, (541) 994-2961 or (800) KOA-2791, p. 76

Depoe Bay: Holiday RV Park, open all year, (541) 765-2302 or (800) 452-2104, p. 76

Newport: Pacific Shores RV Resort, open all year, (541) 265-3750 (800) 333-1583, p. 77

Best private campground for base camping or families with children

Lincoln City: Lincoln City KOA, open all year, (541) 994-2961 or (800) KOA-2791, p. 76

Alternative: Devil's Lake RV Park, open all year, (541) 994-3400, p. 76

Newport: Pacific Shores RV Resort, open all year, (541) 265-3750 (800) 333-1583, p. 77

Alternative: Newport Marina RV Park #1, open Mar.-Nov., (541) 867-3321, p. 77

Alternative: Agate Beach RV Park, open all year, (541) 265-7670, p. 77

Campground Descriptions

Lincoln City

Devil's Lake State Park, open all year, US101/6th St. in Lincoln City, (541) 994-2002 or reservations (800) 452-5687

Location: In a heavily wooded area in Lincoln City on Devil's Lake with a dock for fishing.

Description: This park is like an oasis in the city. It has lots of trees but many of the sites are small. Call first to be sure you can get your rig in. Devil's Lake is surrounded by natural wetlands and marshes creating a haven for wildlife and waterfowl. The lake is one of the primary wintering grounds for migratory geese and ducks. It's quiet and peaceful and right in the center of the action in Lincoln City on Devil's Lake with trout fishing, and a boat dock. A store, restaurant, and laundry are nearby.

100 paved sites, 32 full hookups, (20/30/50 amp), back-ins, max. length 40', 110 acres, mostly shaded, $18.00-$20.00, lower rates in the off-season, restrooms, showers,

no dump, camp host, phone, evening programs in summer, playground, handicap access.

Lincoln City KOA, open all year, AAA, 5298 NE Park Lane, Otis, OR 97368 (541) 994-2961 or (800) KOA-2791
Location: In Lincoln City, off E. Devil's Lake Rd., very close to Devil's Lake.
Description: A lovely park set in a small hollow with lots of wooded hills surrounding it and off Hwy. 101. Excellent facilities and a great playground for the kids. The lower loop which has water and electric only is in a quieter area of the park. When traveling to Lincoln City from the south we recommend using the south end of E. Devil's Lake Road (stoplight at the outlet malls) as the north end of E. Devil's Lake Road has no stoplight, but does have a steep angle from E. Devil's Lake Road onto Hwy. 101. This park is near everything you would want to do in Lincoln City.

50 gravel sites, some shaded, 13 pull-thrus, max. length 60', 9 acres, (30/50 amp), dump station, $19,00-$21.00, lower off-season and weekly rates, Kamping Kabins, restrooms, showers, cable TV, phone, groceries, gift shop, videos, propane, RV supplies, laundry, rec room, large playground.

Devils Lake RV Park, open all year, 4041 NE West Devil's Lake Rd., Lincoln City, OR 97367, (541) 994-3400.
Location: On West Devil's Lake Road in Lincoln City, close to a marina on Devil's Lake.
Description: This is a well-taken care of park but it has no shaded sites. There is a marina across the street and entertainment for the kids. It is close to marina, fishing, boat rental, bumper boats, and golf course.

80 paved sites, 47 pull-thrus, max. length 80', full hookups, (30/50 amps), cable TV, laundry, restrooms, showers, $21.60 to $24.00 daily rate, 7th day free, lower off-season and weekly rates.

Depoe Bay

Holiday RV Park, open all year, P.O. Box 433, Depoe Bay, OR 97341 (541) 765-2302 or (800) 452-2104.
Location: On the Pacific Ocean just off Hwy. 101, one mile north of Depoe Bay
Description: This quiet park is known for its special features as well as its unique surroundings. A large park at the edge of the ocean where you can watch whales swimming in the ocean all year. This park is well taken care of and has friendly management.

110 paved sites (33 ocean-front), 41 pull-thrus, max. length: 55', 110 full hookups, (30 amp), 9 acres, $16.00 to $28.00 daily, lower weekly rates, GS, AAA, restrooms, showers, dump, cable TV, phone, laundry, heated indoor pool, spa, whirlpool, rec room, game room, playground, groceries, gift shop, RV supplies, propane.

Newport Area

Beverly Beach State Park, open all year, 198 NE 123rd St., Newport, (541) 265-9278, reservations (800) 452-5687
Location: Six miles north of Newport (**milepost 134**) on the east side of Highway 101 near the Pacific Ocean.
Description: On the Pacific Ocean just on the other side of the Hwy. 101 in a lovely forest of Douglas fir and Sitka spruce. Beverly Beach State Park is a nice shady place and a great family campground. Spencer Creek runs through the park and has a .75-mile nature trail alongside. Kids have been known to catch a small trout or two here. Beachcombing is particularly enjoyable as you can walk right to the beach through the underpass for Hwy. 101. This park can accommodate all sizes of campers and RVs and is very busy from April through September.

129 paved sites, many shaded, 130 acres. 53 full hookups, 76 partial hookups, (20/30 amp), 32 pull-thrus, max. length 50', $18.00-$20.00, lower rates off-season, restrooms, showers, handicap sites, cable TV, dump, camp hosts, phone, evening activities in summer, playground, beach access, visitors center with books and free coffee. Groceries, videos and laundry available at small store at park entrance. Great place for bike riding, hiking, and beachcombing.
Comments: This is a busy campground during the summer so be sure to make reservations. They are rarely full in the winter. We like G Loop (partial hookups) because it is at the end of this large park and gets fewer drive-throughs. The children's playground is in G Loop.

South Beach State Park, open all year, 5580 S. Hwy. 101, (541) 867-4715, reservations (800) 452-5687
Location: Two miles south of Newport at South Beach, close to the ocean
Description: South Beach is located on a flat, sandy and grassy area between the ocean foredune and wooded hills. It is preferred by those who want to be close to the beach and the pounding surf. Most of the vegetation in the campground consist of short to medium beach pines so the sites stay sunny.

244 sites, 433 acres, 244 partial hookups, (20 amp), back-ins, max. length 50', $17.00-$19.00, lower off-season rates, restrooms, showers, dump, camp host, phone, evening activities in summer, playground, handicap sites. Cooper Ridge Nature Trail (1.75 miles) plus South Jetty Trail and lots of beach hiking.

Agate Beach RV Park, open all year, 6138 N. Hwy. 101, Newport, (541) 265-7670.
Location: On the east side of Hwy. 101, 3 miles north of Newport.
Description: This park is located very close to Newport and right across the highway from Pacific Shores RV Resort. It is well taken care of and has nice grassy sites with ample room between. There are woods around the back side of the park furthest from the highway. Agate Beach RV Park is located close to Agate Beach Wayside where agate hunting on the beach can be good if you are willing to dig a little.

32 paved and gravel sites, 27 full hookups, 5 partial hookups, (20/30 amp), back-ins only, max. length 50', $17.00-$19.00, GS, lower off-season and weekly rates, restrooms, showers, dump, cable TV, phone, laundry. A store is located within one mile.
Newport Marina RV Park #1, open Mar.-Nov., 2301 SE Marine Science Dr., (541) 867-3321
Location: On the Marina, 1.7 miles south of Newport on Hwy. 101. Take the Marine Science Center exit at the south end of Yaquina Bay Bridge
Description: This park is located right at the marina with a view of the Yaquina Bay Bridge. Set along the shore of Yaquina Bay, salmon fishing, marina, boat docks and boat launch are nearby. The sites are located on a parking lot with no grass or shade between them. There is room to park your tow vehicle next to your rig. They have another smaller park next to this one that is open all year. It is very well kept, however, and you can watch the boats come and go. A full-service marina is next to the park with charters, store, cafe and boat rentals. The Oregon Coast Aquarium and Hatfield Marine Science Institute are within walking distance.

100 paved sites, 9 acres, 100 full hookups (30 amp), back-ins, max. length 50', $14.95-$19.25, lower off-season and weekly rates, GS, restrooms, showers, dump, cable TV, phone, laundry, propane, cafe, fishing

Pacific Shores RV Resort, open all year, (541) 265-3750 or (800) 333-1583
Location: 3 miles north of Newport on Hwy. 101, on the Pacific Ocean
Description: This is one of the most luxurious (and most expensive) RV parks on the Oregon Coast. It is, however, a very lovely park with many ocean view sites. The oceanside views of Yaquina Head Lighthouse are breathtaking. Pacific Shores has kept the

bluff natural with many walking paths to picnic tables, gazebos, and paths to the beach. The park has so many planned activities that you will never get bored. They have provided every RV comfort possible. This park receives reservations early in the year for the summer season so get yours in early if you expect to camp during this busy time.

287 paved sites, some shaded, 38 acres, 287 full hookups, (30/50 amp), 100 pull-thrus, max. length 52', daily rate: $22.00-$35.00, extra charge for pets, GS, AAA, lower off-season and weekly rates, restrooms, showers, cable TV, phone, laundry, dump, adult and teen room, store and gift shop, RV supplies, propane, heated indoor pool, whirlpool and sauna, rec room, exercise room, 2 lounges w/fireplace, billiard room, big screen TVs, game room, basketball court, playground, horseshoes, bingo, planned activities. Bus service to Newport Bayfront and Aquarium. The Galley restaurant in the park is open 8 a.m.-8 p.m. in summer, closed Mon. and Tues. off-season and offers fast American choices. Two miles of walking paths with ocean and beach access.

Volunteer/Camp Host Opportunities

Devils Lake State Park, Lincoln City, (541) 994-2002
Beverly Beach State Park, Newport, (541) 265-9278
South Beach State Park, South Beach, (541) 867-4715
Salmon River Fish Hatchery, Otis, (541) 994-8606
Pacific Shores RV Resort, Newport (10 positions), (541) 265-3750

Section 2: Activities in Neskowin/Lincoln City/Depoe Bay Areas

This area includes two tiny towns and one large and bustling one. Neskowin or Depoe Bay is your pick for the slow lane. Lincoln City has the motels, shops, casino, outlet malls, golf courses, and traffic that will keep you entertained for a while. Devil's Lake is a beautiful, relaxing spot. There are some very nice things to do in Lincoln City if you have the time. If casinos are your idea of fun, Chinook Winds will dazzle you.

Don't Miss

- Lincoln City: Regatta Park/Sandcastle Park on Devil's Lake

Regatta Park in Lincoln City has one of the best playgrounds on the coast.

Highly Recommended

- Depoe Bay: Boiler Bay State Park for whale watching

Bike/Auto Tours

Neskowin Scenic Tour is on the original Hwy. 101 road. Start the tour at **milepost 99** on Hwy. 101 between Neskowin and Lincoln City—watch for the scenic tour sign. This tour meanders through the Siuslaw Experimental Forest, the only research program of its kind in the nation. Go slow, watch for bicyclists and share the road on this tour. It is the designated Oregon Coast Bike Trail bypassing the climb over Cascade Head. The tour can be completed by either taking the south fork of the road to Otis on Hwy. 18 or the right fork (Three Forks Road) back to Hwy. 101 at **milepost 104**. It is a lovely ride through beautiful forests.

Bookstores

Robert's Book Shop, 3412 SE Hwy. 101, Lincoln City, (541) 994-4453. Used and antique books. Don't let the outside of the building keep you from using this store. Once inside the door you discover a large collection of "olde" books as well as a large selection of used books, hardcovers and paperbacks. Approximately half the shop is of books that could be termed "collectibles". Robert Portwood, proprietor, is very knowledgeable of the book industry and more than willing to spend the time to assist you.

Annual Events

Check with Lincoln City Chamber of Commerce
4031 NW Logan Rd./Hwy. 101, (541) 994-3070, for specific dates

January
Chamber Super Auction

February
Lincoln Days

April
Gleneden Beach Easter Pet Parade
Oregon Wine Festival, Lincoln City
Classic wooden Boat Show & Crab Feed, Depoe Bay

May
Lincoln City Spring Kite Festival
Annual Fleet of Flowers, Depoe Bay

June
Lincoln City Beach Volleyball
Beachcomber Days

July
4th of July fireworks display, Lincoln City
Summer Kite Festival, Lincoln City
Cascade Head Music Festival, Lincoln City
Lincoln City Sandcastle Festival

August
Siletz Tribe Pow Wow
Flower & Garden Show

September
D-River Ducky Derby, Lincoln City
Oregon Coast Fitness Festival
Depoe Bay Indian Salmon Bake
Lincoln City Fall Kite Festival

November
Lincoln City Beach Lights

December
Lincoln City Winter Garden Party
Winter Whale Watching Week

The estuary at Neskowin Beach.

The Book End, Hwy. 101/Logan Rd. Lincoln City, (541) 994-9393. This large bookstore has all the latest Northwest regional favorites and boasts of having the largest selection of all types of magazines anywhere. They're right!

Cafe Roma Bookstore, 1437 NW Hwy. 101, Lincoln City, (541) 994-6616, open daily 7 a.m. to 5 p.m. A delightful place to browse through a large selection of books and cards while enjoying an espresso or lunch. Nice warm wood interior invites you to sit awhile and relax. They offer sandwiches, salads, soups, lite lunches, kids menu and a wonderful selection of homemade pies and cheesecakes.

Exercise Routes or Leisure Walking

Neskowin Beach Wayside, (day-use park), has good access for RVs. This a good place to take a break, walk to the beach and view Proposal Rock. If you happen to be there when the tide is coming in, watch the water encircle Proposal Rock like a moat. Nice beach walking.

Lincoln City, west end of 51st Street along the beach toward Inn at the Spanish Head where you can watch the brown pelicans, gulls, and sea lions.

Family Activities with Children

Fogarty Creek State Park is a lovely green park with lots of picnic spots, great access to the beach and good access for RVs with pull-thrus. It has a broad beach where kids can build sand castles and a lovely shallow creek that flows to the ocean. An annual salmon barbecue is held here.

Lincoln City Community Center, (541) 994-5208. Enjoy supervised swimming in an Olympic-size indoor pool and warm wading pool at the Lincoln City Community Center. If you would rather swim outside, try a dip in Devil's Lake at Regatta Grounds Park, Sand Point Park or Holmes Road Park.

Catch the Wind Kites, 266 SE Hwy. 101, Lincoln City, OR, (541) 994-9500 will sell you a kite that you can fly from D River State Wayside or Road's End State Wayside.

David's Bicycle Rental, 960 SE Hwy. 101, Lincoln City, (541) 996-6001, is a place you can rent a bicycle

Blue Heron Landing, 4006 West Devil's Lake Rd., Lincoln City, (541) 994-4708. Rent bikes, bumper boats, kayaks, Sea Doos and play on and around Devil's Lake.

Regatta and **Sand Castle City Parks**, on West Devil's Lake Road, Lincoln City, (take 14th street east to the park sign). These two parks are contiguous providing a beautiful place to spend a few hours. Regatta Park is on the lake with ample picnic tables, grassy area, and a fishing dock. Sand Castle Park is a huge playground set built in the shape of a castle. Kids will want to spend hours in this play area. The view of Devil's Lake is spectacular and there is a long dock that can be used for fishing. No parking for larger RVs is available.

Depoe Bay City Park, watch for the sign (by Texaco station) and turn east. Follow the green signs always going downhill. Ample pull-through parking for RVs. Beautiful playground, lots of picnic tables, shaded grassy area. The park is at the end of the marina and is an easy walk to watch the boats unload their daily catch. A good getaway spot when Lincoln City becomes too crowded.

Fishing

***A fishing tale:** Jane Baxter, a well-known Tillamook native in the early 1900s, would walk barefoot through the Salmon River mud flats in waist-deep water until she felt a flounder. Pinning the flounder with her foot, she would then "thrust a spear held between her toes in the fish, and put it in her sack".*

Siletz Bay Park (2 miles south of Lincoln City) for clamming at low tide

Devil's Lake is stocked with trout. Also supports bass, perch, crappie, bluegill. Open

Fogarty Creek meanders on its way to the ocean near Depoe Bay.

Regatta Park has a great fishing pier on Devil's Lake.

year-round. Average depth is ten feet with deepest depth at twenty feet.
Siletz River is popular for salmon and steelhead. Access from the bank is limited.
Siletz Bay: Perch, crab, and flounder
Little Nestucca River is one of the better fishing streams on the coast for trout, steelhead, salmon.

Salmon River offers trout fishing from boat or dock, salmon in season (popular spot is the bridge over Hwy. 101)
The ocean: Surf and bottom fishing is good along the rocky shoreline.

Galleries/Arts

Hawk Creek Gallery, 48460 Hwy. 101 S., Neskowin (503) 392-3879, just off Hwy. 101 next to Hawk Creek Golf Course. Stunning, colorful, soft watercolors by Michael Schlicting, plus metal and cement work for your garden by other artists.

Take a relaxing ride into the country to see the following galleries south of Lincoln City:
Mossy Creek Pottery, Immonen Rd., Gleneden Beach, (541) 996-2415, is a potter's gallery with an imaginative selection of stoneware and porcelain by 25 Northwest potters. From delicate, translucent porcelain to sturdy stoneware and terra cotta, Mossy Creek Pottery offers one of the widest varieties of styles, glazes, and prices on the West Coast. Some would make great gifts to send home and they will package smaller items for shipping. They are open daily 9 a.m. to 5 p.m.

Alder House II, 611 Immonen Rd, Gleneden Beach, is the oldest glass-blowing studio in Oregon and is housed in a geodesic dome nestled in an old grove of alder. Here they practice the 2000-year-old-craft of turning molten glass into goblets, vases, bowls and many other forms. Come and watch the fascinating and dangerous art of glass blowing. Live demonstrations during the day in the artist's studio are especially exciting to watch. Open daily from 10 a.m. to 5 p.m. between March 15 and November 30.

Golfing

Neskowin Beach Golf Course, 48405 Hawk Ave., Neskowin, OR 97149, (503) 392-3377, exit Hwy. 101 to Neskowin wayside. On northeast end of the rest area parking lot is a 350-yard road to the golf course. An easier route is to drive past the rest area on

Salem Ave. making a right onto Breakers Blvd., turn right onto Amity Ave. and drive to the golf course. A nine hole, par 35 course with six par 4, two par 3, and one par 5 holes. This is a beautiful 2,616-yard course in the flood plain of the local creeks. They, of course, close during the winter months (Nov.-April). Clubs are available for rent. Includes a putting green but not a driving range. Snacks are available in the pro shop.

Hawk Creek Golf Course, 48480 S. Hwy. 101, Neskowin, OR 97149, (503) 392-4120, east side of Hwy. 101 on Hawk Creek one-fourth mile north of Neskowin Wayside. Open year-round. A nine hole, par 34 course with one par 5, five par 4, and three par 3 holes in 2,441 yards. Neither a driving range nor a putting green are available. Pro shop includes a restaurant.

Lakeside Golf Course, 3245 Clubhouse Drive, Lincoln City, OR 97367, (541) 994-8442, north end of Lincoln City—turn right at light with DMV sign. An eighteen hole, par 66 course of 4,949 yards consisting of two par 5, eight par 4, and eight par 3 holes. This course is part of a total health club; tennis, basketball, exercise equipment, restaurant, bar and grill. The course is open year-round and includes two putting greens and a limited flight driving range (165 yards). It is one of the more popular and more difficult coast courses.

Salishan Golf Links, Gleneden Beach, OR 97388, (541) 764-9692 or (800) 890-0387. A par 72, eighteen-hole 6,453-yard popular course consisting of four par 5, ten par 4, and four par 3 holes. Includes putting green and putting course, driving range. Part of a resort retreat with lodge and restaurant so reservations are a must. Clubs and carts may be rented.

Hiking

Cascade Head Nature Conservancy Area (7 miles round-trip), Cascade Head is a research preserve just north of Lincoln City. It is owned by the Nature Conservancy, a private non-profit group dedicated to preserving special places. Several trails wind through undisturbed rain forests and lead to a grassy headland. The views of the surrounding lowlands, rivers, beaches and ocean are awesome. The area is open to the public during daylight hours, but please stay on designated trails to prevent damage to the fragile landscape. Dogs are not allowed. There are trailheads off Three Rocks Rd./Hwy. 101 (on the south side) and off Forest Road 1861 (marked Cascade Head Rd.) on the north side.

Cascade Head Nature Conservancy Trail, Located within the Cascade Head Scenic Research Area, this hike is classified as moderate. The trail traverses moderate to steep hillsides in a forest setting. Take Hwy. 101 .5 miles north from the junction with Hwy. 18 to Three Rocks Rd. Turn left and travel approximately two miles to Savage Rd., turn right and travel approximately one mile to the trailhead. There is parking for about 10 cars.

Harts Cove Trail, Located within the Cascade Head Scenic Research Area, Harts Cove is a moderately difficult hike about 5.4 miles round trip. It meanders through a magnificent hemlock and Sitka spruce forest and crosses a couple of rushing streams on footbridges. The trail traverses steep hillsides to a grassy meadow overlooking the Pacific Ocean. The reward is worth it as this hike leads to a grand view overlooking a remote stretch of coastline with breath-taking views of Harts Cove. Take Hwy. 101 3.3 miles north from the junction with Hwy. 18 to Road 1861. Turn left—trailhead is located at the end of the road—4 miles. Call the Siuslaw Hebo Ranger District (503) 392-3161 for trail conditions.

Roads End Wayside, Lincoln City, An easy 2.5-mile (depends on the tide) round-trip hike along a surprisingly quiet stretch of beach. Take Logan Rd. from Hwy. 101 for one mile to Roads End State Park. Go down to the beach and turn right (north). The first mile you will see many unique old cottages along the hill. At the end of the hike

Footprints leading to Proposal Rock at Neskowin Beach.

you will have reached the headland. If it's low tide don't go around the headland or you may have to stay until the next low tide.

Local History/Museums

North Lincoln County Historical Museum, 4907 SW Hwy. 101, (503) 996-6614, free. Features displays of local history including a Japanese mine that washed onto the beach following World War II. Don't miss seeing the blue whale baleen hanging in the pioneer room or the upstairs room of Abe Lincoln pictures and statutes. The best parking is the public parking between 50th and 51st street. Ample room for RVs.
Drift Creek Covered Bridge, on Drift Creek south of Lincoln City. Drive three miles on Hwy. 101, turn left (east) on Drift Creek for 1.5 miles, then turn right for .5 mile. Built in 1914, the bridge is 66 feet long and is no longer in use. There is no parking for RVs.

Photo Opportunities

- Neskowin Beach Wayside: Proposal Rock on the beach
- Boiler Bay State Park has great cliffs and whale watching
- Fogarty Creek flows down to a tiny attractive cove
- Regatta Park has awesome views of Devil's Lake and some friendly resident geese

Restaurants/Espresso

Neskowin

The Hawk Creek Cafe, $$, 4505 Salem Ave., Neskowin, (503) 392-3838, is next to the grocery store and state park wayside and open 7 a.m. to 9 p.m. with a break from 2 p.m. to 5 p.m. This small cafe has a lovely deck overlooking Hawk Creek as it flows to the ocean. It's true—they do have award-winning clam chowder but don't overlook other tasty items like the halibut sandwich. Gourmet pizza and tempting Italian entrees for dinner. A great place to eat and after your meal you can take a romantic walk to Proposal Rock on the beach.

Lincoln City

Audrey's, $$, 1725 S. W. Hwy. 101, (541) 994-6210. Don't miss Audrey's for omelets or hash browns for breakfast. Exciting menu that will satisfy any palate for lunch or dinner. Highly recommended. Small parking lot.

Kyllo's Seafood Grill, $$, 1110 NW First Court/Hwy. 101 at D River, (541) 994-3179, is right on the water with views of the D River and the ocean. This place is very popular with the locals so expect crowds on a summer evening. Their menu is extensive and the portions are generous. We recommend Kyllo's highly for some of the best seafood and atmosphere on the coast.

Mo's Chowder, $, 860 SW 51st St., (541) 996-2535, is world-renowned for chowder. Try the other all-American favorites. They have a breathtaking view of Siletz Bay and the ocean.

Chameleon Cafe, $, 2145 NW Hwy. 101, (541) 994-8422. Mon. to Sat. 11:30 a.m.-9 p.m. serves mostly vegetarian meals in a light airy atmosphere with chameleons painted on the middle table. Middle East, Greek and Italian offerings and there is an occasional fish and chicken dish. They always serve Brazilian black bean soup. Salad dressings are excellent. The restaurant is smoke-free and accepts credit cards for orders over $5.00.

Otis Cafe, $, on Hwy. 18 at the Otis Junction (503) 994-2813, is open for breakfast and lunch every day and Fri. to Sun. for dinner. A tiny cafe, this places serves good food in large portions at reasonable prices. Take home a loaf of their homemade bread. People who know about this cafe's reputation get there early so they don't have to wait in the line on the porch.

Dory Cove Restaurant, $$, 5819 Logan Rd., (541) 994-5180. Hearty American food with seafood the specialty. The parking lot here is always full which should tell you something about the food. The locals here love this restaurant for seafood or burgers. The choices of burgers is mind-boggling. Roads End Wayside is right next door for a relaxing stroll along the beach after your appetite is satisfied.

Special Local Attractions

Chinook Winds: Siletz Tribal Gaming and Convention Center, take Logan Rd. to 44th St. left, (541) 996-5811, is the new attraction at Lincoln City. You can enjoy all types of games: slots, poker, blackjack, bingo, off-track betting, and Keno. Their concerts by the sea bring big-name entertainment to the coast. Open 24 hours, 365 days a year with child care available. The Siletz Room provides 24-hour dining. RVers can park right on the ocean in the casino parking lot for a $10.00 daily permit which includes two free buffet dinners.

Factory Stores at Lincoln City, 1500 SE Devil's Lake Rd./Hwy. 101. You can shop till you drop at 47 large shops in one area, 22 more are being added—the largest concentration of factory outlets in the West. Open daily.

Wildlife Viewing

Siletz Bay Park, in Lincoln City north of Schooner Creek may be accessed from the Taft dock on east end of 51st Street (our preference). Viewing telescopes are available at both Taft dock and the park. View harbor seals, waterfowl, and shorebirds. The variety of species changes by season: brown pelicans in summer, bald eagles, loons, and grebes in winter.

Boiler Bay State Wayside, Depoe Bay, birding is best March through November; black-footed albatross, petrels, horned puffin. Black oystercatchers nest at Boiler Bay. Bald eagles are commonly seen. Don't forget to look for sea lions and whales swimming by. Locals report about 100 gray whales stay year-round. This wayside is one of the best to see them all year. We were fortunate to see about four of them very close to shore in September.

Section 3: Activities in Newport/South Beach

Newport's claim to fame is that it is home to Keiko, the killer whale from the movie "Free Willy", at the Oregon Coast Aquarium. Seeing this huge sea mammal swim by is a thrill that evokes oohs and aahs from young and old alike. Don't forget that Newport is on Yaquina Bay and you can view more marine life in their natural environment by taking a bay tour. The culture of the Performing Arts Center and the Visual Arts Center can be found at historic Nye Beach, where hot baths were a favorite of the "summer people" in the 1920s. The best, however, may be Newport's working waterfront where you can stroll the wide boardwalk and watch the fish come in from the fishing boats and see the fish being processed. The many restaurants and shops will delight you and keep you entertained all afternoon.

Don't Miss

- Newport's working waterfront, Bay Blvd.
- Oregon Coast Aquarium

Highly Recommended

- Yaquina State Park and Lighthouse
- Hatfield Marine Science Center

Bike/Auto Tours

Otter Crest Loop, a 5-mile auto tour between Depoe Bay and Newport over Cape Foulweather. This is a very scenic road along the ocean revealing pounding surf and sheer cliffs. Otter Crest Loop begins and ends on Hwy. 101 with the north end at **milepost 130** and the south end at **milepost 132**. At the middle of the loop is the Cape Foulweather Otter Crest Wayside. There is an old historic building that is now a gift shop with high, breathtaking views of the cliffs and ocean below. This road and wayside are not recommended for RVs of any length.

Yaquina Bay Road from Newport to Toledo along Yaquina Bay. This is a breathtaking drive but we strongly suggest that you make it a bike trip. This route is a great bike trip because of light traffic and a good biking shoulder (mostly 3-4 feet wide). It will be 18 miles round-trip to our turnaround point, but you could make it much shorter and still get the same thrills. The road runs along the bay's edge providing a continuous view of boats on the water, mud flats at low tide, and birds and animals of the wetlands.

To start this tour, drive east on Hwy. 20 from downtown Newport to John Moore

Annual Events

Check with Newport Chamber of Commerce
555 SW Coast Hwy., (541) 265-8801 or (800) 262-7844, for specific dates

February
Seafood and Wine Festival

May
Loyalty Days & Sea Fair, Citywide

June
Red, White, and Blue Kite festival

July
Lincoln County Fair and Rodeo

October
Fisherman's Harvest Festival

Gift shop at top of Cape Foulweather near Depoe Bay.

Rd (stoplight). Go right on John Moore Rd. to Yaquina Bay Rd. Turn left onto Yaquina Bay Road. Drive up the first hill and park on the right at the Port of Newport sign. You will then bike a relatively flat road to the ten-mile marker just before entering Toledo. The views of the bay along this ride are spectacular. For the auto driver you may turn around and return on Yaquina Bay Road or drive into Toledo and return on Hwy. 20.

Bookstores

NYE Book House, 727 NW 3rd, Nye Beach, Newport, (541) 265-6840, has used books in a comfortable house setting. Hunker down in the overstuffed chairs next to the wood stove and enjoy your favorite book. The owner is friendly and so is the resident dog and cat.

Sea Towne Books, 1670 N. Hwy. 101, (541) 265-3827, has a good selection of new books as well as magazines. They also have regional and coast guides and audio books.

Canyon Way Bookstore, 1216 Canyon Way, (541) 265-8319, see restaurant listing

Ecotourism

Marine Discovery Tours, 345 SW Bay Blvd. on Newport's waterfront, (541) 265-6200, (800) 903-Boat, conducts whale watching and bay tours aboard the "Discovery" a 65-foot US. Coast Guard-approved vessel with wrap-around decks which seat 49 people.

Exercise Routes or Leisure Walks

Ona Beach State Park, 3 miles south of Newport is on Beaver Creek with picnicking. A walking bridge to the ocean leads to a lovely small beach that doesn't get much traffic. Views of the Beaver Creek estuary are outstanding. A favorite park for views of the meandering creek and ocean beaches.

Hatfield Science Center Estuary Trail goes from the aquarium to the Hatfield Center. The trailhead can be found east of the entrance to the aquarium. This easy stroll is a one-mile round-trip walk along the estuary. Interpretive signs along the trail explain the ecosystem. At low tide you may see clam diggers working the mud flats. The trail ends at the Hatfield Center and you can either walk the road two blocks back to the Oregon Coast Aquarium or return to your car back down the trail.

Newport Harbor with Yaquina Bay Bridge in background.

Newport's Working Waterfront

Schedule a half day to explore this area of Newport. There is so much to see including watching the fishing charters come and go, enjoying wonderful restaurants and viewing the excellent art in the many galleries. The sea lions on the end of the seawall will keep you entertained. It's an exciting and relaxing way to spend a day. We love to explore Newport's waterfront.

Family Activities with Children

Undersea Gardens, 250 SW Bay Ave., Mariner Square, (541) 265-2206, open 10-5 winter, 9-8 summer. Descend beneath the sea to view a glass-walled chamber of marine creatures with their friendly scuba diver. This is an interesting educational treat for young and old alike. You will learn more about marine life while the diver handles them gently in the tank. An admission fee is charged. There is also the wax museum and Ripley's Believe it or Not across the street in Mariners Square.

Oregon Coast Aquarium: (see "Special Local Activities")

Hatfield Marine Science Center: (see "Special Local Activities")

Yaquina Bay State Park and Lighthouse

At the bottom of the north entrance (Government & Elizabeth St.) there is an excellent children's playground with picnic table.

Fishing/Clamming

Fishing centers around the bustling Newport Bay Marina. Several charters are available for your fishing pleasure. Newport Sportfishing, (541) 265-5435, departs from the Embarcadero Dock at the east end while the Sea Gull Charters, (541) 265-7441, can be found on the bay boardwalk. It is always best to call in advance and schedule your trip. When you bring your bucket of fish back, there are people on the dock ready to clean and filet them for you. Crabbing can also be done right from the dock.

You can also rent your own boat to fish and crab in the bay. Embarcadero Dock Ltd., (541) 265-5435 can provide you with gear for fishing or crabbing.

Galleries/Arts

Oceanic Arts, 444 SW Bay Blvd., (541) 265-5693, original prints, contemporary crafts.

A place where you can pick up gifts to send home.

Rickert Gallery, 640 SW Bay Blvd., (541) 265-5430, has beautiful selections of watercolors and lithographs very carefully and artfully displayed.

The Wood Gallery, 818 SW Bay Blvd., (541) 265-6843, best wood product carvings to be found. The huge wood mushrooms were very interesting.

Newport Visual Arts Center, 839 NW Beach Dr., (541) 265-6540, at Nye Beach, where the art is changed monthly. When we were there there was an incredible display of intricate beadwork.

Golfing

Agate Beach, 4100 N Coast Hwy. 101, Newport, 97365, off Hwy. 101 one mile north of last stoplight, (541) 265-7331. Nine hole, par 36 consisting of one par 5, five par 4 and two par 3. Putting green, chipping green, cafeteria, irons driving range. Open year-round. Golf clubs and carts available for rent.

Crestview Hills Golf Course, 1680 Crestline Drive, Waldport, OR 97394, (541) 563-3020. Situated on the hillside south of Waldport, a nine-hole, par 36 course consisting of two par 5, five par 4, two par 3 holes. Putting green, restaurant. Open year-round. Golf clubs and carts rented.

Hiking

Newport

Yaquina Bay State Park has trails that lead down to the beach. You can walk the jetty trail out and back.

South Beach State Park

Pick up a trail map as you enter the park

South Jetty Trail, one mile one way, start at South Beach State Park day-use area. It ends at the north trailhead at the end of the road out to the south jetty. Walk the road to the end of the jetty. Watch brown pelicans dive for their lunch. Return the same way or make a loop by taking the north trail head inland and turn south at the first trail intersection. A longer loop would be to include the Cooper Ridge Nature Trail.

Cooper Ridge Nature Trail, 1.5 miles one way, start at South Beach State Park northernmost beach access trail and head west. The Cooper Ridge trail sign will be on your right. The trail loops around the campground through the tall pines on the Hwy. 101 side back to the campground entrance.

Beverly Beach State Park

Spencer Creek Nature Trail, a .75-mile trail starting from the hiker/biker camp. It follows along the banks of Spencer Creek and the path is graveled for easy walking. Expect to cross wetlands with skunk cabbage—beautiful in spring. Notice all the new trees that germinated and grew atop old growth stumps. Their roots fall down over the stumps like banyan trees.

Trek under Hwy. 101, through the underpass and cross Spencer Creek and hike north toward Otter Rock. Just past one mile, stairs will lead up to the Marine Gardens tide-pools and a view of Devil's Punchbowl. You may continue to the tide pools by taking the end of the road north of the Marine Gardens day-use parking area. (Marine Gardens and Devil's Punchbowl can both be accessed by driving to the turn to Devil's Punchbowl Wayside off Hwy. 101.)

A hike south on the beach from Beverly Beach State Park is about three miles one-way toward Yaquina Head. The hike ends at a rocky point where shell fossils can be observed. A sea cave similar to Devil's Punchbowl can be seen at trail's end.

Local History/Museums/Lighthouses

Lincoln County Historical Society Museum, 545 SW 9th, Newport, (541) 265-7509, Log cabin and 1895 Victorian house (Burroughs House). Native American, maritime, and coastal settlement history. Open: Tues-Sun 11 a.m.-4 p.m. Donation.

Yaquina Bay Lighthouse, Yaquina Bay State Park, features trails to the lighthouse and museum. The lighthouse is quite different as the light tower is incorporated into a large house where the keepers lived and raised a large family. Tours take you through that early period room by room. Let your imagination wonder about what it must have been like for them on this lonely point. This is a very nicely done park with great views in all directions. Call (541) 265-5679 for tour schedules.

Yaquina Head Lighthouse, (turn at Yaquina Outstanding Natural Area sign off Hwy. 101 north of Newport and follow the signs), is the tallest light on the Oregon Coast at 162 feet above sea level. Call (541) 265-2863 for tour schedules.

Photo Opportunities

- Yaquina Bay State Park
- Newport Harbor and boats
- Newport Marina RV Park
- Cape Foulweather
- Newport's Waterfront

Restaurants/Espresso

Izzy's Pizza Restaurant, $, 5251 N Hwy. 101, (541) 265-3636, is in our humble opinion, the best pizza in Oregon. Don't forget the salad bar or cinnamon rolls or chicken or just about anything in this "all you can eat" restaurant. You just can't beat the prices and variety. A great place to take the family.

The Whale's Tale, $$, Bay Blvd. and Fall St., on the waterfront in Newport, (541) 265-8660, is great for most any meal. Try the eggs Newport with red potatoes for breakfast. The luncheon specials are wonderful. Ask about the spinach salad with chicken and blue cheese.

Newport Chowder Bowl, $, 728 NW Beach, (541) 265-7477, family dining at Nye Beach. Try the delicious fish and chips or their slumgollian soup—a variation on clam chowder with shrimp added. Yum!

Boardwalk Cafe, $, 1000 SE Bay Blvd., Newport, (541) 2563-2108, is a small, cozy place with great views from their deck. Try quiche, soup, sandwiches or pastries for breakfast or lunch.

Port Dock One, $$, 325 SW Bay Blvd. on Newport's Bay Front, (541) 265-2911, Fresh local seafood, outside deck, try chicken teriyaki.

Canyon Way Restaurant, **Bookstore & Deli**, $$, 1216 Canyon Way, Newport, (541) 265-8319, is a nice bookstore with a restaurant that has indoor and garden patio seating. Be sure to have reservations for either lunch or dinner as it is popular. If not, you can order from a limited menu at the deli. It's the same sandwiches and salads as the restaurant. There is a lovely small eating area by the deli with a few tables and lots of windows for a quiet and cozy lunch.

Big Guys Diner, $, 1801 N. Hwy. 101, Newport, (541) 265-5114, is a real 50s monument. If hamburgers are your craving, this is the place. They have many other old favorites also. You can lounge on flamingo pink naugahide booths and look at the pictures of the 50s cars. Open 9 a.m.-9 p.m. daily.

The Daily Grind Coffeehouse, 156 SW Bay Blvd., Newport, (541) 265-6263, espresso, light lunch, open Mon.-Fri. 7 a.m.-5 p.m. Sat.-Sun. 8 a.m.-5p.m. A relaxing place with a nice deck overlooking the waterfront.

Special Local Attractions

Devil's Punch Bowl State Park, 4 miles south of Depoe Bay, formed when the roof fell in on two caves. At high tide, the ocean waves churn in on the cavern walls and with a mighty crash they shoot foam high in the air. The Marine Gardens tidepools are right next door with great exploring of tidepools, rocks, and caves for young and old alike. RV parking is easier in and out at the Marine Gardens parking area.

Yaquina Head Outstanding Natural Area, 3 miles north of Newport off Hwy. 101, this 100-acre preserve offers a stairway down the cliff for exploring tidepools. There are cement walkways to protect the marine life in the tidepools. This gives you a chance to see marine creatures up close. A telescope is available for looking at whales or the Yaquina Head Lighthouse. It's hard to believe that this was once an ugly quarry. This Bureau of Land Management project to reclaim and beautify this area has been underway for 3 years and is still very much in progress. There is limited RV parking.

Oregon Coast Aquarium, 2820 SE Ferry Slip Rd, (541) 867-3123, on the south side of the Yaquina Bay bridge has both indoor and outdoor exhibits, including marine mammals and seabirds. One of the best exhibits of marine life we have ever seen. And of course, the main attraction, Keiko the killer whale of "Free Willy" movie fame. Keiko has a special tank built here from donations to give him a healthier life than he had in Mexico. It is truly a heartfelt thrill to see this giant mammal swim by and nod his head at you as if to say "Thank you". Giftshop restaurant, bookstore, educational programs. South of Newport across the Yaquina Bay Bridge, follow the signs. Open: summer 9 a.m.-6 p.m., winter 10 a.m.-4:30 p.m. Admission fee is charged.

Hatfield Marine Science Center, 2030 Marine Science Dr., south of Newport across the Yaquina Bay Bridge, (541) 867-0100, open 10-4. Displays featuring the natural history of the Oregon Coast. A whale skeleton, a touch pool with starfish and anemones, tidepools teaming with sea life and science films are included. Note: this center was being expanded and redeveloped at this writing and is scheduled to be reopened to the public again in May 1997. The remodeled center will have more exhibits, computer simulations, and a new larger bookstore.

Wildlife Viewing

Otter Crest State Wayside, 8 miles north of Newport. Whales often present all year. Cormorants, pigeon guillemots, tufted puffins nest in this area.

Yaquina Bay, downtown Newport north of Yaquina Bay Bridge. Deck provides close viewing of sea lions and sea birds.

Cape Foulweather on Otter Crest Loop south of Depoe Bay. Walk to the end of the cape on the trail where a telescope allows viewing offshore rocks for sea lions and sea birds.

Yaquina Bar and **South Jetty**, Marine Science Center exit just south of Yaquina Bay Bridge in Newport. Go under bridge and follow road west to jetty. View from rocks. Seals, sea lions, water and shore birds. Killer whales are occasionally spotted.

Section 4: RV Parts & Services in Lincoln City/Newport/Depoe Bay

Diesel

Lincoln City: Shell, Garrison Fuel, 1410 SE Hwy. 101, Lincoln City, (503) 994-2661. Diesel is at the card lock pumps at the south end of the station. Easy access in and out without any overhead obstructions.

Lincoln City: Chevron Car Wash & Food Mart, 2320 NE Hwy. 101, Lincoln City, (503) 994-8448

Depoe Bay: Chevron Liberty Food Mart, 466 NE Hwy. 101, Depoe Bay, (541) 765-2992

Newport: Ron's BP Inc., 1517 N. Coast Hwy., (541) 265-5803, diesel is located on both pump aisles with ample room and clearance for RVs. They also have a large bay car wash for power washing your rig.

Dump Station

Lincoln City, 660 SE Hwy. 101. The dump station is in the parking area of the mall. A $1.00 fee is charged. Access in and out is excellent. Look for the large RV-sized car wash stalls on the intersection of Hwy. 101 and 6th St. The entrance is to the north of the car wash stalls.

Newport: Beverly Beach State Park, 6 miles north of Newport

Newport: South Beach State Park, 2 miles south of Newport

Newport at Visitors Center, 555 SW Coast Hwy. 101, turn east at the visitors center sign. Past the visitor's center you will see the dump station. Drive to the end of the block making a U-turn into the dump station driveway. Easy access. Free

Laundry

Lincoln City: 660 SE Hwy. 101, Lincoln City

Newport: Eileen's Laundry, NE 11th Hwy. 101, Newport

Newport: Beverly Beach Laundromat just off Hwy. 101 on the turn for Beverly Beach State Park next to the grocery store

Library

Lincoln City: Driftwood Library, 801 SW Hwy. 101, (541) 996-1257. Open Mon.-Thu. 9-9, Fri.-Sat. 9-5. A free 30-day temporary membership can be obtained at the library. Children activities include story hours and puppet shows, call for schedule.

Newport Public Library, 35 NW Nye Street, (541) 265-2153. Hours: Mon.-Thur. 10 a.m.-9 p.m. Fri.-Sat. 10 a.m.-6 p.m. Sun. 1 p.m.-4 p.m. An annual membership is available for $1 if you will be in the area for more than a week. Paperbacks can be checked out without a membership. All are welcome to enjoy their "living room setting" with sofas and fireplace; a great place to relax and read if the weather keeps you indoors.

Medical

Lincoln City: North Lincoln City Hospital, 3100 NE 28th St., (541) 994-3661. 24-hour emergency care

Newport: Pacific Communities Hospital, 930 SW Abbey, Newport, (541) 265-2244, 24-hour emergency care

Propane

Lincoln City: A to Z RV Services & Supplies, 660 SE Hwy. 101.

South Beach: Marine & RV Service, Inc., 4352 S. Coast Hwy. 101, South Beach. Propane cylinders can be filled without removal from your rig.

Newport: Amerigas, 18 NE Eads St., (541) 265-2213, cylinders filled and repaired.

RV Parts & Service

Lincoln City: A to Z RV Services & Supplies, 660 SE Hwy. 101, Lincoln City, (541) 994-7447. Located in this convenience plaza is the A to Z RV Services with a small selection of parts and supplies. They are a full-service repair company including dispatching of mobile services. Other stores in this plaza include an RV car wash, Laundromat, pet grooming.

South Beach: Marine & RV Service Inc., 4354 S. Hwy. 101, South Beach, OR 97366, one mile south of Yaquina Bay Bridge, (541) 867-3704. Dale Webster, manager, has stocked the store with a full complement of parts and supplies. If service takes more than

Yaquina Bay Lighthouse near Newport has the light tower built into the keeper's living quarters.

one day, he provides water and electric hookups. They will recommend a towing company if you need towing. They do not provide mobile service.
Newport: Pacific Shores RV Resort, 6225 N Coast Hwy. 101, (541) 265-3750. Has a good selection of RV parts and supplies.
Newport: Wal-Mart has an excellent selection of RV parts and supplies.

Shopping/Groceries

Lincoln City

Lincoln City Plaza, Hwy. 101/NW Logan Rd. Safeway, Bookends Bookstore, photo shop, Salmon Cafe
BiMart, across street from Lincoln City Plaza
The Factory Stores at Lincoln City, Hwy. 101 & South end of E. Devil's Lake Rd., (541) 996-5000. You can shop till you drop at 47 large shops; they are adding 22 more—the largest concentration of factory outlets in the West.

Newport

Safeway, 2220 N Hwy. 101, (541) 265-2930.
Fred Meyer One-Stop Shopping, 150 NE 20th/Hwy. 101 (541) 265-4581, has groceries, variety, pharmacy, clothing, hardware.
Wal-Mart, 160 NW 25th St./Hwy. 101, (541) 265-6560, carries no groceries but everything else.
Namedroppers, 412 SW Bay Blvd. on Newport waterfront, (541) 265-3967, has inexpensive personalized name gifts for family and friends.

USPO

Lincoln City: 1501 SE Devil's Lake Rd. 97367, (541) 994-2148
Depoe Bay: 486 North East 97341, (541) 765-2480
Newport: 310 SW 2nd Street, 97365, (541) 265-5542

Chapter 7

Waldport/Yachats/Florence

Map Grid A4: Waldport/Yachats/Florence Area

Introduction

Waldport is German for "Forest Port" and sits on Alsea Bay. Its biggest claim to fame is probably the fishing in the Alsea River and the Waldport Interpretive Center—in that order. The visitors center tells the story of transportation on the coast and is worth a visit.

Yachats (pronounced: Yah-hots), is derived from the Indian word Yahuts meaning, "at foot of a mountain". It sits at river's end of the Yachats River. Yachats is a jewel of a town with some dynamite views of crashing surf against rocks with blowholes and huge rolling waves. There is a marvelous drive up Yachats River Road to a covered bridge. You can continue on to Cape Perpetua through the forested mountains and past an active beaver pond.

Florence has miles of magnificent beaches, dramatic sand dunes, peaceful freshwater lakes and streams and the Siuslaw River estuary. This seaside city bordered by the Pacific Ocean and the Siuslaw River is rich in early Oregon Coast history. Tour Old Town, Florence's historic bayfront, now being restored to an area of unique shopping, galleries, and restaurants. Florence's average temperature in January is 43° and in July 61°. Rainfall averages 60 inches.

Section 1: Best Campgrounds in Waldport/Yachats/Florence Area

Best Public Campgrounds

Best public campground for base camping

Florence: Carl G. Washburne State Park, open all year, (541) 997-3851, p. 97

Best public campground with full or partial hookups

Waldport: Beachside State Park, open all year, (541) 563-3220, reservations (800) 452-5687, p. 96

Florence: Carl G. Washburne State Park, open all year, (541) 997-3851, p. 97

Alternate: Florence: Honeyman State Park, open all year, (541) 997-3641, reservations (800) 452-5687, p. 99

Best public campground for solitude and scenic beauty

Florence: Carl G. Washburn State Park, open all year, (541) 997-3851, p. 97

Waldport: Beachside State Park, open all year, (541) 563-3220, reservations (800) 452-5687, p. 96

Best public campground for families with children

Florence: Honeyman State Park, open all year, (541) 997-3641, reservations (800) 452-5687, p. 99

Siuslaw River from the dunes near Florence.

Best public campground that accepts Golden Age/Access passes

Yachats: Cape Perpetua Siuslaw NF, open May 15-Oct 15, (541) 563-3211, p. 96
Alternate: Yachats: Rock Creek, Siuslaw NF, open Apr-Oct., (541) 563-3211, p. 97
Florence: Sutton-Siuslaw NF, (541) 268-4473, p. 98
Alternate: Florence: Alder Dune-Siuslaw NF, open Memorial Day to Labor Day, (541) 268-4473, p. 98

Best public campground with low rates

Florence: Harbor Vista County Park, open all year, (541) 997-5987, p. 99

Best Private Campgrounds

Best private campground with low weekly/monthly rates

Florence: B & E Wayside RV Park, open all year, (541) 997-6451, p. 98

Best private campground for solitude and scenic beauty

Waldport: Alsea Bay RV Park, open all year, (541) 563-2250, p. 95
Florence: Heceta Beach RV Park, open all year, (541) 997-7664, p. 98

Best private campground for base camping

Waldport: Alsea Bay RV Park, open all year, (541) 563-2250, p. 95
Yachats: Sea Perch RV Park, open all year, (541) 547-3505, p. 97
Florence: Heceta Beach RV Park, open all year, (541) 997-7664, p. 98

Best private campground for families with children

Florence: Heceta Beach RV Park, open all year, (541) 997-7664, p. 98

Campground Descriptions

Waldport

Alsea Bay RV Park, open all year, 1330 NW Hwy. 101, Waldport, (541) 563-2250
Location: One mile north of Waldport on the west side of Hwy. 101
Description: A nice park under the pine trees and within walking distance to Waldport.

View of the waterfront at Old Town Florence.

Beautiful views of the ocean and the Alsea River can be seen from some of the campsites. This area is a favorite for fishermen because of Alsea Bay. Ona Beach State Park is about 5 miles north on Hwy. 101 with beautiful views of Beaver Creek and the ocean. You can walk to the bay, beach or town in 5 minutes.

69 gravel sites, some shaded, 69 full hookups (30 amp), 10 pull-thrus, max. length: 65', $18.00-$22.00, GS, lower weekly rates, restrooms, showers, dump, cable TV, phone, laundry, groceries, horseshoes, rec hall.

Beachside State Park, open all year, Waldport, (541) 563-3220, reservations (800) 452-5687.
Location: Four miles south of Waldport on the west side of Hwy. 101 on the Pacific Ocean
Description: This park is set in dense pines next to the ocean and is one of the few state parks with oceanfront view sites along the Oregon Coast where you can walk right out on to the beach. The paved interior roads are somewhat narrow but navigable. The park is midway along the eight-mile section of Oregon Coast Trail between Yachats and Waldport, so there is good day hiking in either direction on the nice hard sand. Reservations are advised in summer.

81 total paved sites, some shaded, 31 partial hookups, (20/30 amp), max. length 40', 50 dry camp sites, max. length 30', 17 acres, $16.00-$18.00, lower rates off season, restrooms, showers, dump, camp host, phone, planned activities in summer.

Yachats

Cape Perpetua/Siuslaw NF, open May 15-Oct 15, (541) 563-3211. Call Hoodoo Recreation Services (541) 822-3799 for availability and closure dates.
Location: Central Oregon Coast, approximately 2.5 miles south of Yachats on the east side of Hwy. 101 and 23 miles north of Florence in the Siuslaw National Forest.
Description of area: Located along Cape Creek in a narrow, green and lush coastal forest canyon consisting of Sitka spruce, Douglas fir, cedar and alder. The Cape Perpetua Scenic Area excites the visitor with crashing waves and blowholes that can be seen any month of the year—winter is especially dramatic. You will find an ancient Sitka spruce forest with a 500-year-old tree and plenty of Indian history to keep your interest for

Crashing waves can be seen all year at Shore Acres State Park.

Sunset at Whalehead Beach Cove.

Fishing for salmon on the Tillamook River.

The sculptured sandstone cliffs at Cape Kiwanda are a favorite resting spot for seabirds.

Sunset on the Siuslaw River Bridge at Florence.

The Coquille River Lighthouse, built in 1896, was restored in 1976 and stands today as a museum open daily.

This huge Sitka spruce is the surprise at the end of Cathedral Tree Trail in the heart of Astoria.

Siuslaw River from dunes near Florence.

Dahlias are a favorite on the coast.

View from the Ecola Point picnic area.

Hiking in the dunes can be like a moon walk with beautiful creeks meandering through.

Sunset over Cape Meares Beach.

Colorful flowers line the drive to Blue Heron Cheese Factory near Tillamook.

Relaxing while viewing the other Haystack Rock near Pacific City.

Newport's boardwalk provides an interesting stroll for visitors.

Seagulls viewing 3 Arch Rocks at Oceanside Beach Wayside.

more than just a weekend. Cape Perpetua Visitors Center is the hub for many educational programs, guided hikes and exhibits. It is open daily in summer from 10 a.m.-4 p.m. and weekends after Labor Day. It is walking distance from the campground. The close proximity to numerous day hiking trails of various lengths may warrant a longer stay. Most campsites are along the creek with the Pacific Ocean within walking distance. Cape Perpetua is a quiet place and the last of the campgrounds in the area to fill. This campground has an overflow parking area behind the visitors center at the top of the hill that is used only when the campground is full or closed. There is pull-thru space for 5 RV rigs of any length for overnight only. Camphost is available in this area all year. Donation.

38 paved sites, most shaded, 3 pull-thrus, max. length 30' $11.00, 14 acres. No hookups. Dump station for campers only, restrooms, water, handicap access, camp host, visitor's center nearby, nature trails. Accepts Golden Age/Golden Access passes.

Special Note: Bring warm clothes as the campground canyon is shady and can stay cool. The St. Perpetua Trail is a steep climb but not to be missed. The view at the top is awesome. Wear good hiking boots. For non-hikers, you can also enjoy the view from the top by driving up the overlook road.

Sea Perch RV Park, open all year, Hwy. 101, Yachats, (541) 547-3505

Location: On the central Oregon Coast with oceanside sites, 6.5 miles south of Yachats, **milepost 171**

Description: This campground boasts that it is one of only three campgrounds on the coast to offer oceanside sites. To clarify, they do have oceanside sites where you can walk down to the beach easily. The view is outstanding. Sea Perch is just south of Cape Perpetua with sites directly on the beach or lawn areas. It has its own interesting shell museum and gift shop.

48 gravel sites, 15 pull-thrus, 21 full hookups, 27 partial hookups, (15/20 amps), max. length: 60', $19.00-$22.50, Good Sam, AARP, lower weekly rate, restrooms, showers, cable TV, phone, laundry, groceries, propane, snack bar, deli, gift shop, shell museum.

Rock Creek, Siuslaw NF, open Apr-Oct., (541) 563-3211

Location: On the central Oregon Coast, 10 miles south of Yachats on the east side of Hwy. 101 close to Cape Perpetua Visitors Center.

Description: This is an outstanding campground for those that want peace and quiet. All sites are located in the forest along Rock Creek walking distance to the ocean. They are so far back from the highway that there is no road noise. A real diamond in the rough but alas there are no hookups.

15 paved sites, many shaded, 3 acres, max. length 50', water, restrooms, camp host. No reservations.

Note: Rock Creek Campground is located along a small narrow canyon for the creek. You cannot circle this campground to find a spot. Once you leave, larger rigs will not be able to turn around again at the campground entrance on Hwy. 101 to make another pass through the campground. When entering the campground, park near the camp host if possible and walk the campground to pick a spot first.

Florence Area

Carl G. Washburne State Park, open all year, (541) 997-3851

Location: 14 miles north of Florence, campground on the east side Hwy. 101, day-use on the west

Description: Located in dense coastal woods (1089 acres) with some of the best cover between sites in any Oregon Coast state park affording substantial privacy. A very quiet location with walking access to the ocean and a great trail system through the woods to beaver ponds and the beach. This campground has easy short and longer hikes that lead through the woods and to the ocean. There is also a two-mile beach with tidepools. A herd of elk can be spotted periodically from camp in the meadows. The Sea Lion Caves are three miles south where visitors can take an elevator down into the cavern that gives them a glimpse into seal life in their natural environment.

58 paved sites, mostly shaded, 58 full hookups, (20 amp), max. length 45', $20.00 daily rate, lower off-season rates, restrooms, showers, dump, handicap access, camp host, nature trails, planned activities in summer.

Alder Dune CG: USFS Siuslaw NF, open Memorial Day to Labor Day, (541) 268-4473, no reservations
Location: On Alder Lake, 7 miles north of Florence on Hwy. 101
Description: This campground was really designed for big rigs. A lovely campground with sites spaced wide apart. It is a very dense woodsy area but alas there is some road noise as it is right next to the highway. The day-use is a delightful place right on a little gem of a lake. Alder Dune is near three lakes; Alder Lake, Sutton Lake, and Mercer Lake. Marked hiking trails abound to all the other lakes. There is a boat launch at Sutton Lake. There is no ORVs access on the dunes here which offers quiet hiking opportunities. A nice campground for a stopover. No hookups.

38 paved sites, most shaded, 4 pull-thrus, 15 acres, Golden Age/Golden Access passes accepted, max. length 55', $10.00, restrooms, water, camp host.

Sutton Campground: USFS Siuslaw NF, open all year, (541) 268-4473, no reservations
Location: 5 miles north of Florence off Hwy. 101 on Sutton Beach Road
Description: A large, very nicely designed park with ample woods and cover between the sites. Sutton is on Sutton Creek, not far from Sutton Lake. There is a hiking trail from camp out to the dunes. No ORVs are allowed here for quiet hiking.

80 paved sites, many shaded, 6 acres, Golden Age/Golden Access passes accepted, max. length 60', $10.00, 6 pull-thrus, restrooms, camp host, water, swimming, boat launch, nature trails, fishing, planned activities in summer, playground.

Heceta Beach RV Park, open all year, 04636 Heceta Beach Rd., (541) 997-7664,
Location: Three miles north of Florence off Hwy. 101 on Heceta Beach Rd. From Junction of Hwy. 101 and Hwy 126 in Florence, travel north 3 miles on Hwy. 101 to Heceta Beach Rd. go west 1.8 miles
Description: A very well kept park with good management. The sites have good cover between them and it's away from the highway for peace and quiet. They have very strict rules for pets and they enforce them. This park is in demand for summer so get your reservations in 3 months in advance.

51 gravel sites, some shaded, 25 full hookups, 26 partial hookups, (30/50 amp), 24 pull-thrus, max. length 60', overflow dry camp spaces when available, $17.50-$20.00, GS, lower weekly and off-season rates, dump, restrooms, showers, cable TV, phone, laundry, groceries, RV supplies, large rec hall with pool table, TV and games, restaurant nearby.

B & E Wayside RV & Mobile Park, open all year, 3760 Hwy. 101 N., (541) 997-6451
Location: 1.7 miles north of Florence on the east side of Hwy. 101
Description: This well-groomed park is right off the highway in the heart of Florence so expect some road noise.

59 paved/gravel sites, available: 14 paved, 10 gravel, some shaded, 24 full hookups, (30 amp), dump, no pull-thrus, max. length: 50', $15.00 daily rate, lower weekly/monthly rates, restrooms, showers, cable TV, phone, laundry, rec hall, game room.

Harbor Vista Park (Lane County Park), open all year, N. Jetty Rd./Rhododendron

Dr., (541) 997-5987. Takes reservations.
Location: 3 miles north of Florence on North Jetty Road
Description: This campground has a great ocean view, perched above the north jetty of the Siuslaw River. Whale watching and beachcombing are popular. There is an observation deck that overlooks the jetty and the ocean. This 15-acre park has lush vegetation and has recently been remodeled to accommodate big rigs.

31 gravel/paved RV sites, all partial hookups, (20/30 amp) max. length 60', $13.00-$15.00, dump, restrooms, showers, handicap accessible, camp host, beach access, playground, hiking trails.

Jessie M. Honeyman State Park, open all year, 84505 Hwy. 101 S., (541) 997-3641, reservations (800) 452-5687
Location: Three miles south of Florence on the west side of Hwy. 101
Description: Honeyman is one of the nicest (and most popular) state campgrounds on the Oregon Coast especially for families with children. It has it all—522 acres of freshwater lakes, dunes, and a great day-use park. This popular state park is next to the Oregon Dunes National Recreation Area. Trails wind through the park to the day use area. You can swim or rent boats at Lake Cleawox. A nice playground can be found at the end of L loop. Sites, L24, L25, L26 give children immediate access to the playground. There is some noise here from ORVs (off-road vehicles) at the private dunes next door.

378 total paved sites, many shaded, 66 full hookups (30 amp), 91 partial hookups (20 amp), max. length 60', no pull-thrus, $16.00-$20.00, lower rates off-season, dump, restrooms, showers, handicap access, camp host, nature trails, planned activities in summer. Cleawox Lake, Woahink Lake, trout fishing, swimming, boating, ramp, boat rental, playground.

Volunteer/Camp Host Opportunities

Beachside State Park, Waldport, (541) 563-3220
Jessie M. Honeyman State Park, Florence, (541) 997-3641
Carl G. Washburn State Park, Florence, (541) 997-3851
Rock Creek, summer, (USFS), Yachats, (541) 563-3211
Sutton Campground, all year, (USFS), Florence, (541) 268-4473
Alder Dune Campground, summer only, (USFS), Florence, (541) 268-4473
Harbor Vista Campground, Lane County, Florence, (541) 997-5987
Alsea Fish Hatchery, Philomath, (541) 487-7240

Section 2: Activities in Waldport/Yachats and Vicinity

Waldport and Yachats are both very small towns. There are still many activities in this area that you will enjoy. The Cape Perpetua area is one of our all-time favorite spots on the coast. This is an area where the ocean really makes its presence known.

Don't Miss

- Waldport Interpretive Center,
- Cape Perpetua Visitors Center & auto tour

Highly Recommended

- Sea Lion Caves
- Smelt Sands Trail 804
- Yachats State Park

Bike/Auto Tours

Yachats North Fork Covered Bridge: Drive Yachats River Road north of the bridge in Yachats, for 7 miles (it is best to turn on this road while going southbound on Hwy.

Annual Events

Check with Yachats Chamber of Commerce
3rd Street/ Hwy. 101, Yachats, (541) 547-3530, for specific dates
Check with Waldport Chamber of Commerce
In the interpretive center south of the Alsea Bay Bridge,
(541) 563-2133, for specific dates

March
Arts & Crafts Fair

July
Yachats Smelt Fry

October
Yachats Kite Festival

101). At the road's end, turn left onto a good one-lane gravel road for 2 miles where it ends at the bridge. This is a beautiful, well-maintained, red covered bridge—perfect for photo taking. Watch for the elk crossing signs where elk may be seen in the early morning and late evening hours as they leave the forests to graze in the meadows by the river.
Yachats to Cape Perpetua, (19-mile loop), inland auto tour, drive Yachats River Rd., north of the bridge in Yachats, for 7 miles (it is best to turn on this road while going southbound on Hwy. 101). At the road's end, turn right and follow the signs to Cape Perpetua. This 19-mile tour is a one-lane paved road with many turnouts through young and old forests with interpretive signs. You will pass Keller Creek day-use and picnic area which would make a great lunch stop, and further down the road is a beaver pond in action. When we were there the beavers had just felled trees for their food supply. You will end up at the road that enters the Cape Perpetua Campground. An extra treat would be to turn right and go up to the Cape Perpetua Overlook. Take your camera as the views here are spectacular.

Bookstores

By the Sea Books, 887 Hwy. 101 N., Yachat,s (541) 547-4455, is open from 10 a.m.-6 p.m. daily, closed Tuesday. It has mysteries, metaphysical and more, plus free coffee, cookies and tea. Very friendly proprietors.

Exercise Routes or Leisure Walking

Smelt Sands Wayside (in Yachats) area has a lovely .75-mile (one-way) trail that is easy and gives awesome views of the pounding surf. This trail was preserved only when a group of citizens who had used it as a fishing trail for years fought all the way to the Supreme Court to prevent a private landowner from closing off the trail. This important action saved it forever for all of us and our children to enjoy. Take the time to appreciate the beauty along this bluff by the ocean that their efforts saved.

Family Activities with Children

Yachats Commons playground is a nice secluded park behind the Commons building (5th & Hwy 101).
Yachats River Beach has access from south of the bridge at Yachats Ocean Wayside. There is a large beach where children can play in the sand and wade in the river without the waves of the ocean. Kite flying is also popular here and there are picnic tables for a leisurely lunch.

Fishing

The Alsea Bay and River as well as the Yachats River are noted for freshwater salmon

The trail at Smelts Sands near Yachats was saved by a group of local citizens.

and trout. Upstream the Alsea River Recreation Area from Waldport offers a mix of fishing lodges, small marinas and restaurants.

Galleries

Back Porch Gallery, Hwy. 101 & 4th St., Yachats, (541) 547-4500, has a very nice collection of watercolors, jewelry, weaving, and sculpture. Stop next door at the New Morning Cafe for an espresso.

Hiking

Cape Perpetua Trails: Stop at the Cape Perpetua Visitors Center and ask for a trail guide. Oregon had a very severe winter in 1996 and many of the trails in this area were damaged. Check with the visitors center first to see if your hiking ability is up to the current trail conditions.

St. Perpetua Trail starts at the visitor's center and climbs 600 feet to a stone hut at the top of the cape (2.6 miles round-trip).

Cape Perpetua Shoreline Loop, easy 1.3-mile loop (guided tour from the visitors center) where you will see Indian shell middens, tidal pools, crashing surf and blowholes.

Cook's Ridge, 2-mile loop. Take Cook's Ridge Trail to the mid-trail loop and return to the visitors center.

Cook's Ridge, 4-mile trail through virgin forest. Can combine with Gwynn Creek Trail for a 6.4-mile loop or Cummins Creek Trail for a 9.3-mile loop. These trails will take you through old growth, especially Gwynn Creek Trail.

Giant Spruce, Cape Creek Trail, 2 miles round-trip from visitor's center, one mile round-trip from campground and worth every step.

Carl G. Washburne State Park has 3 great trails. China Creek Trail is a short walk to the beach along China Creek. Valley Trial 1.6 miles one way or a 4-mile loop trial. There is a sign on the entrance road to the campground directing yo, to the trails. Valley Trail winds through coastal forest past creeks and beaver ponds. Trail's end is at the south end parking lot. You may return the same way or cross Hwy. 101, walk to the right to the

Built in 1894, the 49-foot Heceta Head Lighthouse is visible 20 miles out to sea.

sign post on the west side of the Hwy. and take Hobbit Trail to the beach. Walk the beach north back over the dune to Carl G. Washburne State Park day-use area. Across the highway is the campground. Besides lots of small wildlife, you may see elk.

Local History/Museums/Lighthouses

Devil's Elbow State Park, Heceta Head Lighthouse. Walk the short, easy, forested trail which passes through the coastal undergrowth of salal, ferns, and huckleberries to the Heceta Lighthouse and old caretaker's house. The views at the top of this hill are first-rate. Heceta Head Lightstation, a beautifully-kept building now has bed and breakfast accommodations. Call (541) 547-3696 for reservations.

Little Log Church by the Sea Museum, Yachats, 328 Third St., (541) 547-3976, is a rustic little building built in 1930 in the shape of a cross with timber hauled down the Yachats River. It has gone through a couple of different denominations since then and is now a museum housing a rich treasure of local historical artifacts as well as contemporary works on loan as exhibits.

Photo Opportunities

- Cape Perpetua
- Heceta Head Lighthouse is the most photographed lighthouse in Oregon

Restaurants/Espresso

La Serre, $$$, 2nd & Beach, Yachats, (541) 547-3420, considered by the locals to be 4-star dining but pricey. Always an excellent place for seafood for that special occasion.

LeRoy's Blue Whale, $, Yachats, 580 Hwy. 101, (541) 547-3399, is a family restaurant and a great place for fish and chips. A light airy place with vaulted ceilings.

Special Local Attractions

Sea Lion Caves, (**milepost 179** on Hwy 101) one of the world's largest sea caves, is your chance to take an elevator down for a first hand look at the noisy critters. The elevator goes down 205 feet to the grotto and has been hosting visitors since 1932. Visitors peer through screened windows where your chances are good for seeing them barking continuously. Ask if there are any seals to be viewed before you pay. Admission is charged. There is also a gift shop on the premises. RV parking space next to and across the street is very limited. Large RVs might find easier in and out just south of the building in a large gravel parking area.

Alsea Bay Bridge Interpretive Center, in Waldport on the south side of the bridge off Hwy 101, (541) 563-2133, is worth a stop. It traces how we got from place to place on the coast beginning with the Indian canoe and ending with the automobile and the bridges that finally made the trip down the coast so easy. It may not sound like much but it takes you on a journey year by year starting with the 1800s and can be quite interesting as well as educational for both young and old alike. In the summer a ranger does demonstrations of crabbing for visitors. The Chamber of Commerce is also in this building. Free Daily 9 a.m.-5 p.m..

The Little Log church, which is now a museum, was built in 1927 in the shape of a cross.

Wildlife Viewing

Strawberry Hill Wayside, .5 mile south of Cape Perpetua. There are some offshore rocks where you can see many adult harbor seals. Binoculars make the sight more amazing—there are tons of them. A trail leads out to shore rocks where you can get a closer look, but proceed with caution—and of course watch the tide. Look for harbor seal pups in April, May, June. Tidepools are also accessible. There is very limited parking for small vehicles.

Sea Lion Caves, (see "Special Local Activities")

Cape Perpetua Visitors Center, whales, seabirds

Section 3: Activities in Florence and Vicinity

Florence is right in the heart of "dune" country with a dizzy array of campgrounds to choose from in the vicinity. The town is also known for its rhododendrons and the festival in May celebrates them. Florence is doing a credible job restoring its waterfront to make it more tourist friendly, so you may want to spend some time strolling Old Town, Florence.

Don't Miss

- **Heceta Head Lighthouse**
- **Devil's Elbow State Park**

Highly Recommended

Old Town, Florence, on the north bank of the Siuslaw River, restored wood and brick buildings to their 19th century architecture.

South Jetty Road, hike the dune just west of the Siuslaw Bridge (park at the first posted map of the South Jetty Rd. and walk up the dune toward the river). Hikers will be rewarded with high views down to the Siuslaw River, downtown Florence, and the bridge but the going can be slow through the sand.

Bike/Auto Tours

South Jetty Road is a level stretch that can be biked to the Jetty end. You may wish to bypass the ORV staging areas by driving to the "NO ORVs past this point" sign and parking. You can then drive or ride your bike the rest of the road to the jetty end or the fishing dock. The traffic here is light and the views are non-stop. This area can be windy so dress accordingly.

Spend a Day in Mapleton

Getting there: Take Hwy. 126 14 miles east of Florence to the town of Mapleton and enjoy an eye-popping ride along the Siuslaw River. You will see marinas, white egrets, mountains, pastoral farms and best of all the beautiful river. This can be done as an auto tour or bicycle trip. If biking, the bike shoulder is 5'-6' wide most of the time. This is the main highway to Eugene so there is traffic most any time of

Annual Events

Check with Florence Chamber of Commerce
270 Hwy. 101, (541) 997-3128, for specific dates

March
Rhododendron and Azalea Show

May
Rhododendron Festival

July
Stilt Walking Championship

August
Community Salmon Barbecue

The beautifully curved Alsea Bay Bridge at Waldport.

the day. There is not much elevation gain in all 14 miles.

Dining: The **Alpha Bits Cafe** opens at 10 a.m. and is a good stop for a lunch or a Friday night dinner. It's right on main street and a surprise treat for this town. Good food, a lovely gift shop and a large bookstore. This cafe is owed by the Alpha Farm, an intentional community that was started in 1971 that encompasses a simple, self-reliant life for its members.

Sweet Creek Trails: Gorgeous, easy hikes. Stop at the Mapleton Ranger Station and pick up their trail maps. Ask for the Sweet Creek trail map. You will have your choice of four different hikes beginning at the Homestead Trailhead. The beginning part of this trail is wheelchair accessible. You can explore 11 waterfalls. At Hwy. 126 in Mapleton, cross the bridge and immediately turn right and go west on Sweet Creek Road. A beautiful 10.2-mile drive along the Siuslaw River will take you to the first trailhead—Homestead. Watch closely for a small brown sign for Sweet Creek on the left. Hike the Homestead Trail (.75 miles) and then continue on the Sweet Creek Trail (.5 miles) for a real feast for the eyes. Waterfalls everywhere and interesting rock formations. Check your trail guide and see if there are other trails in this area you may want to try.

Bookstores

The Book Trader, 128 Maple, Old Town, Florence, (541) 997-2322, has a good selection of new and used books shelved together. You can buy, sell, or trade. A large selection of children's books.

Ecotourism

Sternwheeler Cruise, Old Town, Florence, (541) 997-9691. Ride the paddle boat up the Siuslaw River to Mapleton. Includes a narrated history while viewing wildlife in the tidal river estuary.

Darlingtonia Botanical Wayside, 4 miles north of Florence on Mercer Lake Rd., Botanical Gardens with a large garden of *Darlingtonia californica* or Cobra-Lily (a fly-eating plant.

One of 11 waterfalls along Sweet Creek, a new handicap accessible trail near Mapleton.

Exercise Routes or Leisure Walking

Obtain a "Walking Map of Old Town Florence" from the Florence Chamber of Commerce, 270 Hwy. 101

Miller Park, 18th St. West, Florence, has a great .75-mile walking path that goes all around this lovely green park. The path is a nice, soft bark and sometimes sand surface. Great place for your morning exercise.

Family Activities with Children

Jessie M. Honeyman Park, south of Florence. Visit this park even if you are not staying there for swimming in the freshwater lakes, hiking, and exploring the sand dunes or playing at the playground.

Central Coast Watersports, 1560 2nd Street, Florence, 1-800-789-DIVE. Kayak, canoes, surf boards, wet suits, etc. rentals. Decide how adventurous you want to be; rent a canoe and paddle across the calm estuary to view the wildlife, or rent a wet suit and surf kayak and head for the ocean.

Sandland Adventures, 85366 Hwy. 101 S., (541) 997-8087, has miniature golf, bumper boats, go-karts, dune buggy tours, dune vehicle rentals. They will take you on a guided tour to the most scenic parts of the dunes.

Seahorse Stagecoaches, (541) 999-0319, has horse-drawn wagons that make trips on the beach.

Sea Lion Caves, 91560 Hwy. 101 N., (541) 547-3111

Westward Ho Sternwheeler, docks at Mo's in Old Town (541) 997-9691, has 90-minute guided historical time warp tours, 30-minute bay rides, sunset (2 hour) dinner cruises.

Sand Dunes Frontier and Theme Park, 4 miles south of Florence on Hwy 101, (541) 997-3544. Miniature golf, shooting gallery, sand dune buggy rides

Florence City Parks

Miller Park, 18th St. West, Florence. Twenty-acre park with six ball fields, basketball courts, walking path, enclosed area with playground equipment. Picnic tables are available both in the open areas and under cover. Restrooms are next to the parking area.

Rolling Dunes Park is for the tennis buff. Two courts at 35th Street and Siano Loop, Florence (go west on 35th.)

Fishing/Clamming

Fish or crab the **Siuslaw Estuary** from the dock at Laurel St. & Bay St. in Florence (Old Town Park).

South Jetty, Florence. A dock over the jetty is a popular place for crabbing and fishing.

Siltcoos Lake, six miles south of Florence take Westlake Road east to a boat ramp and fishing dock. This large freshwater lake contains trout, bass, bluegill, crappie, yellow perch.

Galleries/Arts

Wind Drift Gallery, 125 Maple St., Florence, (541) 997-9182, in old town. Specialty is marine art and gifts.

Blue Heron gallery, 1385 Bay St., Florence (541) 997-7993. Collection of jewelry, paintings, sculptures, wood carvings, glassworks

Golfing

Sandpines Golf Links, 1201 35th St., Florence, west on 35th, (541) 997-1940 or (800) 917-4653. Public 18-hole course voted best new public golf course by Golf Digest in 1993. A par 72 with four par 5, ten par 4, and four par 3 holes. Four putting greens, coffee shop, driving range. This course is built in the dunes with very little level ground. You will want to test your skills on this one.

Ocean Dunes Golf Links, 3345 Munsel Lake Rd., Florence, (541) 997-3232 or (800) 468-4833. Public 18-hole course advertising themselves as "a wee bit o' Scotland on the Oregon Coast". This par 70 course built in the dunes has two par 5, twelve par 4, and four par 3 holes. Putting green, deli, driving range (irons only)

Heceta Head Lighthouse caretaker's house near Florence.

Cape Creek Bridge from Devil's Elbow State Park.

Hiking

Sutton Creek Sand Dunes: 2.5 miles north of Florence take Sutton Road west to Sutton campground. Several trails begin at this campground from .2 mile to 2.4 miles in length. Trails lead to Sutton Lake, a boardwalk over a bog, Holman Vista overlooking the estuary, or the sand dunes. Obtain trail maps at the campground from the camp host.

Sand Dunes Trail, Honeyman State Park, 4-mile round-trip. This trail passes through the dunes, goes around Cleawox Lake and past the playground, plus it goes across Hwy. 101 to Woahink Lake and the Honeyman day-use area. You can pick up the trail at the registration booth for the campground.

Sweet Creek Trails (see "Spend a Day in Mapleton")

Local History/Museums/Lighthouses

Siuslaw Pioneer Museum, 85294 Hwy. 101 S, Florence, (541) 997-7884. Pioneer and Indian exhibits. Hours: 10 a.m.-4 p.m. Tue-Sun. Volunteers will assist and explain the history behind the photographs and donated pioneer furnishings from the Florence area. A well done museum for a small community. Donation

Heceta Head Lighthouse is the most photographed of the many Oregon beacons. Tours are available at Heceta Head Lighthouse through the summer.

Photo Opportunities

- The Dunes
- Florence Beaches; especially sunsets
- Sunset behind the Siuslaw Bridge from the dock at Old Town, Florence
- Heceta Head Lighthouse
- Cape Perpetua
- Devil's Elbow State Park

Restaurants/Espresso

Florence

Bridgewater Seafood, $$, 1297 Bay St. in Old Town, Florence, (541) 997-9405, has a good variety on its menu in an attractive setting.

Travelers Cove, $$, Gourmet Cafe & Import Shop, Florence, 1362 Bay St., (541) 997-6845, an excellent place to eat. Try the Thai chicken salad or the BBQ chicken. Open daily.

Blue Hen Cafe, $$, 1675 Hwy. 101, Florence, (541) 997-3907. As the name implies, the specialty is breakfast. The portions are very generous and all homecooked. Smoke-free.

Morgan's Country Kitchen, $, 85020 Hwy. 101 S, Florence, (541) 997-6991, good home-cooking for breakfast, lunch or dinner. Chicken is their specialty. Smoke-free.

Mapleton

Alpha Bits, $, downtown Mapleton, (541) 268-4311. Open 10 a.m.-6 p.m. serves a luncheon menu of mostly American food. This interesting spot has a large book display, as well as crafts and gifts for sale. Definitely worth a stop if you are in Mapleton.

Special Local Attractions

Florence's waterfront (Bay St.) is being revitalized. It's a pleasant place to stroll, look at the shops, and catch a meal.

Old Town Park located at the end of Laurel on Bay Street, the site of the old Siuslaw River Ferry. It has a fenced dock for fishing or crabbing. Enjoy the gazebo and benches on the lawn.

Gallaher's Park, Hwy 126/Spruce St., is a little (3.5-acre) gem in the city which has trails through the forest with both native and cultured rhododendrons to Munsel Creek. Bring your lunch and enjoy this quiet oasis on the picnic table and if it's May you'll get a real floral display.

Wildlife Viewing

Devil's Elbow State Park is a popular destination for day-trips and picnics. It is named for the distinctly shaped sea rocks just offshore. A short trail from the park leads to the headlands above and to one of the Oregon Coast's most spectacular settings—Heceta Head Lighthouse. Watch for whales and seabirds

Siuslaw River Estuary (Old Town Florence), seals, sea lions

South Jetty Road, Florence. Drive across the dunes to marshy lakes and finally the jetty. Great place for shorebird watchers. In the winter a high concentration of swans and Canadian geese can be seen.

Sutton Recreation Area, milepost 185.4. on Hwy. 101 then two miles to the day-use area where you will find trails and a view of the Sutton Creek estuary from Holman Vista.

Section 4: RV Parts & Services from Yachats to Florence

Diesel

Yachats: Texaco,(935 N Hwy. 101, Yachats, (541) 547-3882. Diesel pump is located on the south side corner of station—not along the gasoline pump aisles. There is ample room to drive behind the station to position your rig for filling.

Florence: Bob Miles Texaco, 813 Hwy 101N, Florence, (541) 997-9737. Intersection of Hwy. 101 and Hwy. 126. Diesel on outside bay. Excellent access in and out.

Florence: Chevron Foodmart, 1839 Hwy. 101, Florence, (541) 997-3351. Diesel in the outer bay. Excellent access.

Dump Station

Yachats: Carl G. Washburne State Park
Florence: Honeyman State Park

Laundry

Yachats: Suds R Us, 2nd St./Hwy. 101, (541) 547-4440, has commercial washers for big loads. Snacks, magazines and change makers.
Florence: 37th Street Coin Laundry & Showers, 37th Street and Hwy 101, (541) 997-5111. TV sitting area, attendant on duty, drop off laundry, has a play yard for the kids while you do the laundry.

Library

Yachats Public Library, 7th Street, Yachats, (541) 547-3741, is open Mon.-Fri. 10 a.m.-4 p.m., Sat. 12 p.m.-4 p.m.. Fill out their free membership card to become a member and check out books immediately. They have some periodicals which are free and they also sell some paperbacks. They take donations.

Florence: Siuslaw Public Library, 9th & Maple, Florence, (541) 997-3132. Hours: Sun. 1-5 p.m., Mon.-Thur. 10-8 p.m., Fri-Sat 10-5 p.m.. One of the nicest libraries we've seen. They have a large, comfy reading area with a very nice selection of periodicals and newspapers. The sunken children's area with its stuffed animals, toys, and games is a delight. A great place to hang out on a rainy day.
A one month membership can be purchased for $2 at the library with checkout privileges the same day.

Medical Services

Florence: Peace Harbor Hospital, one mile west of Hwy. 101, 400 9th Street, (541) 997-8412, 24-hour emergency care

Propane

Yachats Texaco, 935 N Hwy. 101, Yachats, (541) 547-3882, on the north side of the station.
Florence: Chevron Foodmart, 1839 Hwy. 101, Florence, (541) 997-3351. Propane on south of station.

RV Parts & Service

Florence RV & Automotive Specialists, 4390 Hwy. 101 N, Florence, (541) 997-8287. Full service company and AAA authorized towing for the area. Will provide water and electric hookup if service requires overnight. Full selection of parts and a limited amount of RV supplies in stock.

Shopping/Groceries

Florence: Safeway, 700 Hwy. 101, (541) 997-2204, groceries, deli, floral, bakery, takes credit cards
Florence: BiMart, 4310 Hwy 101, (541) 997-2499

USPO

Yachats: 141 Beach Street, 97498, (541) 547-3512
Florence: 770 maple, 97439, (541) 997-2533

Chapter 8

Dunes City to Coos Bay

Map Grid A5: Dunes City to Coos Bay

Introduction

Reedsport is the center hub for "Dune City" where people come to drive their ORVs (off-road vehicles) on the great sand dunes. For fishing enthusiasts, however, nothing beats the Umpqua River, one of the prettiest rivers on the coast. Winchester Bay is known as the largest sport-fishing marina on the coast with nearly 1,000 boat slips.

North Bend marks the transition from dunes to the rugged south coast. Combined with Coos Bay, this is the largest urban community on the coast. The three towns of North Bend, Coos Bay, and Charleston seem to almost run together and at one time North Bend and Coos Bay discussed merging but the individuality of each town won out and they decided to stay separate. It's still hard to tell where one ends and the other begins. Charleston, however, is a little farther away from the other two and with its harbor and boats has a distinction all its own. Charleston leads you to the wildly beautiful Pacific Ocean and Cape Arago, Shore Acres State Park and all the beauty to be had in this part of the coast. This town is also the third largest commercial port on the coast, and includes fish-processing for tuna, oysters, salmon, and shrimp.

Coos Bay is slowly making the changes necessary for many timber-based towns that want to increase tourism as part of their economic base. Their biggest opportunity now is to spruce up the town and lead the tourists who come to see this area to their natural jewels like Mingus Park, Empire Lakes and of course Sunset Bay, Shore Acres and Cape Arago. Coos Bay is fixing up the downtown wharf area just as Newport and Florence are doing. The boardwalk is very pleasant and has some interesting interpretive signs about the importance of their watershed. The bay area enjoys a relatively mild marine climate. Rainfall averages about 60 inches a year. Average temperatures range from 40° in January to 57° in July. The elevation is nearly sea level.

Section 1: Best Campgrounds

Best Public Campgrounds

Note about ORVs: Because so much of this area's fun involves the Oregon Dunes Recreation Area, you may hear the buzz of ORVs (off-road vehicles) zipping around on the sand dunes. ORVs can be rented or brought only to the designated campgrounds in the area. If you are interested in riding an ORV, check with the Oregon Dunes Recreation Area Visitors Center in Reedsport for a map showing which areas and timeframes are open to these vehicles. The campgrounds we list in this grid do not allow ORV staging and are a quieter place to stay.

Best public campgrounds for base camping

Winchester Bay: Umpqua Lighthouse State Park, open all year, (541) 271-4118, reservations (800) 452-5687, p. 114

Lakeside: Tugman State Park, open all year, (541) 759-3604, reservations (800) 452-5687, p. 115

Fisherman enjoying the pier on Eel Lake at Tugman State Park.

Charleston: Bastendorff Beach County Park, open all year, no reservations (541) 888-5353, p. 116

Best public campgrounds for solitude and scenic beauty

Lakeside: Tugman State Park, open all year, (541) 759-3604, reservations (800) 452-5687, p. 115
Charleston: Sunset Bay State Park, open all year, (541) 888-4902, reservations (800) 452-5687, p. 117
Alternate: Charleston: Bastendorff Beach County Park, open all year, no reservations (541) 888-5353, p. 116

Best public campgrounds for families with children

Lakeside: Tugman State Park, open all year, (541) 759-3604, reservations (800) 452-5687, p. 115
Charleston: Bastendorff Beach County Park, open all year, no reservations (541) 888-5353, p. 116

Best public campgrounds with low rates

Winchester Bay: Windy Cove County Park A & B, Park A (541) 271-4138, Park B (541) 271-5634), p. 115
Charleston: Bastendorff Beach County Park, open all year, no reservations (541) 888-5353, p. 116

Best public campgrounds that accept Golden Age/Golden Access passes

Dunes City: Lagoon Campground, Siuslaw NF, open all year, no reservations (541) 271-3611, p. 113
Alternate: Carter Lake Campground Siuslaw NF, Dunes City, open: 4/30-11/1, no reservations (541) 271-3611, p. 113

Alternate: North Eel Creek Campground, Siuslaw NF, Lakeside, open all year, no reservations (541) 271-3611, p. 115

Best Private Campgrounds

Best private campground with luxurious facilities

Lakeside: Osprey Point RV Resort, open all year, (541) 759-2801, p. 115

Best private campground with Good Sam discount or low weekly rates

Charleston: Charleston Marina RV Park, open all year, (541) 888-9512, p. 116
Reedsport: Coho RV Resort, open all year, (541) 271-5411, p. 113

Best private campground for solitude and scenic beauty

Charleston: Oceanside RV Park, open all year, (800) 570-2598, or (541) 888-2598, p. 116
Reedsport: Surfwood Campground, open all year, (541) 271-4020, p. 114

Best private campground for base camping

Coos Bay: Lucky Loggers RV Park, open all year, (541) 267-6003 or (800) 267-6426, p. 117

Best private campground for families with children

Reedsport: Surfwood Campground, open all year, (541) 271-4020, p. 114
Charleston: Oceanside RV Park, open all year, (800) 570-2598, or (541) 888-2598, p. 116

Campground Descriptions

Dunes City Area

Lagoon, Siuslaw NF, open all year, no reservations, (541) 271-3611
Location: 7 miles south of Florence on Hwy. 101 within the Oregon Dunes National Recreation Area. Turn west at the Siltcoos Recreation Area sign.
Description: This is a beautiful campground circled by a nice lagoon where egrets and blue herons can be spotted. A beautiful trail (Lagoon Trail) goes around the campground. There are no hookups. Some pull-thru sites can be tight. The access roads are somewhat narrow. ORV access is half mile away. Waxmyrtle Campground (across the road) would be an alternative but it is closed after November.

40 paved sites, some shaded, Golden Age/Golden Access passes accepted, max. length 45', 8 pull-thrus, $10.00, flush toilets, water, camp host, swimming, ocean access, trails, fishing, amphitheater.

Carter Lake, Siuslaw NF, open: 4/30-11/1, no reservations, (541) 271-3611
Location: 8.5 miles south of Florence off Hwy. 101, on Carter Lake within the Oregon Dunes National Recreation Area.
Description: This campground is set along the north shore of Carter Lake, however the campsites do not have lake views. Boating swimming and fishing are permitted on this long, narrow lake, and there is a nice swimming beach area. The campground is set among dunes overgrown with vegetation and beach pines. Hiking is peaceful and quiet as there is no ORV access here. Taylor Dunes Trailhead is close to camp.

23 paved sites, some shaded, max. length: 45' (approximately 50% of the sites), $10.00, Golden Age/Golden Access passes accepted, restrooms, water, camp host, no hookups.

Reedsport

Coho RV Park, open all year, 1580 Winchester Ave., Reedsport, (541) 271-5411
Location: .5 miles south of Reedsport just off Hwy. 101
Description: This RV park is a well taken care of and has a secured marina for people

Kayaking the surf at Sunset Bay near Charleston.

who want to bring their boat. It is right on Hwy. 101 so it gets some road noise.

49 paved sites with patios, 13 pull-thrus, max. length 50', 49 full hookups, (30 amp), cable TV $, $12.00 daily rate, lower weekly rates, GS, restrooms, showers, phone, Scofield Creek, salmon fishing, clamming, crabbing, boat ramp, secured marina.

Surfwood Campground, open all year, 75381 Hwy. 101, Reedsport, (541) 271-4020
Location: Near Winchester Bay, this park is .5 miles from the marina. Located at the center of the Oregon Dunes National Recreation Area where the Smith and Umpqua rivers empty into the Pacific Ocean making this a fisherman's paradise.
Description: Surfwood has left the trees and shrubbery between the sites so you will have plenty of privacy here. The owner is very friendly and helpful. In the back of the park is a secluded area for children to play or adults to play tennis. The pool is only operational in the summer. Being close to the marina, it makes for a good fishing spot. There are many trails nearby, leading west across the dunes to the ocean and east to lakes in a wooded area. Wildlife watchers will enjoy the Dean Creek Elk Preserve 10 miles east off Hwy 38.

163 gravel sites, many shaded, 40 partial hookups, 101 full hookups, (20/30 amp), 78 pull-thrus, max. length: 60', $12.00-$16.00, lower weekly/monthly rates, GS, restrooms, showers, cable TV, phone, laundry, heated pool, store, sauna, horseshoes, playground.

Winchester Bay

Umpqua Lighthouse State Park, open all year, (541) 271-4118 reservations (800) 452-5687
Location: Near Winchester Bay, off Hwy. 101, 6 miles south of Reedsport on Lighthouse Road. On the Umpqua River near Lake Marie with trout fishing and swimming.
Description: Located in a wooded basin between the ocean and Hwy. 101, this camp-

ground is on Discovery Drive which leads to the Umpqua Lighthouse. Umpqua Lighthouse is still operational and is worth a visit. There is a whale watching station with interpretive signs across the street. Umpqua Lighthouse State Park is walking distance to Lake Marie and adjacent to the miles of sand dunes in the Oregon Dunes National Recreation Area. You can take a trail from the campground to Lake Marie where there is an easy one-mile trail that follows the shoreline of the lake. The dunes in this area can be as high as 500 feet with hiking trails leading from the park to the Umpqua Dunes Scenic Area. Dean Creek Elk Viewing Area is nearby off Hwy. 38.

64 total paved sites, some shaded, 450 acres, 22 full hookups, (20 amp), max. length 45', no pull-thrus, $20.00, lower off-season rates, restrooms, showers, handicap access, camp host, phone, nature trails, planned activities in summer.

Windy Cove Douglas County Park A & B, open all year, no reservations, 380 Salmon Harbor Dr., Winchester Bay, Park A (541) 271-4138, Park B (541) 271-5634
Location: On Salmon Harbor Rd. off Hwy 101 south of Reedsport
Description; Across the street from Winchester Bay with good views of the boats, harbor and marina. Both parks are situated in a flat grassy 10-acre area. Park A has better shade against the hill but both parks are nice being so close to the water and the bustling activity of the marina. A fee dump station is located across the street at the Salmon Harbor RV Park at the back.

97 total paved sites between A & B, some shaded, 64 full hookups, (20 amp), 4 electric only hookups, 29 tent sites, max. length 60', $11.55-$14.70, Cable TV $, restrooms, showers, handicap access, 24-hour attendant, phone, marina, restaurants nearby, playground, fishing, crabbing, whale watching.

Lakeside

William M. Tugman State Park, open all year, (541) 888-4902, reservations (800) 452-5687
Location: Off Hwy. 101, 8 miles south of Reedsport on Eel Lake
Description: Tugman is one of the most beautiful state parks on the coast. It is set along the shore of Eel Lake, which offers almost five miles of shoreline for swimming and trout fishing. There is a boat ramp, and a 10 mph speed limit for boats. The Oregon Dunes National Recreation Area is just across the highway for great hiking. The beautiful and large grassy day-use area invites you to relax and gaze at lovely Eel Lake. It's a picture perfect setting for a picnic or boat ride. The sites in the campground are spaced nicely and have ample cover between them for privacy. One of our favorite parks.

115 paved sites, many shaded, 560 acres, 115 partial hookups, (20 amp), max. length 50', no pull-thrus, $19.00, lower off-season rates, dump, restrooms, showers, handicap access, camp host, phone, nature trails, playground, wheelchair accessible fishing pier.

North Eel Creek/Siuslaw NF, open all year, no reservations (541) 271-3611
Location: On Eel Creek in the Oregon Dunes National Recreation Area, 12.1 miles south of Reedsport on Hwy. 101.
Description: This campground is set along Eel Creek, near both Eel Lake and Tenmile Lake. In a thick forest of beach pines, it has well spaced sites. It provides quiet as it is well off the highway and the interior access roads are nice and wide. Some of the sites will fit RVs up to 50'. Water-skiing is allowed at Tenmile Lake, but not at Eel Lake. There are trails nearby that access the Oregon Dunes Scenic Area. There is no ORV access from this campground.

52 sites, mostly shaded, 12 acres, accepts Golden Age/Golden Access passes, most sites; max. length 30', some up to 50', no pull-thrus, $10.00, restrooms, water, amphitheater.

Osprey Point RV Resort, 1505 N. Lake Rd., Lakeside, (541) 759-2801
Location: In the small quiet town of Lakeside (south of Winchester Bay) on Tenmile Lake for great fishing.
Description: This is one of the top 5 parks we've seen on the coast. Osprey Point is a large park, very well designed and managed. The quiet spot and views of Tenmile Lake (187 miles of shoreline) make it a wonderful place to stay for a week or more. A Camper Clubs of America Park open all year to the general public. They give Escapees members a 10% discount (see Resource List). They are new and still developing the rec. room and swimming pool. Don't let that stop you, this is a first-rate park with some dynamite lake views.

132 grassy sites, on 65 acres, paved interior roads, all full hookups, (30/50 amp), 70 pull-thrus, max. length 65', $18.00-$27.00, lower off-season and weekly/monthly rates, dump, restrooms, showers, store/deli, laundry, arcade, meeting hall, telephone, cable TV, children's fishing pond, propane.

Charleston

Bastendorff Beach County Park, open all year, no reservations, (541) 888-5353
Location: On a bluff above Cape Arago near Charleston. From Charleston (near Coos Bay) travel 2 miles on Cape Arago Hwy., turn right at sign. The drive up the hill is steep.
Description: A beautiful park nestled in a secluded setting on a bluff above the ocean but none of the sites have ocean views. The park is nicely designed and sites are spaced wide apart. There is a large day-use area close to the ocean with a great playground for kids. Near Cape Arago State Park, nearby activities include clamming, crabbing, fishing, swimming and boating. Don't miss the Shore Acres Botanical Gardens about 3 miles away.

81 paved sites, most shaded, 25 dry camp, 56 partial hookups, (20/30 amp), max. length 60', 1 pull-thru, $13.00-$15.00, lower off-season rates, 2 dump stations, restrooms, showers, camp host, phone, great playground.

Charleston Marina RV Park, 7984 Kingfisher Dr., open all year, (541) 888-9512
Location: On Coos Bay in Charleston off Boat Basin Dr., from junction of Hwy. 101 and Ocean Beaches/Charleston sign, west 9 miles on Empire Blvd./Cape Arago Hwy. across Charleston Bridge to Boat Basin Dr. right, 2 blocks to Kingfisher Dr.
Description: As with most RV parks on a marina, this one is in a paved parking lot style arrangement. It is right on the bay with good access for fishing and crabbing. They even have a crab room where you can clean your crabs and cook them. Nearby activities include hiking, swimming, clamming, crabbing, boating, and fishing.

110 sites, 110 full hookups, (30 amp), 25 pull-thrus, max. length: 50', $14.00 daily rate, lower weekly/monthly rates, restroom, showers, dump, handicap accessible, cable TV, phone, laundry, propane, play area. A store, cafe, laundry, boat docks, launch, restaurants and boat rentals are nearby.

Oceanside RV Park, open all year, 9838 Cape Arago Hwy,. (800) 570-2598), (541) 888-2598
Location: On the Pacific Ocean off Cape Arago Hwy. From junction of Hwy. 101 and Ocean Beaches/Charleston sign, west 9 miles on Empire Blvd./Cape Arago Hwy. across Charleston Bridge then west 2 miles to the park.
Description: Presently a small park right between the county park and the state park in a very pleasant park setting with just a short walk to the beach. It is being enlarged and will have 70 sites even closer to the beach by May 1997. A very nice park and friendly managers.

20 gravel sites, some shaded, 20 full hookups (30 amp), 4 pull-thrus, max. length: 60', $16.00, lower weekly rates, restrooms, showers, dump, cable TV, phone, laundry,

propane, playground, hiking trails, surfing, tidepooling. A store, good restaurants, boat docks, launch, golfing, and boat rentals are nearby.

Sunset Bay State Park, open all year, (541) 888-4902, reservations (800) 452-5687
Location: On the east side of Cape Arago Hwy. at Sunset Bay, day use is on west side of highway right on the prettiest bay you will ever see. From junction of Hwy. 101 and Ocean Beaches/Charleston sign, west 9 miles on Empire Blvd./Cape Arago Hwy. across Charleston Bridge then west 3.2 miles to the park (follow the signs).
Description: This campground is near Sunset Bay, a small picturesque, well-protected cove with a great beach for swimming. At Shore Acres, a short distance south, visitors will enjoy beautiful views of rugged cliffs, crashing surf, exquisite floral gardens, and sea lions barking on offshore reefs. A wonderful place to stay and relax for a week. Set in dense woods with Big Creek running right through the campground, it is in a very sheltered and quiet location. Sunset Bay Campground is lovely but the highlight is across the highway at Sunset Bay day-use. This bay is tiny but so beautiful. Bring your camera and lots of film for the "knock your socks off" sunsets here. A 9-hole golf course is within walking distance of the campground.

137 total sites, some shaded, 387 acres, 34 partial hookups, 29 full hookups, (30 amp), max. length 50', 1 pull-thru, $17.00-$20.00, lower off-season and weekly rates, restrooms, showers, handicap access, camp host, phone, planned activities in summer.

Coos Bay

Lucky Loggers RV Park, open all year, 250 E. Johnson, Coos Bay, (541) 267-6003 (800) 267-6426
Location: On Coos Bay, right in town, Hwy. 101/E. Johnson Ave., 2 blocks on Johnson.
Description: Beautifully maintained grounds and facilities right on the waterfront. A few sites have a view of the bay. One block to major shopping area and downtown Coos Bay. A good place to stay in town close to the casino.

78 paved sites, some shaded, 4 acres, max. length: 50', 78 full hookups, (30/50 amp), 13 pull-thrus, $20.00-$22.00, GS, lower weekly/monthly rates, restrooms, showers, handicap accessible, cable TV, phone, laundry, propane, game room and lounge, gift shop. Free shuttle bus to the casino.

Volunteer/Camp Host Opportunities

Oregon Dunes National Recreation Area, (541) 271-3611
Tugman State Park, Reedsport, (541) 888-4902
Umpqua Lighthouse State Park, Winchester Bay, (541) 271-4118
Sunset Bay State Park, Charleston, (541) 888-4902
Bastendorff Beach County Park, Charleston, (541) 888-5353

Section 2: Activities in Reedsport/Charleston area

Be sure to stop in at the Oregon Dunes National Recreation Area Headquarters, 855 Hwy. Ave., Reedsport (541) 271-3611, across from the chamber of commerce for tips on hiking trails and where to spot wildlife. A publication called "Sand Tracks" lists the interpretive programs, overlooks, campgrounds, dune buggy staging areas, hiking and other information. A handy strip map helps guide you through the area.

Don't Miss

- Dean Creek Elk Viewing Area, Reedsport east on Hwy 38

Highly Recommended

- Discovery Drive
- Umpqua River Lighthouse

Bike/Auto Tours

Siltcoos Recreation Area sign off Hwy. 101. The road to Waxmyrtle and Lagoon Campgrounds (7 miles south of Florence) is a good biking tour. Bike to the end of the road to the large day-use area. Walk across the dunes to the ocean for some nice flat beach hiking. ORVs go north, beach hikers go south.

Smith River Road is a good short, level bike tour. Smith River Road runs east from Hwy 101, (**milepost 210**), north of Reedsport. Park at the Douglas County Bolon Island Boat Landing or at the abandoned weigh station. It is three miles to a bridge over the river to Stowe Marsh with wildlife viewing on both sides of the road. The bike lanes are wide and the incline slight.

Bookstores

Reedsport Books & Tapes, 439 Fir Ave, Reedsport, (541) 271-2555. Butch Haines says he has over 15,000 used books to choose from. We didn't count but we believe him. He also has a nice selection of CDs and cassettes.

Ecotourism

Umpqua Discover Center, 409 Riverfront Way, Reedsport, (541) 271-4816 or (800) 247-2155, opened in mid-1993 and features the "Umpqua Experience" which examines the region's human and natural history. The other attraction is the 300-ton wood-hulled research vessel *Hero*, a retired Antarctic vessel that has some scars from the ice. Admission is charged.

Annual Events

Check with Coos Bay Chamber of Commerce
50 E. Central, (800) 824-8486, (541) 269-0215, for specific dates

February
Charleston Merchant Crabfeed

March
South Coast Dixieland Clambake Jazz Festival
Dune Musher's Mail Run

May
Rhododendron Show, Shore Acres State Park, Charleston
Youth Festival
Whalefest

June
Oregon Hover-In, Hovercraft Race
Father's Day Rose Sunday, Shore Acres State Park

July
Oregon Coast Music Festival
Fireworks over the Bay, July 4th
North Bend Air Show
Sandblast in the Dunes

August
Farwest Gemcraft Show
Charleston Seafood Festival
Salmon Barbeque, Charleston
Blackberry Arts Festival, Coos Bay

September
Bay Area Fun Festival, Coos Bay
Sand Dune Sashay Square Dance Festival
Prefontaine Memorial 10K Race
Oregon Shorebird Festival
Bay Area Fun Festival
Scandinavial Day

December
Holiday Lights at Shore Acres

View of Cape Arago Lighthouse on Gregory Point near Charleston.

Exercise Routes or Leisure Walking

Champion Park, Juniper Ave., Reedsport, 2 blocks west of Hwy 101, is a nice park with a walking path, kids playground, restroom, and picnic tables. Many of the locals choose a longer route by walking the dike to the visitor's center.

Family Activities with Children

Lions Park, On Hwy. 101 and 21st. Reedsport, a full block of play area for kids, two picnic tables, large playground equipment for children and a separate fenced area with smaller playground equipment for the toddlers. Fenced-in basketball court, large grass area, restrooms.

Highland Park, Ranch Road and Hwy. 101 (best access is Longwood Drive), Reedsport. Two tennis courts and several ball fields provide a large play area when games are not being played.

Highland School swimming pool, Longwood Dr., Reedsport, (541) 271-9222. Call for schedule of public hours for this olympic sized pool.

Umpqua Jet Adventures, 423 Riverfront Way, old town Reedsport, (541) 271-5694 offers 2-hour jet-boat trips for adults and children

Fishing/Clamming

Tenmile Lake County Park, Lakeside, gives access to Tenmile and N. Tenmile lakes and is a great park for picknicking, boating, or fishing from the long dock out into the lake. Fishing here can net bluegill and large-mouth bass. Located east of Lakeside (Hwy. 101) and northeast of Oregon Dunes Recreation Area. Take the exit from Hwy. 101 to Lakeside (**milepost 222**) and continue to Lakeside. Turn at Park and 8th St.

Siltcoos Lake: Turn on Pacific Ave. (**milepost 197**) and drive to the Westlake area at the end of the road and fish at the dock on Siltcoos Lake.

Tahkenitch Fishing Village, 80135 Hwy. 101, Gardiner, OR 97441, (541) 271-5222, **milepost 202**. If you get the urge to fish and you are not prepared, go to Tahkenitch

View from Waxmyrtle Campground in Oregon Dunes National Recreation Area near Dunes City.

Fishing Village. Here you can rent a boat with motor, fishing tackle, purchase bait, buy a license, and get free advice. Fishing on Tahkenitch Lake's 1500 acres may net you largemouth bass, rainbow trout, cutthroat trout, yellow perch, bluegill, crappie, coho salmon, or steelhead.

Douglas County Wayside on Discovery Drive, Winchester Bay. Drive past Salmon Harbor to **milepost 1**. Douglas County has provided a large parking area with picnic tables and restrooms for those wishing to use the 600-foot dock for crabbing and fishing. Don't miss watching for the brown pelicans, cormorants, and harbor seals.

Reedsport Discovery Center, Old Town Reedsport, fish or crab from the dock next to the Artic ship *Hero.*

Galleries/Art

Mindpower Gallery, 417 Fir Ave., Reedsport, OR 97467, (541) 271-2485. Tamara and Tara Szalewski operate this excellent gallery and gift shop combination. Paintings are artfully displayed, both wood and bronze sculptures are included in the viewing rooms.

Golfing

Forest Hills Country Club, #1 Country Club Drive, Reedsport, (541) 271-2626. A 9-hole course located on the west end of town. A par 36 consisting of two par 5, five par 4, and two par 3 holes on 3,108 yards. Putting green, driving range, clubs rented, restaurant.

Hiking

Note: Before starting out on your hike, pick up the booklet "Hiking Trails in the Oregon Dunes National Recreation Area" from the Siuslaw National Forest Service, Oregon Dunes National Recreation Area Visitors Center in Reedsport. This will give you specifics about mileage and sights on the hikes. Some are marked with posts and some are not. Be sure to talk to the ranger about orienting yourself on a hike in the dunes. The landscape is so vast that it can be a puzzling experience to get back to your car if you don't fix on a landmark. Listed are a few of our favorites. Most are very easy, but if you feel up to it don't pass up the Oregon Dunes Overlook Trail, taking the Takenitch Creek Trail back. Just remember, hiking in the dunes can be hard work.

Taylor Dunes Trail, 1-mile round-trip, to a viewing deck with great vistas of sand dunes, marsh-like deflation plains and the ocean. The forests are full of rhododendrons which are beautiful in bloom in May. An easy stroll and handicap assessible to the deck. There is a small bench below the deck for contemplating the dunes.

Oregon Dunes Overlook trail, 3.5-mile loop, take the Oregon Dunes Trail to the ocean marked by posts going west through the dunes. It is 1 (easy) mile to the beach but to see some really awesome scenery, continue by walking south 1.5 miles on the hard beach sand to the Tahkenitch Creek Loop. There is a brown hikers sign on the foredune marking where to turn back into the dunes for the hike back. Tahkenitch Creek Loop trail is more difficult because so much of it is on soft sand. Follow the blue banded posts to find your way back to the overlook. Be sure to walk over to see the broad sweep of the creek with the steep dunes falling to its edge—and bring your camera. This is a wholly different world—the large rolling dunes and towering tree islands are exciting and vast. Don't worry, the trail is well marked with the blue banded posts.

Siltcoos Recreation Area, off Hwy 101 (**milepost 198**)

Waxmyrtle Trail, easy, 1.5 miles. The trail can be picked up at the entrance to Waxmyrtle CG just across the bridge. This is a lovely hike next to the Siltcoos River Estuary. Outstanding views of the lower estuary and ocean highlight this trial. Chances are good that you will see blue herons, cormorants, ducks, and egrets. Take the right fork to the estuary and find a secluded beach area with gulls surfing the intertidal area. A nice easy hike right next to the campgrounds.

Lagoon Trail, 1 mile, pier at Waxmyrtle Campground sign. This is another easy relaxing trail with a feast for the eyes. The trail meanders across wooden boardwalks and paths alongside the Siltcoos River Lagoon for close-up viewing of plants and wildlife. It was once known as "The River of No Return" nature trail because it follows an old arm of the Siltcoos River that was cut off when the Siltcoos Beach Road was built. The lagoon is soft shades of green and there are many birds to be seen all along the trail. Watch for the blue herons. They are so graceful in flight. Egrets are a common sight also. Bring your camera.

Local History/Museums/Lighthouses

Coastal Visitor Center, Old Lighthouse Rd., Winchester Bay, (541) 440-4500, is an attractive museum containing photos and artifacts of the early days of settlement along the Umpqua River. A special exhibit focuses on the gray whale and its amazing yearly 12,000-mile round-trip past the Oregon Coast.

Umpqua River Lighthouse, Umpqua Lighthouse State Park, (541) 440-4500, built in 1894 is open for tours inside by appointment but the grounds can be viewed any time. This site is also a prime whale watching place, being 100 feet above sea level. Check out the Umpqua River Whale Watching Station across from the lighthouse.

Photo Opportunities

- Tugman State Park
- Oregon dunes
- Umpqua Lighthouse State Park

Restaurants/Espresso

Pizza Rays, & Suzy's, $, 2165 Winchester Ave. Reedsport, (541) 271-4100, for breakfast, lunch or dinner

The trail around Lagoon Campground near Dunes City is a beautiful place to see all types of wildlife.

Bayfront Bistro, $$, 208 Bayfront Loop, Winchester Bay, (541) 271-9463, has a nice light interior. Only one table in the back allows smoking, the rest is smoke-free. Mostly American with seafood. Ask for their "special of the day"

Harbor Light Family Restaurant, $$, 390 Hwy. 101, (541) 271-3848 has a good selection on their menu, especially breakfast and friendly waitresses.

Special Local Attractions

Kleo the Krab Bounty Hunt occurs from mid-August to Labor Day in the bay. Live crabs are tagged and released into the harbor and whoever catches them is eligible for various prizes. The special crab (Kleo) gets you $2500.00 and if no one lands him by Labor Day, a winner is chosen by lottery. You should see lots of crabpots in the bay during this event.

Coho Point Promenade, Salmon Harbor Recreation Area, Winchester Bay a 600-foot-long wooden promenade along the waterfront on Coho Point in the harbor.

Wildlife Viewing

Be sure to stop in at the **Oregon Dunes National Recreation Area** headquarters 855 Hwy. Ave., Reedsport, (541) 271-3611, for tips on hiking trails and where to spot elk, osprey, and other wildlife.

Dean Creek Elk Viewing Area, 3 miles east on Hwy. 38 from Reedsport. Several pull-offs are along Hwy. 38 with the O.H. Hinsdale Interpretive Center at about the half way point. Ample pull-thru parking for RVs, restrooms and displays are at the interpretive center. Don't miss the Wetland Viewing Area just west of the center where you will learn of the habits of the inhabitants of the marsh. Elk may be seen year-round, especially early or late in the day. Wetlands mixed with the meadows offer viewing of heron, osprey, waterfowl, beaver, and muskrats.

Section 3: Activities in North Bend/Coos Bay/Charleston

Coos Bay is gearing up to attract more tourists but it has a long way to go to compete with the draws in tiny Charleston. The three state parks in this area are some of our all-time favorites. The ocean will speak to you here of the respect you should have for its power. Shore Acres Botanical Garden willl delight gardeners. Bring your camera.

Don't Miss

- Sunset Bay State Park, Charleston
- Shore Acres State Park, Charleston
- Cape Arago State Park, Charleston

Highly Recommended

- Coos Art Museum, Coos Bay
- Mingus Park, Coos Bay
- The Oregon Connection (Myrtlewood tour), Coos Bay

Biking

If you would like more strenuous bike rides than mentioned in this section, stop by the Coos Bay Chamber of Commerce in Coos Bay and pick up the booklet, "Coos County Ride Guide" for information on recommmended bike rides in the area.

BLM North Spit Boat Launch, on Trans Pacific Parkway, is an easy biking route. This road is a dead-end and is 4 miles long from the beginning so it gets very little traffic. It's flat and there are sand dunes, wetlands, and the bay to be seen. From Hwy. 101 (**milepost 232.7**) turn at the Horsefall Campground sign and continue to the fork. Stay left and stay on the Trans Pacific Parkway Rd. Follow it to the boat launch where there is ample parking. You can then bike the road for approximately 8 miles round trip.

Coos Bay River Rd.: At the south end of Coos Bay turn left from Hwy. 101 at sign for Alleghany. Drive 2.2 miles and park at the closed weigh station next to the river. From here you can bike up Coos Bay River Road or the Catching Slough Road across from the weigh station. Both roads are fairly level running alongside rivers. On Coos Bay River Road, go under the bridge staying next to the river. You could ride for miles on this relatively flat route and still get the benefit of the river view on one side and the pastoral green farms on the other.

The gardens at the old Simpson estate in Shore Acres Botanical Garden are a relaxing place to stroll.

Bookstores

North Bend: House of Books, new, 1611 Virginia Ave, Pony Village Shopping Center, (541) 756-322

North Bend: Pirates Cove, 1987 Sherman Ave., (541) 756-6163, new and used books very well organized. Some gift items.

Ecotourism

Betty Kay Charters, whale watching cruises, P.O. Box 5020, Charleston Boat Basin, (541) 888-9021 or (800) 752-6303, daily afternoon whale cruises (Jan. thru June) reservations required.

Wavecrest Discoveries, 470 Golden #1795, Coos Bay, (541) 267-4027. Marti Giles gives custom interpretive tours of the area which allow small or large groups to experience nature in meaningful ways. This could include beachwalks, clam-digging (equipment provided) or full-day excursions.

Exercise Routes or Leisure Walking

North Bend: Pony Point Recreation Area is an urban waterfront park adjecent to the existing two-lane boat ramp. Broadway & Virginia Ave., North Bend. From Hwy 101, take Virginia Ave. west, turn right on Marion Ave. (public boat landing sign) and follow it to the parking lot. It has a dock for fishing, a .5-mile walkway with interpretive signs, overnight primitive camping ($4.00), vault toilet, ample RV pull-thru parking, one-mile bikepath/walking.

Mingus Park, 10th & Commercial St., Coos Bay, (541) 269-1181, is an exceptionally lovely place offering a lake with fountains, beautiful Japanese gardens, picnic areas, hiking trails, tennis courts, large swimming pool, and two separate playground areas. The Japanese gardens honor their sister city, Choshi, and are not to be missed. Be sure to take the extra trails through the woods. Around the lake you can expect the ducks to hound you for a handout. Bring your camera.

Millicoma Marsh Trail, across from Millacoma Middle School, Coos Bay, from Hwy. 101, take Allegany Road one mile and turn left on D St. Follow the brown binoculars signs. Park at the school and walk down the steps across the street to the running track. The trailhead starts by the scoreboard and the loop trail is approximately 1.25 miles. It follows the dikes that were built when Coos Bay was dredged. It is grassy, flat and easy with continuous views of the bay. There are interpretive signs along the first part of the trail explaining the wetlands and the dredging of the bay. A nice, peaceful, easy walk. It is handicap accessible.

Family Activities with Children

Sunset Bay State Park, Cape Arago Hwy., (541) 888-4902, is a great place for kids to wade or swim in the lovely little bay. It is so sheltered here, that it is generally calm, even during winter when a raging surf is just offshore.

Pacific Coast Recreation, 4121 Hwy. 101, North Bend, (541) 756-7183, open daily 9 a.m.-dusk. Half track tours are made inside authentic WWII military transport vehicles. Pacific Coast Recreation also conducts free showings of the coast's largest inventory of WWII and Korean war military equipment.

Empire Lakes Park, Ackerman St. & Newmark, or Hull St. & Newmark, Coos Bay (541) 269-1181 is a surprising jewel in the city for a peaceful getaway. It consists of a 120-acre lush forest and two large lakes inviting hikers, naturalists, and fishermen. This is a wonderful area left natural and full of a wide variety of plants, trees, and animal life. The parks easy trails (over 1.25 miles) are paved or graveled and provide relaxing walks around the lakes and woods.

Hiking in the dunes near Dunes City can be like a moon walk with beautiful creeks meandering through.

Fishing/Clamming

Empire Pier Restoration, Empire & Newmark Ave., Coos Bay. From the 210-foot-long pier you can view the bay while landing crab and fish. At the intersection, follow the boat landing signs to the parking lot. Interpretive sign, picnic tables, restroom.
Charleston Boat Basin, fishing pier, fish-cleaning station.

Galleries/Arts

Coos Art Museum, 235 Anderson St., Coos Bay, (541) 267-3901, is the one of the biggest surprises in this town. It has 3,500 square feet of exhibit space and houses a first-rate permanent collection of American prints, oils, watercolors, and sculpture. If art is your interest, don't miss this gallery. Open most afternoons. Donation.

Golfing

Kentuck Golf Course, 675 Golf Course Lane (3.5 miles on East Bay Drive, North Bend, (541) 756-4464. A par 70, 18-hole golf course with four par 5, eight par 4, and six par 3 holes on 5,393 yards. Open year-round weather permitting. Clubs and carts can be rented.

Sunset Bay Golf Course, 11001 Cape Arago Hwy., Coos Bay, (541) 888-9301. A 9-hole, par 36 course next to Sunset State Park consisting of two par 5, five par 4, two par 3 holes on 3,020 yards. Big Creek runs through the middle of this course giving it good drainage even for the winter months. Clubs and carts may be rented. The pro shop has coffee and some snacks.

Hiking

Coos Bay: Blossom Gulch Trail, park at Blossom Gulch School, map can be obtained at Coos Bay Chamber of Commerce. The trail starts at the back of the school. Register at the school before taking the trail. This easy, short loop (approximately .3 mile) trail winds along Blossom Creek and the wooded hill above and is a lovely jaunt in the city (one small steep spot). There are sitting benches and boardwalks to make the short hike easier. Funded by the Oregon Lottery and implemented by a variety of public agencies it helps you understand how important watersheds and wetlands are to clean water and the plants and animals that depend on them. Blossom Creek is part of the former Mill Slough watershed which was sent underground into a tunnel in the 1920s so the town could be built on top. Before the slough was sent underground, small boats used to deliver goods and passengers up Mill Slough as far as 9th Street. That was only one block away from where the school stands today.

Sunset Bay State Park: Cape Arago Shoreline Trail, 4 miles round-trip, look for trail-head post near the restrooms at the south end of the day-use parking area. Wear boots, it's muddy in places.

Cape Arago State Park: Cape Arago North Cove Trail, .2 mile, park at the parking loop watch for trail marker on north side. It drops down to a large cove with a sandy beach and excellent tidepooling.

Umpqua Dunes Trail is an easy, 4-mile round-trip hike that takes you into some of the more spectacular dunes and away from the constant buzzing of the ORVs. From Eel Creek Campground, 11 miles south of Reedsport, you will find the trailhead. Take the trail west through a forest of tall rhododendrons, and evergreens and then step out onto massive 500-foot-high dunes in .2 miles. Blue banded posts guide your way to the beach from the deflation plain. You will feel like you are in the Sahara Desert.

South Slough Trails, 4 miles south of Charleston on Seven Devil's Road. Pick up a trail guide at the visitor's center. A quarter mile to 3 miles of trails in this area. The Estuary Study Trail gives you the best exposure to the areas and the wildlife that this preserve protects. (See Wildlife)

Local History/Museums/Lighthouses

Coos County Historical Museum, in Simpson Park, North Bend, near the visitors center (541) 756-6320, contains the usual pioneer artifacts and collections. Lots of photos and artifacts about shipping and logging. Open Mon.-Sat 10 a.m.-4 p.m. and Sun.. 12 p.m.-4 p.m. in summer, Tues.-Sat. 10 a.m.-4 p.m. the rest of the year. Admission is charged.

Cape Arago Lighthouse, 12 miles southwest of North Bend and Coos Bay off Hwy. 101. It stands 100 feet above sea level just off Gregory Point, 2.5 miles southwest of entrance to Coos Bay. Listen for unique fog horn. Not open to public, but good views available from trail at Sunset Bay State Park south of the lighthouse or the first turnout after Sunset Bay Campground going south. Managed by the BLM, (Bureau of Land Management), (541) 756-0100 or 888-3778.

The Marshfield Sun Printing Museum, Coos Bay, (541) 269-1363. Between Front St. and northbound Hwy. 101 across from the Timber Lodge. Watch for the blue sign "Marshfield Sun" on the Fir St. post. Phone for tour in off-season. Walk in the door of this historic newspaper and take a step back in time. Things are just as they were in the 1900s. During the summer there are demonstrations that start at setting the type, proofing the copy, and printing the newspaper on their antique press. Children who use computers will marvel at what it took in the "old days" to do what they now consider commonplace.

Photo Opportunities

- Cape Arago State Park
- Sunset Bay State Park
- Shore Acres State Park
- Mingus Park

Restaurants/Espresso

North Bend

Hilltop House Restaurant & Lounge, $$, 166 North Bay Drive, North Bend, (541)

756-4160. Lunch and dinner daily. One of the area's finest restaurants with a great view of the bay, especially at sunset. A very nice restaurant. The same management runs the Portside in Charleston.

Pancake Mill & Pie Shoppe, $, 21390 Tremont, North Bend, (541) 756-2751. Breakfast and lunch only. Big tasty pancakes and three egg omelets. Smoke-free, great food. The locals love it!

Coos Bay

Blue Heron Bistro, $$, Hwy. 101 & Commercial St., Coos Bay, (541) 267-3933, serves breakfast, lunch, and dinner every day. This bistro has an airy feel with indoor and outdoor tables and an innovative menu. One of our personal favorites.

Kum-Yon's, $$, 835 S. Broadway, Coos Bay, (541) 269-2662, serves up truly great South Korean dishes. Don't be afraid to try some of the hot dishes. Just be sure to tell your waiter what hot means to you. Get there early on weekends.

El Puerto Mexican Restaurant, $, 252 Broadway, Coos Bay, (541) 269-7754, serves hearty Latino fare; some with a seafood twist. They also have some old-favorite American dishes on the menu.

Gourmet Coastal Coffee, $, the "little red building", 4th & 273 Curtis Ave., Coos Bay, (541) 267-5004. Espresso, tea, juice, homemade pastries and sandwiches, outdoor patio seating. A very nice place off the main drag to stop for espresso or even lunch with lots of newpapers for catching up. Try the veggie sandwich or chicken pita. There is space for RV parking in the gravel lot on the northwest side of Curtis Ave. and public parking across the street from the cafe.

Kaffe 101, **$**, 134 S. Broadway, Coos Bay, one block from the visitors center (541) 267-4894, is open at 7 a.m. for espresso, bagels, pastries or ice cream. Nice living room area with comfy chairs around a fireplace.

Charleston

Portside Restaurant & Lounge, $$, 8001 Kingfisher Rd., Charleston, (541) 888-5544, has lighted tanks with live crabs and lobsters. One of them may be your dinner. On Friday's there is a great seafood buffet. Just over the Charleston Bridge, off Boat Basin Rd. American, mostly seafood. The bay area's best seafood, seasoned right, great service—a highly recommended restaurant with the best view in town.

Special Local Attractions

House of Myrtlewood, The Oregon Connection, 1125 S. First St., Coos Bay, (541) 267-7804 or (800) 255-5318, provides a free 20-minute tour of the myrtlewood factory where you can see woodturners, carvers, and finishers in action. A very worthwhile stop to see an interesting process. They have a gift shop and snack bar.

Q. What's a myrtlewood?

***A.** A very hardwood tree that only grows in a small area of the Pacific Coast.*

Shore Acres State Park, 13030 Cape Arago Hwy., Charleston, (541) 888-3732, is part of a 1,000-acre coastal preserve of the former home of lumber baron Louis J. Simpson. All that remains now is a gardener's cottage, formal gardens, and stunning views from the top of the cliffs. The power of the ocean here takes your breath away with the booming of its incessant pounding on the cliffs. The photo opportunites are endless here. One of the loveliest beaches in Oregon. Admission to the gardens is free and it's open during daylight hours year-round. Don't miss it.

Cape Arago State Park, (541) 888-3732, just offshore from this rugged cape, rocky islands offer shelter for hundreds of elephant seals and sea lions. Bring your binoculars, the barking can be heard from a long ways away. The best viewing spot is Simpson Reef Viewpoint. Tidepools along these beaches offer hours of fun observing marine critters.

Shore Acres State Park has high bluffs and crashing surf near Charleston.

Sunset Bay State Park, (see "Family Activities")

Bastendorff Beach County Park, north of Sunset Bay at the mouth of Coos Bay, has a long, wide beach that's popular with surfers.

Oregon Dunes National Recreation Area, north of North Bend where the ocean disappears behind 40 miles of massive sand dunes. About half of the 14,000 acres of "unvegetated" dunes are open to off road vehicles (ORVs). You can rent one yourself if you would like to try dune-riding, or avoid them altogether by choosing a campground that does not allow them. One of the better places for peace and quiet and foot traffic hiking only is the Oregon Dunes Overlook just north of Reedsport. Another good spot is North Eel Creek Campground near Lakeside. A publication called "Sand Tracks" lists the interpretive programs, overlooks, campgrounds, dune buggy staging areas, hiking and other information. A handy strip map helps guide you through the area. The publication is available at the visitor's center in Reedsport.

Waterfront Revitalization, Coos Bay, three interpretive structures with exhibits, a viewing platform and two 312-foot-long floating docks for moorage. One of the exhibits is a tug pavilion with a real tug boat inside.

The Mill, Resort & Casino, Hwy 101 between North Bend & Coos Bay, (541) 953-4800, (800) 953-4800, has slots, bingo, blackjack, poker, free RV parking at the edge of their parking lot, along the bay, waterfront dining. Open 24 hours.

Wildlife Viewing

Cape Arago State Park overlooks the Oregon Islands National Wildlife Refuge, home to sea lions, birds, and seals. The Oregon Coast trail connects you with Shore Acres and Sunset Bay State Parks. Shell Islands and Simpson Reef are the largest haul-out spots on the Oregon Coast for northern elephant seals, harbor seals, and California sea lions.

South Slough National Estuarine Preserve, P.O. Box 5417, Charleston, OR 97420, (541) 888-5558. This is Amerca's first federal estuarine reserve created in 1974. The visitor's center occupies a wooded rise where you can see the slough below. Exhibits and a video explain the value of a tidal estuary and how it is one of nature's richest habitats. This Research Reserve protects 4,500 acres of tidal habitat, mudflats, woodlands, and salt marshes which is set aside for research, education and recreation. Obtain maps at the interpretive center and take hikes and watch birds. Open Monday-Friday.

Watershed Trail allows the visitor to explore an entire watershed ecosystem, culminating at the estuarine and wetland shoreline. Includes an observation deck and 500 foot boardwalk which winds its way through a tidal marsh.

Estuary Study Trail is a 3-mile round-trip hike beginning at the center and following Hidden Creek down to the slough. At the bottom of the marsh is an observation lookout for viewing birdlife.

The Wasson Creek Trail, down Seven Devils Rd. from the reserve, is only .75 mile with easy walking through meadow and forest.

Sunset Bay State Park, tidepools, interpretive programs in summer.

Section 4: Reedsport/Coos Bay
RV Parts & Services

Diesel

Reedsport: Henson Texaco, 2118 Winchester Ave. (Hwy. 101), (541) 271-4912. Diesel pump in both bays. A little tight access from the south but ample room from the north.

North Bend: Shell, Marion & Virginia Ave., (bypass Hwy 101 to Cape Arago). Diesel is in the inside bay.

North Bend: Texaco, 1700 Sherman (Hwy. 101), (541)756-5731. Great access even for big rigs.

Coos Bay: Bassett-Hyland Chevron, 1059 Evans Blvd. (Hwy. 101 south end of Coos Bay). Vehicle diesel in with the gasoline pumps. Easy access in and out as you go south on the one-way Hwy. 101.

Coos Bay: Davis Oil Texaco, 1670 Ocean Blvd., (on the way to Cape Arago Hwy. from Coos Bay city center). Pump is located by itself with easy access.

Dump Station

Lakeside: Tugman State Park
Winchester Bay: Salmon Harbor Marina, dump is located at the far end of the marina. Drive down the road past the marina office. Fee is charged for non-campers.
Reedsport: Coho RV Park & Marina, 1580 Winchester Ave., (541) 271-5411. Fee is charged for non-campers.
Coos Bay city RV dump station, located on Front St. from northbound Hwy 101 in downtown Coos Bay, turn right on Alder St. Watch for the blue sign for the dump station on Hwy 101, turn right for 1 block, turn right again on Front St. Dump is one block on right.

Charleston: Bastendorff Beach County Park, fee is charged
Charleston: Oceanside RV Park, fee is charged

Laundry

Reedsport Coin Laundry, Umpqua Shopping Center on 14th St., (541) 271-3587
North Bend: Wash a Lot, 1921 Virginia Ave., (541) 756-5439. Open 24 hrs.

Library

Reedsport Public Library, 395 Winchester Ave., Reedsport, (541) 271-3500. Hours: Mon. & Thur. 2-8:30 p.m., Tue.-Wed. & Fri.10-6 p.m. Sat. 10-1 p.m. A small library with a children's area. Annual temporary membership is $10. All visitors welcome to come and read at the library. Excess paperbacks are sold.

North Bend: North Bend Public Library, 1800 Sherman Ave., (541) 756-0400. A very nice library with a separate room for children with a sunken play area. Paperbacks can be checked out by non-members. There is a very large periodicals section with comfy chairs and couches for reading. Mon.-Wed. 11 a.m.-9 p.m., Thurs.-Sat. 11 a.m.-5:30 p.m., Sun. 1 p.m.-5 p.m. Sept.-May only.

Coos Bay: Coos Bay Public Library, 525 Anderson, (541) 269-1101, is a medium size library with a helpful staff. Paperbacks are on the honor system. Membership card if over 30 day resident. Videos and audio tapes. Separate children's area with scheduled story times. Two free computers for public use and an Internet terminal for reading your E-mail. Open Mon.-Thurs. 10 a.m.-8 p.m., Fri.-Sat. 10 a.m.-5:30 p.m.

Medical Services

Reedsport: Lower Umpqua Hospital, (541) 271-2171. 24-hour emergency care
Coos Bay: Bay Area Hospital, 1775 Thompson Rd. (541) 269-8111. 24 hour emergency care

Propane

Reedsport: Chevron, 1399 Hwy. 101, Reedsport, (541) 271-3221
North Bend: Empiregas of North Bend, 425 Virginia Ave., (541) 756-5614 (east of Hwy 101 & Virginia). Mon.-Fri. 8 a.m.-5 p.m. Cylinders filled and repaired.
Coos Bay: Bassett-Hyland Chevron, 1059 Evans Blvd., (Hwy. 101 south end of Coos Bay).
Coos Bay: Davis Oil Texaco, 1670 Ocean Blvd., Coos Bay, (on the way to Cape Arago Hwy. from Coos Bay city center).
Charleston: Oceanside RV Park, on Cape Arago Hwy.

RV Parts & Service

Reedsport: Smith River Trailers Sales, Inc., 909 Winchester Ave., Reedsport, OR 97467, (541) 271-3107, full complement of parts and adequate selection of supplies. Call and they will arrange towing if needed. They will set you up with water and electric if repairs exceed one day.

Oregon Dunes trail has posts for navigating the trail through the dunes.

Coos Bay: Bert's RV Supplies & Service, 810 S. Broadway, (541) 269-1338, has an excellent choice of RV supplies in a very well organized store. A good supply of RV guide books also.
Coos Bay: Gib's RVs sales, service, parts, 1845 Ocean Blvd., (800) 824-4388.

Shopping /Groceries

Reedsport: Safeway, 1499 Hwy. 101, (541) 271-3142, in the Umpqua Shopping Center
Winchester Bay Market, 8th St. & Hwy. 101, (541) 271-2632
Lakeside: McKay's Market, 200 S. 8th St., (541) 759-3411
North Bend: Pony Village Mall, 1611 Virginia Ave., boasts over 80 shops where there are several toy, hobby, and candy shops.
North Bend: Safeway, 1659 Virginia, North Bend, (541) 756-4717
North Bend: Bi-Mart, 2131 Newmark, North Bend, (541) 756-7526
North Bend: Albertson's Food Center, 2121 Newmark, North Bend, (541) 756-2588
Coos Bay: Safeway, 550 South 4th, Coos Bay, (541) 267-3512
Coos Bay: Fred Meyer, One-Stop Shopping 1020 1st St., Coos Bay, (541) 269-4008
Coos Bay: Wal-mart, 2051 Newmark, Coos Bay, (541) 888-5488
Coos Bay: K Mart, 3111 Ocean Blvd., Coos Bay, (541) 267-2151

USPO

Reedsport: 301 Fir St., 97467, (541) 271-2521
Lakeside: 8th St., 97449, (541) 759-3504
North Bend: 1835 McPherson, 97459, (541) 756-6610
Coos Bay: 470 Golden, 97420, (541) 267-4514

Chapter 9

101

RVer's Best Guide

Bandon to Port Orford

Map Grid A6: Bandon to Port Orford

In this stretch of the coast you will leave the larger urban areas behind for two tiny towns, Bandon and Port Orford. Port Orford is considered by some to be the western-most point of the US and because of it, it can get ferocious winds. The charm of the town of Bandon is not to be missed. Fortunately for RVers, you can park your RV at the waterfront and just walk the whole downtown area. Bandon has a quiet appeal with great galleries, restaurants, and of course, cranberries. They have been included in almost any kind of edible concoction that you can think of. Bullards Beach State Park, one of our top 5 state parks on the coast is here at Bandon.

Section 1: Best Campgrounds

Best Public Campgrounds

Best public campground for base camping

Bandon: Bullards Beach State Park, open all year, (541) 347-3501, reservations (800) 452-5687, p. 134

Best public campground with full or partial hookups

Bandon: Bullards Beach State Park, open all year, (541) 347-3501, reservations (800) 452-5687, p. 134

Port Orford: Humbug Mountain State Park, open all year, (541) 332-6774, reservations (800) 452-5687, p. 136

Best public campground for solitude and scenic beauty

Bandon: Bullards Beach State Park, open all year, (541) 347-3501, reservations (800) 452-5687, p. 136

Port Orford: Cape Blanco State Park, open all year, (541) 332-6774, reservations (800) 452-5687, p. 136

Port Orford: Humbug Mountain State Park, open all year, (541) 332-6774, reservations (800) 452-5687, p. 136

Best public campground for families with children

Bandon: Bullards Beach State Park, open all year, (541) 347-3501, reservations (800) 452-5687, p. 134

Best public campground with low rates

Langlois: Boise-Cope Curry County Park, Floras Lake, (541) 247-7074, p. 134

The colors of the cliffs are what give Cape Blanco State Park its name.

Best Private Campgrounds

Best private campground with low rates

Port Orford: Elk River Campground, open all year, (541) 332-2255, p. 136
Port Orford: Port Orford RV Trailer Village, open all year, (541) 332-1041, p. 136

Best private campground for solitude and scenic beauty

Port Orford: Elk River Campground, open all year, (541) 332-2255, p. 136
Port Orford: Arizona Beach, open all year, (541) 332-6491, p. 137

Best private campground for base camping

Langlois: Port Orford KOA, open all year, (541) 348-2358, (800) 562-3298, p. 134

Best private campground for families with children

Langlois: Port Orford KOA, open all year, (541) 348-2358, (800) 562-3298, p. 134

Campground Descriptions

Bandon

Bullards Beach State Park, open all year, (541) 347-3501, reservations (800) 452-5687

Location: 1 mile north of Bandon on the west side of Hwy. 101, close to the Pacific Ocean and the Coquille River

Description: This beautiful, heavily wooded campground is on the Coquille River which offers good fishing in season and miles of shore access. Sites are spaced wide apart with ample privacy because of the tall beach pines and huckleberry bushes. There are also several hiking and walking trails. Bullards Beach is one of our top favorite parks on the coast. For bikers, it can't be beat as it has a long access road to the north jetty that is perfect for leisurely biking and has little traffic. The lovely lighthouse at the end of the road is a special bonus. For the wildlife viewer, Bandon National Wildlife Refuge is just across the river from the park. Bring your camera for the sights around this park. Bandon "by the sea" is located close by and is one of the most quaint and inviting towns on the coast. Their Old Town is made for walking and the stroll along the waterfront is relaxing.

191 total paved sites, most shaded, 1226 acres, 92 full hookups, 99 partial hookups, (20/30 amp), max. length 65', no pull-thrus, $19.00-$20.00, lower off-season rates, dump, restrooms, showers, handicap access, camp host, phone, playground, evening activities in summer, boat ramp, fish-cleaning station, crabbing, clamming. C loop with partial hookups is sunnier. A & B loops are shadier.

Langlois

Bandon-Port Orford KOA, open all year, Langlois, (541) 348-2358, (800) 562-3298

Location: 16 miles south of Bandon on the west side of Hwy. 101 (**milepost 291.3**)

Description: This private campground is so wooded it reminds us of a state campground as it has extra large secluded sites among big trees and coastal ferns. A very well taken care of park. We especially liked the picnic and playground area that had large grassy lawns and was well away from traffic areas. Pet rules are strictly enforced. Even though this campground was just off Hwy. 101, the back loop had very little road noise. The manager was very friendly and takes great care of the place. Elk River and Sixes River are nearby and offer good fishing. Cape Blanco State Park is close by.

72 gravel sites, many shaded, 5 acres, max. length: 80', 16 full hookups, 38 partial hookups, (20/30 amp), 30 pull-thrus, $19.00-$20.50, lower off-season and weekly rates, GS, cable TV, dump in summer, restrooms, showers, phone, laundry, groceries, propane, horseshoes, game room, playground, free miniature train rides in summer.

Boise-Cope Curry County Park at Floras Lake, open all year, no reservations, Floras Lake Rd., (541) 247-7074

Location: On the shore of Floras Lake, a freshwater lake very near the Pacific Ocean. Take Hwy. 101 to Floras Lake Loop, (watch for brown sign to county park), continue for 1.1 miles to Floras Lake Rd. and turn right, continue 1.4 miles to Boice-Cope Rd. to the park.

The Coquille River Lighthouse in Bandon was built in 1896 and restored in 1976. It stands today as a museum open daily.

Description: This park is a real sleeper. Not advertised in most of the travel guides, it is a lovely, quiet place right next to Floras Lake. Sites are spaced wide apart and are quite large. There are woods surrounding the whole inside grassy campground. For a stopover, or even a few days, this would be a nice place to stay. Windsurfers love it here as there is usually good wind on the lake.

30 graveled sites, no hookups, max. length 45', $8.00 daily rate, water, restrooms, showers, dump, firewood, camp host, hiking trails to beach, phone, boat launch.

Port Orford

Cape Blanco State Park, open all year, (541) 332-6774, reservations (800) 452-5687
Location: On Cape Blanco near the Pacific Coast. From Port Orford 3.7 miles north on Hwy. 101, turn west on Cape Blanco Rd., travel 5 miles to the park.
Description: Cape Blanco is named for the white (blanco) chalk of the sea cliffs, which rise 200 feet over the ocean. Wildlife enthusiasts will be able to watch the sea lions on the offshore rocks. History buffs will enjoy the Hughes House which is located in the lovely grassy day-use area along the Sixes River estuary in the park. This is a very heavily wooded campground that affords a lot of privacy between each site. The bushes between are over 6 feet tall in some loops. By being so far off Hwy. 101 the only thing you will hear here is the wind—and there's lots of that.

58 paved sites, many shaded, 1880 acres, 58 partial hookups, (20 amp), max. length 70', no pull-thrus, $16.00-19.00, lower off-season rates, dump, restrooms, showers, handicap access, camp host, phone, nature trails. Hikers will enjoy the trails and the road that leads to the black sand beach below the cliffs.

Elk River Campground, open all year, 93363 Elk River Rd., (541) 332-2255
Location: From Port Orford, travel 1.5 miles north on Hwy. 101, then east 1.8 miles on Elk River Road
Description: Elk River is just what it says, a campground on a lovely bend of the Elk River with good fishing for salmon and steelhead in season. It is set amidst farming fields well off Hwy. 101 for a quiet camping experience. Elk River Campground has one mile of private river access on Elk River known for its excellent salmon fishing. The manager is friendly and helpful. Elk River Road is a country road that would make a good biking road from the campground. Call early for reservations if you plan to stay during the summer.

50 gravel sites, some shaded, 10 acres, max. length: 60', 50 full hookups (30 amp), 16 pull-thrus, $14.00 daily rate, lower weekly/monthly rates, GS, cable TV, restrooms, showers, phone, laundry, boat ramp.

Port Orford RV Trailer Village, open all year, 2855 Port Orford Loop, Port Orford, (541) 332-1041
Location: Off Hwy. 101 at Port Orford: from Hwy. 101 in Port Orford, drive on block east on Madrona Ave., then .5 mile on Port Orford Loop.
Description: This is a very friendly campground where the owners make you feel welcome. There is an informal group campfire and happy hour every evening. Coffee is available at the gazebo and patio in the morning. Fishing enthusiasts will enjoy trying their luck on the Elk and Sixes rivers in the fall and winter—only 1.5 miles away. The campground has a freezer, smokehouse, canner, and fish-cleaning station for their guests' convenience.

30 available gravel sites, some shaded, 2 acres, max. length: 65', 21 full hookups, 9 partial hookups, (30 amp), 10 pull-thrus, $15.00, lower weekly rates GS, Escapees, cable TV, restrooms, showers, phone, laundry room with TV, rec. room, gazebo room with TV, fish-cleaning station, propane.

Humbug Mountain State Park, open all year, (541) 332-6774, reservations (800) 452-5687
Location: At the base of Humbug Mountain on the east side of Hwy. 101, 6 miles south of Port Orford
Description: In a densely wooded area at the base of Humbug Mountain right next to

Hwy. 101. This park is named after the mountain that rises almost 2,000 feet above the coast. There is a three-mile trail that leads to the summit with a picturesque viewpoint.

105 total paved sites, some shaded, 1,840 acres, 30 partial hookups, (30 amp), max. length 50', no pull-thrus, $18.00, lower off-season rates, dump, restrooms, showers, handicap access, camp host, phone, nature trails.

Arizona Beach, open all year, 36939 Hwy. 101, (541) 332-6491
Location: On the Pacific Ocean, 12.2 miles south on Hwy. 101 from Port Orford
Description: This nice campground has a large strip of campsites right on the ocean. It is nestled in a quiet, wooded area of the coast not far off Hwy. 101. A great place to stay if you like to hear the roar of the ocean just a few feet from your door.

127 sites, some shaded, max. length: 60', 10 full hookups, 117 partial hookups, (20/30 amp), 20 pull-thru, $17.00-$19.00, lower weekly rates, GS, cable TV, dump, restrooms, showers, phone, laundry, groceries, giftshop, pool table, rec hall, security gate.

Volunteer/Camp Host Opportunities

Bandon Fish Hatchery, Rt. 2, Box 418, Bandon, OR 97411, (541) 347-4278
Elk River Fish Hatchery, 95163 Elk River Rd., Port Orford, OR 97465, (541) 332-7025
Bullards Beach State Park, Bandon, (541) 347-3501
Cape Blanco State Park, Port Orford, (541) 332-6774
Humbug Mountain State Park, Port Orford, (541) 332-6774

Section 2: Activities in Bandon

Bandon is a charming town with a lovely downtown area perfect for strolling. Old Town on the Coquille River estuary has been transformed to a quaint and quiet area to visit. It doesn't have the glitz of some of the coast towns further north but what it does have is understated style and grace. Everything in town is within walking distance and the walk along the waterfront with its new docks is relaxing. Great restaurants, a terrific gallery, and lots of crashing surf on the rocks and sea stacks. We love Bandon.

Don't Miss

Coquille Point, Oregon Islands National Wildlife Refuge, at the end of 11th St., with the 1.25 miles of paved walkways

Annual Events

Check with Bandon Chamber of Commerce
300 SE 2nd St., (541)347-9616, for specific dates
Pick up a copy of "Coffee Break" and a handy walking tour map of town

January
Bandon Stormwatchers seminars

May
Stormwatcher's Seafood and Wine Festival
Sandcastle and Sculpture Competition

June
Native American Salmon Bake

July/August
Coquille River Lighthouse, living history demonstrations

October
Cranberry Festival, parade, and food fair

December
Festival of Lights

At Coquille Point, Elephant Rock is a big island shaped like a big-eared elephant.

Highly Recommended

- Bandon Old Town, stroll the shops, galleries and waterfront promenade
- Bullards Beach State Park and the day-use area on north jetty for the Coquille River Lighthouse
- Beach Loop Drive, with all its waysides and stunning views of the ocean and sea stacks

Bike/Auto Tour

Beach Loop Drive, off Hwy. 101 west on 11th Street, is a lovely drive (or biking road) with many waysides affording ocean views of rocks and sea stacks. Bring your camera for Face Rock Wayside and Bandon State Park.

Coastal Rivers Scenic Loop, Bandon inland on Hwy. 42S then down to Gold Beach then back up Hwy. 101. Ask the Bandon Visitors Center about the booklet guiding you on this loop. They can make copies ($) of the map in the booklet. It is a 170-mile round-trip auto tour through some of the most remote areas of the inland areas of the coast.

"Biking Bullards Beach" is a very helpful guide that can be obtained from the Bandon Visitors Center. Bullards Beach State Park is one of the greatest parks for biking because of the miles of roads leading to the north jetty and Coquille River Lighthouse. Families with children will especially like this park.

Hwy. 42S to Coquille is a beautiful 18-mile drive along the Coquille River.

Bookstores

Winter River Books, 170 2nd St., Bandon, (541) 347-4111, is a very nice, large bookstore with one of the best selections of Northwest regional guides and gifts.

Ecotourism

Nature Seminars from the Bandon Stormwatchers, P.O. Box 1693, (541) 347-2144, conducts seminars about the local flora and fauna at the Bandon Community Center in the city park on Beach Loop Dr. from Jan.-Apr. Seminars are generally on Saturday.

Shoreline Education for Awareness, Inc., provide wildlife interpreters to help you view marine mammals and birds. It also takes groups on walks through the intertidal zones around Bandon's sea stacks—part of the Oregon Islands National Wildlife Refuge. Activities are scheduled from May to Sept. P.O. Box 957, Bandon, OR 97411 (541) 347-3683. Call for scheduled or customized tours.

Exercise Routes or Leisure Walking

Coquille River Boat Basin walkway on 1st street in Old Town gives you a wonderful, relaxing look at the boats and activities along the docks.

Coquille Point at the west end of 11th Street, has 1.5 miles of paved walkways along the ocean with interpretive signs.

Family Activities with Children

Bandon City Park and Russ Sommers Memorial Playground, is a great place to take the kids to work off some energy. A super playground, picnic tables, lots of grass, basketball, restrooms, and baseball diamonds. The Senior Center is there also.

West Coast Game Park Safari, petting park, lions, tigers and elk (7 miles south of Bandon on Hwy. 101, **milepost 280**, (541) 347-3106, where you will get a chance to pet the tamer animals. It can be quite surprising to walk around a corner and have 20 or more goats coming at you. There are lots of goats, deer, donkeys, hens, peacocks and others running loose trying to chew on anything you may have flapping around. The kids will love it.

Fishing/Clamming

Coquille Sport Basin Dock and Breakwater, floating dock system to provide access for crabbing and fishing. It is part of the waterfront revitalization activities in historic Old Town.

Surfperch are popular with people who fish the north and south jetty of the Coquille River as well as from the jetties and rocks near the lighthouse.

In early fall, salmon begin moving into the Coquille River and are active until December when steelhead season starts.

The lower Coquille River offers superb crabbing from the bar to the bridge. Many keepers can be taken from the piers and boat basin docks.

There are fishing charter offices on 1st Street in Old Town where you can rent fishing gear and crabpots that you can take right out on the pier and use.

Galleries/Arts

Second Street Gallery, 210 Second, (541) 347-4133. Don't miss this one. It truly is one of the finest on the whole coast and features many local artists as well. Artfully arranged in a large setting, it was a real surprise in such a small town. Expect to see the finest quality original art of the Northwest.

Klahowya Native American and Nature, 175 2nd St., Continuum Plaza, features a beautiful collection of unique art including jewelry, pottery, and framed art.

Golfing

Bandon Face Rock Golf Course, 3235 Beach Loop Dr., south of town, (541) 347-3818, offers a very challenging 9 holes, not far from the famous Face Rock, in a very scenic setting.

Hiking

Bullards Beach State Park, hiking, biking and equestrian trails. Try the 1.5-mile trail to the beach. A 3-mile trail wanders through woods and fields to the historic Coquille River Lighthouse, located on the north jetty.

Local History/Museums/Lighthouses

Coquille River Lighthouse in Bullard's Beach State Park is 2 miles north of Bandon on the north bank of the Coquille River. Commissioned in 1896 and decommissioned in 1939 following improvements to the river channel. Restored in 1976 as an interpretive center and open to the public. Open year-round during daylight hours with tours to tower watch room guided by park staff upon request (541) 347-2209. In spectacular wildlife viewing area.

Bandon Historical Society Museum, Hwy. 101 & Filmore St., (541) 347-2164, is housed in the old city hall building and has artifacts and graphics that recall the town's yesteryears. There are also displays of pioneer relics and a large presentation about the Coquille Indians. Donation.

Photo Opportunities

- Face Rock Viewpoint, Bandon, on Beach Loop Rd. Good beach access
- Coquille Pointe, west end of 11th Street
- North Jetty, Coquille River Lighthouse, Bullards Beach State Park

Restaurants/Espresso

Andreas, $$, 160 Baltimore, Bandon, (541) 347-3022, no credit cards, breakfast, lunch Mon-Sat, dinner every day, brunch Sun. Breakfast is first-rate; try the omelets. This place is known by the locals as the best. Smoke-free.

Harp's, $$, 130 Chicago, (541) 347-9057, dinner only every day starting at 5 p.m., try their salads with garlic balsamic vinegar dressing

Lord Bennett's Restaurant, $$$, 1695 Beach Loop Rd., (541) 347-3663. Exceptionally beautiful place with dramatic ocean views. Try the blackened fish or sole stuffed with mushrooms. For an elegant and romantic dinner with the best view in town, this is the place to go.

Minute Cafe, $, 145 N. 2nd St., (541) 347-2702, for a $2 breakfast. Open from 5 a.m.-8 p.m. every day. The prices here are reasonable and the food is so good. They make all their own soups and usually have three or four different ones on the menu. Good old American cooking. Salad bar. Smoke-free.

Station Restaurant, $$, east of Old Town on Hwy. 101, (541) 347-9615, has a great menu selection with good service. This is a good family restaurant featuring mostly American food. They also have a very nice gift shop where the kids will enjoy watching the German-made LGB trains run around the track at the ceiling.

Complements Bakery & Coffee Shop, $, 60 2nd St., (541) 347-9440, has a great assortment of their own homemade pastries and cookies to go with your espresso. Soup and sandwiches for lunch also.

Special Local Attractions

Bandon Cheese Factory & Store, 680 Second, (541) 347-2456, dates from 1939 where you can watch a video explaining how their cheese is made. Try the many varieties of their flavored cheeses as samples are always plentiful. We especially like the smoked salmon cheese. This is the second largest factory of its kind. Guess where the first is? If you have followed the book, you've already been there.

Cranberry Sweets, 1st & Chicago, has an enticing aroma and makes homemade candies many of which contain cranberries, of course. They are generous with their samples and almost all candies are available to tempt you. Try to get out of here with just one bite.

Bullards Beach State Park is 1,226 acres of beauty along most of the north side of the Coquille River Estuary. The lighthouse is in this park. Don't miss this stop.

51st Annual Cranberry Festival in September, Faber Farms tours and tasting room, Hwy. 42S east from Bandon, then right on Morrison Road for one mile. Call (541) 347-1166 for more information.

Vitra Glass Blowing Studio, Hwy. 101, 6.5 miles south of Bandon, open Mon.-Fri. 9 a.m.-5 p.m., (541) 347-4723, demonstrating the amazing craft of glass blowing. There are usually at least three people working together as a team to create stunning glass creations. The studio is very well organized and it is fascinating watching people practicing this potentially dangerous craft. They offer many of their incredible glass-blown creations for sale at the studio.

Wildlife Viewing

Coquille Point Oregon Islands National Wildlife Refuge, tidepooling, seals and sea lions, seabirds, located at the west end of 11th St. Access to intertidal area is from either the south bank of the Coquille River or the trail down the bluff off 11th St. Many seabirds can be seen on the offshore rocks.

Bullards Beach State Park, 1 mile north of Bandon on Hwy. 101. Explore dunes, jetty, river, woods on foot. Turnstones, surfbirds, oystercatchers visible on jetty. Herons and shorebirds feed on mudflats along riverbank. View Bandon Marsh National Wildlife Refuge from picnic area and boat ramp.

Bandon Marsh National Wildlife Refuge, Coquille River, especially in the fall to see this prime birding site on the coast. Mongolian plovers join migrating shorebirds during October. Outstanding salt marsh and coastal estuary. Access is via unmarked trails off River Road bordering the Coquille River east of Bandon. Immediately southwest of Coquille River bridge on the north edge of Bandon.

Bandon Offshore Rocks, viewing sites along Scenic Beach Loop Dr., Beach Loop and 11th St. SW, Bandon Ocean State Wayside, and Face Rock Viewpoints. Nesting murres, gulls, tufted puffins, and cormorants on offshore rocks in spring and summer. Brown pelicans in summer and fall. Canada geese are present during migration.

Section 3: Activities in Port Orford

Port Orford is the western-most town on the mainland US which also makes it famous for its wind. It is also one of the best places on the coast for whale watching. Oregon's coastal "banana belt" which has brought so many retirees to the southern coast starts just south of here. This means warmer winter temperatures but not necessarily less rain. Port Orford's average temperature in July is 65° and in 45° in January. Port Orford's average rainfall is 73 inches per year. There is not much in the downtown area to attract tourists except for the views at Battle Rock Wayside—most of the attractions can be seen at the state parks nearby.

Don't Miss

- **Humbug Mountain State Park**
- **Battle Rock State Wayside**

Highly Recommended

- **Cape Blanco State Park**

Bike/Auto Tour

Elk River Road is a nice road for biking. It goes through farms and fields and doesn't get much traffic.

Family Activities with Children

Buffington Park, on the west end of 14th St., Port Orford, is a 20-acre park with something for everyone. Picnic tables, ball field, tennis and basketball courts, and playground equipment. There is a small lake here that has a swimming beach in summer. Plenty of trails with many places for children to run and play, it makes a great place for a family afternoon.

Boice-Cope County Park is on fresh-water Floras Lake, popular with boaters, anglers, and board sailors because of the consistent wind here. This park has a good trail system for hiking to the beach and around the lake.

Annual Events

Check with Port Orford Chamber of Commerce
Battle Rock Information Center, (541) 332-8055, for specific dates

May	July
Port Orford Arts Festival	4th of July Jubilee Celebration

Elk River Fish Hatchery, 7 miles off Hwy. 101 on Elk River Road, Port Orford, (541) 332-7025, daily 8-4 (July-Sept.)

Prehistoric Gardens, 36848 Hwy. 101 S., Port Orford, (541) 332-4463, is located in a rain forest area that has been known to get 110 inches of rain in one year. This park was developed by sculptor E.V. Nelson who has recreated life-size replicas of the dinosaurs in a natural forest setting. Younger children especially will enjoy this exhibit. Open daily from 8:00 a.m. to dusk. Admission is charged.

Fishing

Visit the **Elk** and **Sixes** rivers for the salmon and steelhead runs.

Hiking

Humbug Mountain Trail, moderate difficulty, 6 miles south of Port Orford, has a 5.5-mile loop trail, elevation change: 710 feet, trail to the top of the mountain with dazzling views to the south of Nesika Beach. Look for the large brown sign for Humbug Mountain Trail.

Grassy Knob, easy, 1.6 miles round-trip, 4 miles north of Port Orford, tun east on Grassy Knob Road for 3.9 paved miles then 3.8 miles (FR5105) of one-lane gravel road to a parking area. From the summit there is a great 180° view.

Cape Blanco State Park has many hiking trails. Pick up a trail guide at the park entrance.

Local History/Museums/Lighthouses

Cape Blanco Lighthouse towers above the western-most point in Oregon, 9 miles north of Port Orford off Hwy. 101. Oldest standing lighthouse on Oregon Coast; commissioned in 1870. Open for tours May-Oct. Call Cape Blanco State Park (541) 332-6774 for current times.

Hughes House at Cape Blanco State Park, is a restored Victorian home built in 1898 for rancher Patrick Hughes. It has a beautiful view of the Sixes River estuary and the surrounding farm fields. It now serves as a museum and is operated by the State of Oregon. Open May 1-Sept. 30, Thurs.-Sat. and Mon. 10-5, Sun. 12 p.m.-5 p.m.

Photo Opportunities

- Battle Rock State Park
- Cape Blanco State Park and day-use area

Restaurants/Espresso

Whale Cove, $$, Hwy. 101 & Battle Rock Beach, (541) 325-7575, has a great view and the food lives up to its setting.

Crazy Norwegians, $, Hwy. 101, downtown Port Orford (541) 332-8601, for lunch they have good soup and fish and chips.

Special Local Attractions

Cape Blanco State Park, Hwy. 101, 11 miles north of Port Orford the (much debat-

Propeller from the wreck of the Cotoneva schooner, Port Orford.

ed) western-most point of land in mainland U.S. On top of the cape is the oldest and highest lighthouse that has been in continuous use in Oregon. It uses the same French-made lens that was installed in 1870. This is a very windy point so dress accordingly.

Wildlife Viewing

Port Orford, tidepooling, picnicking, in Port Orford, go west on 9th St. off Hwy. 101. Main intertidal area is north of the boat dock
Cape Blanco State Park, whale watching, seabirds
Battle Rock State Park, whale watching, beautiful views of sea stacks
Paradise Point State Park, (Paradise Point Rd. **milepost 290.8**) offers miles of nice secluded beach for walking or hunting for agates

Section 4: RV Parts & Services Bandon to Port Orford Area

Diesel

Bandon Texaco, 465 2nd St., diesel, propane, water, and air on the north side of the station. No overhead obstructions, easy access
Port Orford: Chevron, 12th St. & Hwy. 101, has diesel in the front bay with great access from both directions.

Dump Station

Bandon: Bullards Beach State Park
Port Orford: Cape Blanco State Park
Port Orford: Humbug Mountain State Park,

Laundry

Bandon: Hwy. 101/Hwy. 42S, Bandon Shopping Center
Port Orford: Duds & Suds, 2040 Hwy. 101, (541) 332-8575

View from Battle Rock with sea stacks looking south.

Library

Bandon: Bandon Library, on Hwy. 101 in the City Hall Building, (541) 347-3221, is a small library with a one on one paperback exchange. It has a separate children's area with storytimes. Mon., Fri., Sat. 10:30 a.m.-5 p.m., Wed.-Thur. 10:30 a.m.-8 p.m.

Port Orford: Port Orford Library, 555 W. 20th, (541) 332-5622, is a small library with lots of magazines and paperbacks that are free. They have two computers available for word processing. Mon., Tues., Thurs. 1 p.m.-8 p.m. Wed., Fri. 10:00 a.m.-5 p.m., Sat. 1 p.m.-5 p.m..

Medical Services

Bandon: Southern Coos General Hospital, 640 W. 4th, (541) 347-2426, 24-hour emergency care

Propane

Bandon Texaco, 465 2nd St. Cylinders can be filled without removing them from rig.
Port Orford Chevron, 12th & Hwy. 101

RV Parts & Service

Port Orford: Budwyn's Custom Shop, 92765 Silver Butte Rd., (541) 332-1895

Shopping /Groceries

Bandon: Ray's Food Place, 66 Michigan, Bandon Shopping Center, (541) 347-2011
Port Orford: Buck's Sentry Market on Hwy. 101, downtown Port Orford, (541) 332-1185

Dandelions in the Dunes on Oregon Dunes Trail.

USPO

Bandon: 105 12th St., 97411, (541) 347-3406
Port Orford: Jackson & 7th, 97465, (541) 332-4251

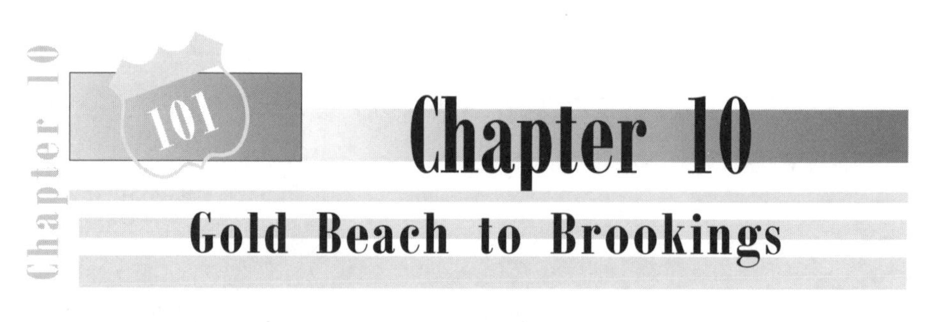

Map Grid A7: Gold Beach to Brookings

Introduction

Mention Gold Beach and most people think of the Rogue River, but the name came from the gold-laden black sands of the Rogue River estuary that spurred a gold rush in the 1850s and '60s. The black sands of the Rogue River in the early days were high in gold and all they had to do was scoop it up off the beach—but the gold soon played itself out.

The Rogue River is one of the few remaining wild and scenic rivers in the country. That is one of the reasons that the fishing here is so good. During the last several decades, white-water rafting and jet-boats provide a more ecological look at the area. Things wind down quite a bit in the winter due to the torrential rains and the seasonal nature of many of the businesses. Spring however, brings warm weather and the wildflowers tourists like to see.

Brookings and Harbor combine to make a large town on the coast. Just 6 miles from the California border, Brookings beckons to California and Oregon retirees with its mild year-round climate. Brookings is a busy port town with one of the safest harbors on the coast. And like other successful coast towns trying to attract tourists, it too is putting in a waterfront boardwalk at the marina with a host of new shops. Brookings boasts that it is the "banana belt" of Oregon. It does stay milder here all year but check the rainfall amounts before you get too excited. Brookings' temperatures in January range from a high of 54° to a low of 42°. July ranges from 68°-51°. Rainfall averages here are 81 inches per year.

Section 1: Best Campgrounds

Best Public Campgrounds

Best public campground for base camping

Brookings: Harris Beach State Park, open all year, (541) 469-2021, reservations (800) 452-5687, p. 150

Best public campground with full or partial hookups

Brookings: Harris Beach State Park, open all year, (541) 469-2021, reservations (800) 452-5687, p. 150

Best public campground for solitude and scenic beauty

Gold Beach: Quosatana Siskiyou NF Campground, open all year, (541) 247-6651, p. 150

Brookings: Loeb State Park, open all year, (541) 469-2021, p. 150

Best public campground for families with children

Brookings: Harris Beach State Park, open all year, (541) 469-2021, reservations (800) 452-5687, p. 150

Best public campground that accepts Golden Age/Access passes

Gold Beach: Quosatana Siskiyou NF Campground, open all year, (541) 247-6651, p. 150

The Gold Beach Bridge stretches across the mighty Rogue River.

Brookings: Winchuck Siskiyou NF, open 5/1-10/1, (541) 469-2196, p. 150

Best public campground with low rates

Gold Beach: Curry County Fairgrounds, open all year, (541) 247-4541, p. 150

Best Private Campgrounds

Best private campground with luxurious facilities

Gold Beach: Honey Bear Campground, open all year, (541) 247-2765, (800) 822-4444 (OR only), p. 148

Alternate: Gold Beach: Kimball Creek Bend RV Resort, open all year, (541) 247-7580, p. 149

Brookings: Whaleshead Beach Resort, open all year, (541) 469-7446, (800) 943-4325, p. 152

Best private campground for solitude and scenic beauty

Gold Beach: Four Seasons RV Resort, open all year, (541) 247-4503, (800) 248-4503, p. 148
Alternate: Indian Creek Recreation Park, open all year, (541) 247-7704, p. 148
Brookings: Riverside Campground, open all year, (541) 469-4799, p. 151

Best private campground for base camping

Gold Beach: Ireland's Ocean View RV Park, (541) 247-0148, p. 149
Alternate: Oceanside RV Park, open all year, (541) 247-2301, p. 149
Brookings: Harbor Beachfront RV Park, open all year, (541) 469-5867, (800) 441-0856 (OR only), p. 151

Best private campground for families with children

Gold Beach: Kimball Creek Bend RV Resort, open all year, (541) 247-7580, p. 149
Brookings: Harbor Beachfront RV Park, open all year, (541) 469-5867, (800) 441-0856 (OR only), p. 151
Alternate: Riverside Campground, open all year, (541) 469-4799, p. 151

Campground Descriptions

Gold Beach and Vicinity

Four Seasons RV Resort, open all year, 96526 N. Bank Rogue, Gold Beach, (541) 247-4503, (800) 248-4503
Location: 7 miles from Gold Beach. At the north end of the Rogue River Bridge, travel 3.5 miles east on N. Rogue River Road to N. Bank Rogue southeast for 3 miles.
Description: This park advertises itself as the RV park on the Rogue with river-front sites and it's true. They have a row of sites with breathtaking views of the Rogue. You can watch the jet-boats come and go or they will stop here and pick you up if you want to take a trip up the river. Deer commonly walk through the park. This park is well taken care of with a friendly manager. They have their own fishing dock, moorage and guide service. You can come in with no gear and get a license, guide, go fishing and they will clean, smoke or can the fish for you. There is also an 18-hole golf course about 15 minutes away.

43 sites, 3 acres, max. length 55', 43 full hookups, (30/50 amp), $15.00-26.50, lower weekly/monthly rates, GS, AAA, cable TV, restrooms, showers, dump, phone, laundry, groceries, propane, salmon fishing, tackle, boat ramp, dock, game room.

Honey Bear Campground, open all year, 34161 Ophir Rd., Ophir, OR, (541) 247-2765, (800) 822-4444 (OR only)
Location: 6.5 miles north of Gold Beach off Hwy. 101. Turn east on Ophir Road for two miles and follow signs to campground
Description: Honey Bear Campground is a nicely wooded park that has sites with a few ocean views as well as forest settings. It is the home of the Black Forest Sausage Kitchen with deli products that are made in the park for sale. The owners have built a lovely chalet containing a German deli, a large recreation area, outdoor deck and a big dance floor. Enjoy their German hospitality with family-style dinners and live music for dancing 6 nights a week during the summer, and weekends in winter. Their Octoberfest occurs the last weekend in September and the first weekend in October. A very nice campground to stay at in the Gold Beach area.

64 sites, some wooded and shaded, 100 acres, max. length: 60', 50 full hookups, 14 partial hookups, (30 amp), 25 pull-thrus, tent sites and overflow dry camp sites, $14.95-$17.95, 7th night free, lower weekly rates, GS, AAA, cable TV, restrooms, showers, dump, phone, laundry, walking access to the beach.

Indian Creek Recreation Park, open all year, 94680 Jerry's Flat Rd., Gold Beach (541) 247-7704

Location: Near Gold Beach, at south end of the Rogue River bridge, east .5 mile on Jerry's Flat Road to campground
Description: This campground is set across the road from the Rogue River close to Gold Beach. Indian Creek Trail Rides next door can take you on a horse ride and there are jet-boat trips on the Rogue River. Grant's Pancake House is also next door for a delicious, quick breakfast or they will make you breakfast or lunch to go if you are fishing. This park has a nice play area and large rec. room with pool tables and game machines.

100 grassy sites, some shaded, 2 acres, max. length: 60', 100 full hookups, (20/30 amp), 7 pull-thrus, $20.00-$22.00 daily rate, lower off-season and weekly/monthly rates, AAA, cable TV, restrooms, showers, sauna, phone, laundry, rec room, pool tables, free coffee and tea, store, cafe, and playground.

Ireland's Ocean View RV Park, open all year, 29272 Hwy. 101, Gold Beach, (541) 247-0148
Location: Just off Hwy. 101 in downtown Gold Beach, follow sign
Description: This is a small, very well taken care of park right in downtown Gold Beach just over a small dune to the ocean. All sites are paved with grass in between. This park is only a mile from some of the best fishing on the famous Rogue River. It is also right across Hwy. 101 from the U.S. Forest Service office and chamber of commerce making it convenient for obtaining information about the area. Early reservations are recommended.

32 paved level sites, max. length 60', 32 full hookups, (20/30 amp), 4 sites with 50 amp, 9 pull-thrus, $20.00 daily rate, lower off-season and weekly rates, cable TV, restrooms, showers, phone, laundry.

Kimball Creek Bend RV Resort, open all year, 97136 N. Bank Rogue, Gold Beach (541) 247-7580
Location: 8 miles from Gold Beach on the north side of the Rogue River, from Hwy. 101 at the north end of Gold Beach Bridge, turn up-river, follow North Bank Rogue River Road, keeping right, follow the river for 8 miles (look for signs).
Description: One of the largest and prettiest parks we've seen right on the "sunny side" of the Rogue River. Lots of green lawns and manicured landscaping within a forest setting. They have 14 acres of spacious grounds where deer roam free. Sites are spaced nicely apart. Their light and airy rec room with couches and TV is one of the largest and nicest around with lots of indoor and covered outdoor dining. A very well maintained facility, this resort is set right along the wild and scenic Rogue River. It's far enough away from the highway to provide peace and solitude. Extras include an 18-hole golf course 15 minutes away, hiking trails, and launch and tie-up boating facilities. Truly a family vacation resort where children and adults alike have room to play.

63 paved or gravel sites, some shaded, 14 acres, max. length 60', 63 full hookups, (30/50 amp), 16 pull-thrus, $20.00-$25.00, lower off-season and weekly/monthly rates, cable TV, restrooms, showers, dump, phone, laundry, groceries, propane, rec room w/kitchen, gifts, gameroom for children, separate library room, board jet boats at their dock, play area with equipment, fishing and guide service.

Oceanside RV Park, open all year, 94040 South Jetty Rd., Gold Beach, (541) 247-2301
Location: In Gold Beach on the ocean, .3 miles south on Hwy. 101 to the Port of Gold Beach entrance
Description: This park is right on the ocean with boating and beachcombing. It is a wide open, graveled area where the Rogue River meets the ocean, close to town and restaurants.

96 gravel sites, 14 acres, max. length: 55', 36 full hookups, 60 partial hookups (20/30 amp), 25 pull-thrus, $19.00-$20.00 daily rate, lower off-season and

weekly/monthly rates, cable TV, restrooms, showers, dump, phone, laundry.

Quosatana CG, Siskiyou NF, open all year, (541) 247-6651
Location: Off Jerry's Flat Road on the south end of the Gold Beach Bridge. From Gold Beach, take Jerry's Flat Road 4.2 miles, then NE on CR595 to FR33 NE 10 miles. (Hint: After the 4 miles on Jerry's Flat Road, follow the brown Forest Service signs to the campground instead of looking for road names).
Description: You will have to look long and hard to find a prettier, more spacious Forest Service campground than this one. Some of the campsites are nestled in a beautiful myrtle grove. This is a large park with good paved interior roads for larger RVs to maneuver. Some of the sites are directly overlooking the Rogue River. There are large grassy areas large enough for playing baseball. Lots of room for kids to run. We were really impressed by this park and how nice the facilities were for RVers.

44 paved sites, many shaded, 37 acres, Golden Age and Golden Access passes, max. length 40', no slide-outs, $7.00, restrooms, water, dump, boat ramp, fishing.

Curry County Fairgrounds, open all year, 950 S. Ellensburg, (Hwy. 101) Gold Beach, (541) 247-4541
Location: In downtown Gold Beach, with many sites right on the ocean with great views. This is a real camper's secret for the price in Gold Beach. They are expanding the ocean view sites with more partial hookups.
Description: Behind the offices for the fairgrounds, these sites offer unobstructed views of the ocean. The area is open gravel and grass. Interior roads are good gravel and level as are all the sites.

50 sites, some oceanfront, 10 partial hookups, 40 dry camp, $5.00-$10.00, max. length: any, restrooms, showers, phone, fishing.

Brookings

Harris Beach State Park, open all year, (541) 469-2021, reservations (800) 452-5687
Location: 2.2 miles north of Brookings on the west side of Hwy. 101
Description: This park has a large day-use area right on the beach but the campground is uphill in a densely forested area with good cover between all the sites. For wildlife watchers, Goat Rock, a migratory bird sanctuary is just off shore. The Chetco River has some of the best salmon and steelhead fishing around. There are many nature trails around the park and to the beach.

152 total paved sites, many shaded, 141 acres, 34 full hookups, 52 partial hookups, (30 amp), 66 dry campsites, max. length 50', no pull-thrus, $16.00-$20.00, lower off-season and weekly rates, dump, restrooms, showers, handicap access, camp host, phone, playground, planned activities in summer, ocean, fishing, nature trails.

Loeb State Park, open all year, (541) 469-2021
Location: 8 miles east from Brookings on North Bank Chetco River Road, follow signs
Description: This park is a sleeper and well off the beaten path. Set back into the woods with a Redwood old-growth trail nearby and on the banks of the Chetco River, you couldn't find a nicer place for peace and quiet. Loeb has partial hookups only with no dump but it does have gray water disposal making it easy to spend a week here. A very nice secluded spot nestled in an old-growth myrtlewood forest with lots of hiking.

53 paved sites, many shaded, 320 acres, 53 partial hookups, (20 amp), max. length 45', most 35', no pull-thrus, $18.00, lower off-season and weekly rates, restrooms, showers, handicap access, camp host, nature trails, fishing in Chetco River, swimming, planned activities in summer.

Winchuck CG, Siskiyou NF, open 5/1-10/1, no reservations, (541) 469-2196
Location: 5.5 miles south of Brookings, 8 miles east on Winchuck Road, follow brown Forest Service signs

View north from Otter Point near Gold Beach.

Description: This park is on the Winchuck River in the Siskiyou National Forest. It's a very quiet and secluded camp not far from the coast. Campsites on the left of Winchuck Rd. (sites 1-9) are the only ones suitable for medium or large RVs. There are a few pull-thrus but some are tight. You may want to verify by calling to see if your rig is suitable.

9 gravel sites suitable for RVs, many shaded, 5 acres, accepts Golden Age and Golden Access passes, max. length: 45', no pull-thrus, $7.00, water, improved vault toilets, handicap access, camp host, nature trails.

Harbor Beachfront RV Park, (Port of Brookings), open all year, (503) 469-5867, (800) 441-0856 (OR only)
Location: Right on the ocean in Brookings at the marina on Boat Basin Road
Description: This spacious park faces the ocean with the south jetty of the Chetco River on its edge. Views here are great with lots of walking along the beach or jetties. The frontage road and the areas around the marina would also be good places for bicycle riding.

136 available gravel sites, max. length 60', 48 full hookups, 36 partial hookups (20/30 amp), 36 pull-thrus, $9.00-$18.00 daily rate, lower weekly/monthly rates, Cable TV $, restrooms, showers, dump, phone, large laundryroom, ocean, fishing, swimming, boating, ramp, dock, marina, rentals. There are also several good restaurants nearby.

Riverside RV Campground, open all year, 97666 North Bank Chetco River Rd., Brookings, (541) 469-4799
Location: On the banks of the Chetco River very close to Brookings. Take North Bank Chetco River Road turn-off and drive 500 yards east.
Description: This is a lovely campground right on the Chetco River in a beautiful setting. This river is famous for salmon and steelhead.

25 gravel sites, 25 full hookups, (30/50 amp), 7 pull-thrus, max. length back-ins 45', $20.00, lower off-season and weekly/monthly rates, cable TV, restrooms, showers, dump, phone, laundry, rec room with TV and library, pool table, boat launch, river fishing.

Whaleshead Beach Resort, open all year, 19921 Whaleshead Rd., Brookings, (541) 469-7446, (800) 943-4325
Location: Off Hwy. 101, 9 miles north of Brookings, **milepost 349.5**
Description: This park gets our vote as one of the top 5 private parks on the coast. If you plan to stay a while, check their weekly/monthly rates against other parks—you may find them very competitive. Whaleshead is designed to fit well with the surrounding forest in tiers all the way down to the beach. They even have their own tunnel going under Hwy. 101 directly to the beach at Whalehead State Park. There is a lovely creek flowing through the park with grassy areas and picnic tables in secluded spots. The facilities are top notch. The laundry room has an additional room with table and indoor phone so you can catch up with home while doing your laundry. They also have one of the largest and best lodge rooms with fireplace and TV that we have seen. Mail slots are assigned to each camper for easy pickup at the office. Don't miss a stop at this campground.

65 available gravel sites, some shaded, back-ins: max. length 60', 57 full hookups, 8 partial hookups, (30/50/100 amp), $20.00-$25.00, GS, lower off-season and weekly/monthly rates, cable TV, restrooms, showers, phone, laundry, rec hall, groceries, propane, cedar decks on each site, beach access, horseshoes, game room, free coffee, hot chocolate, snack bar, cabins.

Volunteer/Camp Host Opportunities

Harris Beach State Park, (541) 469-2021
Loeb State Park, (541) 469-2021
Winchuck Siskiyou National Forest Campground, (541) 469-2196
Quosatana Siskiyou National Forest Campground, (541) 247-6651

Section 2: Activities in Gold Beach and Vicinity

The two most famous activities in this area are the jet-boat rides up the Rogue River and the fishing. The Rogue River has been designated a Wild and Scenic River preserving its ecosystems and beauty for all to see. If you have time take the drive up to Agness to get the full impact of this lovely river.

Don't Miss

- Rogue River jet-boat rides

Highly Recommended

- Auto tour up the Rogue River
- Fishing the Rogue River

Bike/Auto Tours

Biking: Drive north across the bridge and park in the gravel view area on the left side of Hwy. 101. Ride your bike down Wedderburn toward the jetty. Bike the asphalt road north along the coast. The road starts as Wedderburn Loop, turns into the old Hwy. 101 and finally into a single-lane asphalt road. Along the way you will have ocean beaches on your left with many accesses. Otter Point State Park will be near the end of the three-mile one-way trip. There are no restroom facilities along this ride.

Auto Tour to Agness: Scenic drive up south bank of Rogue River. Travel Jerry's Flat Road (paved but bumpy in spots) for 34 miles to Agness a small pioneer community. Terrific river views especially where the Illinois River meets the Rogue, with birdwatching, picnic areas, hikes, and campsites. You may see some of the many guided fishing boats or one of the jet-boats go by. There is still a mail-boat delivery to Agness, a tiny town with a store, museum, and post office.

Bookstores

The Bookworm Bookstore, 29401 S. Ellensburg, (541) 247-9033, is predominately a used bookstore with 7,000 used books, a few new and audio books. They have espresso, tables and a small gallery of regional artists.

Ecotourism

Jerry's Rogue River Jet boats, Box 1011, Gold Beach, (800) 451-3645, (541) 247-4571 or Mail Boat Trips, Mail Boat Dock, Rogue River Rd., (541) 247-7033, (800) 458-3511, both offer a 64-mile round-trip excursion which interprets the various sights and wildlife on the Rogue River. There are many stops along the way to explain the history and wildlife.

At the Chamber of Commerce obtain the booklet "Self-guided Ecology Driving Tour". A short and long tour will be described including interpretive stopping points. The short tour is 31 miles. that includes views of the Rogue River, a short walk into a Myrtlewood grove, a drive through old growth forest. Be aware that 11 miles of this tour is on one lane gravel road with turn outs. After completing the gravel road portion of this tour we suggest you stay on the north side of the Rogue River. It has several nice turn outs for viewing the river and its wildlife. If you prefer to stay on asphalt roads, this is still an excellent 20 mile loop tour.

Exercise Routes or Leisure Walking

Walk the beach south of Rogue River. See if you can find some of that flour gold that gave this town it's name.

Annual Events

Check with Gold Beach Chamber of Commerce
29279 Ellensburg Ave., (541) 247-7526, (800) 525-2334, for specific dates

January
Whale of a Wine Festival

February
Fish Fry, Squaw Valley, North Bank RFPD

March
Western Fun Night
Sea Lion Suds Fest

April
Wildflower hikes

May
Clam Chowder Festival, Art & Flower Show

June
Rogue River Jetboat Marathon

July
Jetboat races
Baseball, apple pie, 4th of July
Gold Beach Summer Theater

August
Cedar Bend Invitational Golf Tournament

September
Curry County Fair
Festival of Quilts

October
Fall Crafts & Collectibles Sale

November
Calico Country Bazaar
Festival of Lights

December
Community Christmas Bazaar

Gold Beach constructs a new fantasy playground for the kids.

Rotary Club Fitness Trail at Buffington Memorial Park (see "Family Activities with Children").

Family Activities with Children

Collier Buffington Memorial Park has the largest set of playground equipment on the coast. The park also has a basketball court, tennis court, large grassy areas for running, covered picnic pavilion, restrooms, with a babbling brook thrown in. On the east end of the parking area is the Rotary Club's Fitness Trail. The signs for the park are on Turner Street.

Fishing/Clamming

Clamming: Meyers Creek Beach, south of Gold Beach.
Fishing: South jetty, west on Moore St. to south jetty. Restrooms, seals, sea lions, crabbing. No license is required for surf fishing for perch, smelt, but one is required for salmon or steelhead.
Rogue River along the bank for salmon or steelhead where access is permitted.

Galleries/Arts

Crow Gallery, 29957 Harbor Way, (541) 247-0105, has a small collection of lovely Native American art.
Gray Whales, 455 N. Ellensburg, (541) 247-7514, fine art.

Golfing

Cedar Bend Golf Course in Ophir, 34391 Squaw Valley Rd., (541) 247-6911, 11 miles north of Gold Beach. Turn on Ophir Road and follow it to Squaw Valley Road and turn right at the Old Ophir Store and continue until you see the course. This is the only golf course in Curry County. It is a par 36, 9-hole course in low, rolling hills, sheltered from the wind. It is unique in that each hole has two tee locations and two holes on each green for diversity in playing 18 holes. Carts and clubs can be rented, and they have a driving range and putting green.

Hiking/Waterfalls

Hikes up **Jerry's Flat Road** on the south side of the Rogue

Schrader Old Growth trail, 8-miles up Jerry's Flat Rd. near the Lobster Creek Campground. Easy .8-mile loop. Watch for signs. Brochure available at the chamber of commerce.

Myrtlewood Trail, easy, .5-mile round-trip hike. Follow Lower Rogue River Trail signs, turn left on Rd. 3310 across a scenic one-lane bridge at Lobster Creek and then turn right on Rd. 3533 for one mile. The steep .25mile trail that begins here switch-backs up to the massive myrtlewood tree beside a picnic table and a lovely creek. This is one of the best areas to view old-growth myrtlewood trees.

Local History/Museums

Curry County Historical Museum, 920 S. Ellensburg, Gold Beach, (541) 247-6113, has a small collection of exhibits on Indian and pioneer life, mining, logging, fishing, and agriculture. Don't miss looking at the black sand with the flour gold that gave Gold Beach its birth and name. Another interesting feature is the realistic mock-up of a miner's cabin, vintage photos, and Indian petroglyphs. Free June-Oct. Tues-Sat 12 p.m.-4 p.m., Oct-May Sat. 12 p.m.-4 p.m.

Jerry's Rogue River Museum and Gift Shop in the ticket office of Jerry's Rogue River Jet boats, Port of Gold Beach has a large collection of artifacts, photos and illustrations depicting the Rogue River's geologic formation, early man, early river travel, and local history. There is also a natural history exhibit of birds, fish and animals native to the Rogue River area displayed in a simulated natural environment. This is a worthwhile museum to visit and follow the events along the Rogue from the early 1800s to the present. Free

Photo Opportunities

- Otter Point State Park
- Gold Beach Bridge from the north jetty
- Gold Beach Bridge from Mail-Boat Trips dock
- Cape Sebastian

Restaurants/Espresso

Grant's Pancake and Omelet House, $, 94680 Jerry's Flat Rd., Gold Beach, (541) 247-7208. Open 5:30 a.m. to 2:00 p.m. 7 days a week. Great menu for breakfast and the service can't be beat. They will make breakfast and lunch deli sandwiches to go. The locals love it here.

Spada's, $$, 1020 S. Ellensburg, Gold Beach, (541) 247-7730, has a good menu selection reasonably priced.

The Chowderhead Restaurant, $$, 910 S. Ellensburg, Gold Beach, (541) 247-7174, has ocean-view dining and a very imaginative menu. Bon Appetit Magazine considers the Chowderhead "one of America's best restaurants." Excellent food.

Rod & Reel Restaurant, $$, 97491 Wedderburn, Gold Beach, (north of the bridge on ocean side), Gold Beach, (541) 247-6823. Open for all three meals, formal dining area used for evening meals, with a large menu selection. Lunch may be served in the sports bar lounge area. Very nicely arranged and decorated.

Norwester Seafood Restaurant, $$, Port of Gold Beach, (541) 247-2333. American mostly seafood. For that elegant dinner with a view—it's right on the marina. Excellent choices of seafood and steak. Dinner from 5 p.m.

Gold Beach with Humbug Mountain in the distance.

Special Local Attractions

Jetboat rides up the Rogue River

Mail-Boat Trips, Mail-Boat Dock, .25 miles inland from Rogue River Bridge, Rogue River Rd., (541) 247-7033, (800) 458-3511. Their new glass-enclosed excursion boats make trips for groups comfortable no matter what the weather. Mail-boats run 64- 80- and 104-mile trips up the Rogue. Besides tourists, these boats actually do carry mail to Agness and other towns.

Jerry's Rogue Jets, Gold Beach Boat Basin, (541) 247-7601, (800) 451-3645. Jerry's runs 64- and 104-mile round-trips up the Rogue and has a great museum right across from their ticket building.

Wildlife Viewing

Cape Sebastion State Park, seals and sea lions, whale watching, seabirds on the trail out at the point.

Just west of Mail Boat Trips on North Rogue River Road there is a herd of elk that can be seen on the dry hills above the road. Bring your binoculars as they blend in with the dry grass in fall.

Section 3: Activities in Brookings, Harbor and Vicinity

Brookings and Harbor are the southern-most communities on the Oregon Coast. You will see many plants growing here that would never make it in colder areas. Loeb State Park has the largest grove of coast redwoods. Brookings is sprucing up its waterfront area with a boardwalk and new shops much like Newport and Florence.

Don't Miss

- Samuel H. Boardman viewpoints
- Lone Ranch Beach and Natural Bridges Cove
- Redwood Nature Trail

Highly Recommended

- Whalehead Beach
- Azelea Park
- Harris Beach day-use

Biking

Lower Harbor Road has a nice, wide bike lane for easy biking.

Bookstores

The Book Dock is a very organized store at the marina that has new and used books. 16364 Lower Harbor Rd., (541) 469-6070, (800) 230-3591. Open daily, closed Monday in winter.

Words & Pictures Art Gallery & Bookstore, South Coast Center, 16261 Hwy. 101 S. (541) 469-7067, is a very nice bookstore with a wonderful little gallery next door that has excellent art. Open Mon.-Sat.

Ecotourism

Self-guided forest ecology tour (Bombsite Trail), stop by the chamber of commerce and pick up the booklet, "Self-Guided Forest Ecology Tour". This tour takes you on a 37-mile round-trip tour past 20 plaques that explain the forest around you. You will also have an opportunity to hike the Bombsite Trail, where incendiary bombs landed in W.W.II. This is a 5-mile paved road and 13-mile gravel road—one way.

Exercise Routes or Leisure Walking

Brookings Marina, Lower Harbor Road, is building a boardwalk at the marina as well as many more shops and places for visitors to linger and just enjoy the wharf. This is scheduled to be open in 1997.

Azalea Park has many walking paths among the tall azalea bushes and is in a quiet part of town.

Family Activities with Children

Azalea Park is a great place for families to picnic. It has a kid's fantasy playground that will entertain them for hours. (There is a debate as to whether this one or the one in Gold Beach is bigger). Take the short path up to the gazebo to see the beautifully landscaped grounds and the tall azalea bushes which bloom April through June. Take North Bank Road and turn left at the stop sign. Park entrance is just a short distance on your right.

Lone Ranch Beach State Park, 5 miles north of Brookings on the west side of Hwy. 101, is a great place to bring the kids for an afternoon. There is a lovely little creek for them to wade in while the adults enjoy a picnic on one of the many tables facing the ocean. The views here of the rocks, driftwood and little cove are outstanding. Reports are that agate hunters love it here.

Fishing/Clamming

Chetco Fishing Pier, off Boat Basin Road next to the Coast Guard Station, has a paved parking lot right next to the pier. The small pier over the Chetco River is a popular, no-

Annual Events

Check with Brookings/Harbor Chamber of Commerce
16330 Lower Harbor Rd., (800) 535-9469, (541) 535-9469, for specific dates
Check with the Chetco Ranger District, (541) 469-2196, for trails into the Kalmiopsis Wilderness

March
Beachcomber's Festival

May
Annual Azalea Festival

July
Fireworks display
Southern Oregon Kite Festival

Enjoying the day-use area at Harris Beach State Park near Brookings.

fee facility used extensively by the physically challenged and the elderly as it has a picnic table and benches. Crab, salmon, steelhead, smelt can be caught.

Galleries/Arts

See Words & Pictures Bookstore & Gallery under "Bookstores"

Hiking

Whalehead Beach: Milepost 349, trailhead at turnoff is a 0.2-mile walk to overlook **Whalehead Island.** Take a walk down to the beach for a look at a delightful cove with a little creek entering the ocean.

Redwood Nature Trail and Riverview Trails provide a 3-mile round-trip hiking experience from Loeb State Park. From the north end of the bridge in Brookings, turn inland on North Bank Road along the Chetco River. This is a beautiful drive along the wide, lazy river. Turn into Loeb State Park, there is trailhead parking straight ahead. Redwood Nature Trail if done separately can be accessed from North Bank Road. It winds through a pristine redwood grove with trees up to 350 feet tall.

Bombsite Trail, 18 miles east of Brookings, a two-mile round-trip hike through old growth redwoods to where two Japanese incendiary bombs landed during World War II. Hwy. 101 to South Bank Road of the Chetco River. At 5 miles turn right onto gravel Mt. Emily Road and follow "Bombsite Trail" signs for 13 miles (a twisting uphill drive). Obtain a brochure for this auto tour and hike from the Brookings Chamber of Commerce.

Samuel H. Boardman State Park. Several good trails, most short from waysides to beach. There are seven viewpoints in the park with short rewarding hikes. The Oregon Coast Trail winds in and around many of these viewpoints.

Local History/Museums/Lighthouses

Chetco Valley Historical Society Museum, 15461 Museum Rd. (541) 469-6651, housed in an 1857 clapboard cottage. Site of world's largest Monterey cypress tree. Open Wed.-Sat.

Photo Opportunities

- Samuel Boardman State Park viewpoints
- Lone Ranch Beach
- Arch Rock
- Natural Bridges Cove
- Whalehead Beach

Restaurants/Espresso

Flying Gull, $$, 1153 Chetco, (541) 469-5700, part of the Bookings Best Western, has an excellent menu. Try their dinner buffet and great salad bar.

Hog Wild Cafe, $$, 16160 Chetco Ave., (541) 469-8869, has excellent breakfast with unique menu choices. Smoke-free.

Rubio's Mexican Restaurant, $$, 1136 Chetco Ave., (541) 469-4919. Known for their homemade Salsa Rubio; try the chile rellenos and chile verde on their patio.

The Tea Room Cafe, $, 434 Redwood in the Abbey Mall, (541) 469-7240. Breakfast and lunch only. The desserts are to die for. They have received many awards that they will be glad to show you. Friendly waitresses and just plain good food at reasonable prices. Look around and you will see over 700 teapots around the cafe. Superb, home-made food. Only open M-F from 7 a.m.-2:30 p.m. No credit cards.

Espresso Gallery, $, Boat Basin Rd., on the marina, Port of Brookings, (541) 469-3161, has a cozy cafe with outdoor deck where you can watch the boats on the wharf. Coffee, tea, pastries, muffins and art. Open daily 6:30 a.m.-5 p.m.

Special Local Attractions

Natural Bridges Cove Viewpoint is a photographer's delight. Outstanding views of sculpted natural arch bridges are revealed by taking a short boardwalk to a wooden over-look. Don't miss it.

Azalea Park, 76-acre park with Azaleas 20 feet tall and 300 years old. Access is on North Bank Road.

Enjoying the day-use area at Harris Beach State Park near Brookings.

Natural Bridges Cove in Samuel Boardman State Park near Brookings.

Lone Ranch Beach has a well marked turnout to great picnic area and fabulous beach. Agates.

Wildlife Viewing

Lone Ranch Beach, tidepooling, located 5 miles north of Brookings, off Hwy. 101.

Harris Beach, tidepooling, restrooms, picnicking, seabirds, interpretive programs in summer, located just north of Brookings, west of the campground. Access is from the main parking lot by walking south along the beach.

Samuel Boardman State Park viewpoints, whale watching, seabirds.

Sea lions, seals, and river otters at the mouth of the Chetco Rivers.

Section 4: RV Parts & Services in Gold Beach to Brookings and Vicinity

Diesel

Gold Beach: Howard's Excel Services, (Shell), 1025 S. Ellensburg (Hwy. 101), (541) 247-6010. Diesel is the red pump in front of the large white tanks south of the station.
Brookings: Harbor Shell & Foodmart, 16021 Hwy. 101, (541) 469-4113, has good access with diesel in both bays. No overhead obstructions.

Dump Station

Gold Beach: 5th and Hwy. 101 turn toward the ocean. Past the fire department about 100 yards you will see a sign with the dump on the left side of the road. Free
Brookings: Harris Beach State Park, on Hwy. 101, 2 miles north of Brookings
Brookings Rest Area, on Hwy. 101, 2 miles north of Brookings, **milepost 356**

Laundry

Gold Beach: Coin-op Laundry, 29734 Hwy. 101. Open 24 hours.
Brookings: Laundromat, Brookings Harbor Shopping Center.

Library

Gold Beach: Curry Public Library, 330 Colvin St., (541) 247-7246. Large parking area

on north side with 24-foot pull-thrus. Small library open M-Th 10-8 p.m., F 10-6 p.m., S 10-5 p.m. Free periodicals in the foyer, paperbacks may be purchased for 10 cents. Three month, $15 membership required to check out catalog books.
Brookings: Chetco Public Library, 405 Alder, (541) 469-7738, is a new library building open Mon-Sat. Mon. 10:00 a.m.-6 p.m., Tues. and Thurs. 10 a.m.-7 p.m., Wed. 10 a.m.-8 p.m., Sat. 10 a.m.-4 p.m. Free periodicals in the foyer. Paperbacks available without a membership.

Medical Services

Gold Beach: Curry General Hospital, 220 East Fourth St., (541) 247-6621, (800) 445-8085. 24-hour emergency care

Propane

Gold Beach: Howard's Excel Services (Shell), 1025 S. Ellensburg, (Hwy. 101), (541) 247-6010.
Gold Beach: Rogue River RV, 94144 Wedderburn Loop, (541) 247-5004 or (800) 249-5004.
Brookings: Blue Star Propane & Repair, 16160 Hwy. 101 S., (541) 469-7827.

RV Parts & Service

Gold Beach: Rogue River RV, 94144 Wedderburn Loop, (541) 247-5004 or 800-249-5004. A full-service repair facility for RVs. There are no supplies at this facility but Rich Tetzlaff can order parts needed if he does not have them in stock. Call if you need towing and they will make the arrangements. You may stay in your rig with water and electrical hookup if repair takes longer than one day.
Brookings: Don's RV Repair, 99070 W. Freeman Lane, (541) 469-6476.

Shopping/Groceries

Gold Beach: McKay's Market, 320 S. Ellensburg, (541) 247-7144
Brookings: Fred Meyer One-Stop Shopping, (541) 469-1610
Brookings: Ray's Food Place, 906 Chetco Ave., (541) 469-3742

USPO

Gold Beach: Hwy. 101, 1 block west on Moore, 97444, (541) 247-7610
Brookings: 711 Spruce St., 97415, (541) 469-2318. In the Brookings Harbor Shopping Center.

Samuel Boardman State Park near Brookings.

Chapter 11

RVer's Best Hints

How to prevent becoming a camping horror story

Introduction

This chapter was written for all the RVers out there who may have some apprehensions about driving a large land yacht. When we first got our 29' fifth-wheel, the tension was noticeable as we drove off the dealer's lot. With a little more experience, we figured out that we really could control our destiny and not become an RV horror story.

When you hit the road with an RV you are taking a trip with a combination motor vehicle and house. The maintenance and upkeep you perform on your automobile and your residence at home are also required on the equipment you take on the road. In our travels we have heard many horror stories, from water running out of RVs with broken water lines to getting stuck on a road with no room to turn the rig around. This chapter is provided to help keep you from having an RV horror story of your own.

Planning

Planning is one of the most important steps an RVer can take. A thoroughly planned trip and execution of the plan provides its own self satisfaction, confidence, and a lower level of stress and tension. Besides, planning builds anticipation and is half the fun of the trip. We spend many hours planning and re-planning although we are experienced RVers. We do it to be prepared, of course, but we do it as much for the excitement and building of anticipation for the trip that it creates.

Road Selection and Research

Recently the state of Washington considered passing a law requiring RV drivers to be trained and tested the same as truck drivers. There has been lots of debate on this subject. When you hit the road with a large RV, the driving skills required are different than driving a car. It takes much longer to stop that much weight. You have a wider turning radius, and based on your rig you need to know which roads you can and cannot navigate. We heard a story from an RVer who ended up on a two-lane road facing an underpass too low for their fifth-wheel. Talk about raising the stress level!

One of our first scary experiences was getting on a road that was winding and too steep for our rig. After eight miles of white knuckles, we reached the summit doing 5 miles per hour and blowing black smoke all the way. We were both nervous wrecks. Fortunately for us we were ascending and not descending. Going downhill is far riskier than the uphill battle. A road such as the one we were on with no turnouts can quickly overheat the brakes and brake failure is an experience none of us want as a horror story. We've learned to take roads with easier grades even if we have to drive extra miles to get to our destination.

Research your route to find out what the (%) grades are. Is the road winding with curves requiring speeds below 40 mph? If it is a rural road are the lanes standard size or narrow. Besides travel guides, we use two visual guides; if the truck drivers don't use it we generally don't use it. An old RV friend once told us, "Follow the rivers". If you have the luxury of time in your travels, research whether the roads following rivers would be good RV roads for you. They generally do not have steep grades and the scenery is lovely. Of course, we do have the luxury of taking more time in traveling and do enjoy the scenic routes.

Fuel and Rest Stops

With an RV you will need to fuel up more often. Since you are in a larger rig, the space for entering and exiting fuel stations becomes critical. It was just this year that we saw a new fifth-wheel with one side crushed in. They had hit the edge of the pump's concrete island. Also this year a service station attendant pointed out a pump turned 30 degrees where an RV had hit it while trying to navigate into position for refueling.

As we plan our routes we also take the time to plan the refueling stops. Since we pull a fifth-wheel, we can make a decision to refuel with or without the RV attached. First we determine the distance we will travel each day. If it does not exceed the distance we can travel without refueling we plan to refuel after the fifth-wheel is disconnected. If it does exceed the distance we can travel without refueling we then identify a station (first choice is truck stops) for refueling. Our preferences are stations directly on our route with name brand products (especially for diesel). This way we do not waste time traveling away from our route and the name brands provide less worry of getting contaminated fuel.

We also believe that frequent rest stops are important to both the driver and the RV. We try to plan a 15-30 minute rest break for every 1-2 hours of driving even if all we do is stop at a closed weigh station. This gives the driver a chance to check out the RV for potential problems, and gives everyone a chance to walk around and stretch, increasing the alertness for the next hour or so. Stopping also allows the RV or tow vehicle a chance to cool down so that parts affected by heat are not overly stressed. Some would argue that this reduces the miles that can be covered in a day. Our arguments are two; first, you will arrive at your destination fresher and relaxed, and second, you are on this trip for the enjoyment so why not take the time and enjoy it.

Packing the RV

Whether you are taking a weekend trip or a trip of several months you will have to decide what you want to take with you; clothes, outdoor camping equipment, food, cameras, cooking utensils. Planning on how the gear will be packed is important. The portion of the RV above the axles has less vibration for jarring and shaking your cargo. We store the heavy utensils and gear at floor level as close to the axles as possible. This includes canned goods. We then plan the rest of the packing to distribute the other weight evenly throughout the rig. Each storage area needs to be either fully filled or the empty space packed. It does not take much of a bump to dislodge your stored goods. Even experienced RVers have opened their door to find goods scattered through the interior. We have found the rig handles better with the weight evenly distributed.

You should know how much weight you are carrying with your RV. Your owner's manual will tell you the maximum weight limit (GVW—gross vehicle weight). When we noticed some RVers pulling a large fifth-wheel with a truck that was laboring, we asked how much their trailer weighed loaded. Their reply was, "we don't want to know". Well, we do, it gives us the confidence to know that we are driving safely. If you want to know how much you weigh, stop at any closed weigh station and check it. In Oregon, the stations leave the scales on even when they are closed. Record these weights periodically and you too will have the knowledge necessary to travel safely.

Campgrounds

We have the most fun when it comes to planning the campgrounds where we will stay. There will be campgrounds for just an overnight stay and there will be the campgrounds that are our final destination for base camping. Our selection criteria differs for the two types of camping.

The overnight campground needs to be close to the route we are traveling but far enough off the road to reduce traffic noise. Hook-ups are not important to us and unless we need to fuel, often we will not even disconnect. We look for a site with privacy and easy access as far from the road noise and other campers as possible. Our objective is a quiet and relaxing rest getting prepared for the next day of travel.

The base camp selection (1-2 weeks) is a decision that takes into account environmental beauty, close proximity to activities we enjoy, type of hook-ups (example; dry-camp, or 20 amp versus 30 amp versus 50 amp power connection), as well as accessibility for our size of rig. We have seen several campgrounds we thought were great only to find we would not be able to get our rig out easily once we got it in because the interior roads were tight around trees. Look around at the next campground you are in and count the number of trees scarred by passing rigs. Ask yourself "I wonder how that rig looked after this encounter?" There has been many a time when we backed into a pull-thru campsite for this reason.

Preparing For the Trip

Once the planning is completed it is time to start getting prepared for the trip. In most cases, RVs spend more time parked than being used. Before getting them on the road, preventative maintenance will make the trip less worrisome and safer.

• **Insurance:** Is the equipment under insurance coverage including roadside service and towing? Before the trip starts is the time to make the decision on the amount of insurance coverage versus risk you are willing to take. Seeing an RV precariously parked at the side of the road broken down is not a picture you want to see, especially with you in it.

• **Wheels and axles:** Have the wheel bearings been inspected and packed, brakes inspected and adjusted, springs and shocks inspected within the last 12 months?

• **Tires:** Are the tires in excellent condition, balanced, and with the proper air pressure (carry a gauge)? Are the lugs tight?

• **Lube and oil:** By now you can estimate the total miles for your trip. If your maintenance schedule calls for fluid changes during the trip you may wish to do it prior to the trip at facilities you have used and are confident with. Now is the time to make certain that the vehicle has had all the periodic maintenance needed.

• **Under the hood:** The engine components will be stressed pulling the heavy load. Any weakness will be uncovered at the most inopportune time. Radiator hoses, belts, pumps, and filters all need inspection, if necessary repair or replace them prior to the start of the trip and you will do well to carry extras with you.

• **Warranties:** If your RV is under warranty you should carry the warranty information with you including the hotline phone numbers. Regardless of the warranty status, carry the name, address, and phone number of mechanics that know your RV, and road services you plan to use in an emergency. We have called the dealership where we bought our RV several times while traveling when we had a mechanical problem. In every case, they provided a solution that kept us on the road enjoying our vacation. The Good Sam Club has a list of Good Sam resources in many cities that can be called on in an emergency for advice.

• **Food:** Not all food needs to be carried with you. In fact, the more food and cooking containers you carry, the more weight you will be pulling and storage space problems you might have. Invariably, we pack too much food, hauling half of it back home after our trip. Like most RVers, we eat out more often than planned. We also find we have more leftovers that make another meal than we planned. Creating a list of the food basics, seasonings, pots and pans, paper plates, and other utensils you prefer simplifies the preparation and can be used trip after trip. We keep bulk food items like oatmeal stored in clear plastic storage containers that go from house to RV and back to the house again after the trip.

• **Non-food items:** Again, a list is almost a must. Items that might be on this list are flashlights, medical supplies, hiking gear, fishing gear, sewing kit, writing material, children's toys, clothing for all weather, generator, air pump, paper towels, dish washing material, bathroom towels and toiletries. We use the same list and just keep adding or subtracting things.

The Week Before Your Trip

The day you have been waiting for is almost here. But there is a list of things to do prior to departure day that will make getting on the road smoother.

• Does the freshwater tank need to be sanitized? This is a two-day process. First, partially fill the tank. Dilute 1/4 cup chlorine bleach per 15 gallons of holding tank capacity and pour into the fill spout. Finish filling the tank and run water through all faucets. Let sit for four hours before draining (don't forget to drain the hot water tank). To remove the chlorine taste use 1/2 cup dissolved baking soda or vinegar poured into the fresh-water tank. Fill the tank. Again, open all faucets and flush the lines. Let this solution sit overnight. Flush the tank and lines twice with freshwater. One time we skipped the flushing with fresh water. It was a trip with our granddaughter, Sondra. Boy, did we hear about it when she was the first to get a glass of water. It really does take two tanks to flush out the vinegar smell and taste.

• Check and fill propane cylinders? Some RVers we know choose to travel with one propane cylinder full and the other cylinder empty for the same reason we don't fill the freshwater tank. Our preference is to start the trip with both cylinders full. Once we are on the road we will let one cylinder empty and not fill it until the second cylinder is half empty (unless we are using the furnace).

• How full to fill the fresh-water tank? Water is heavy and traveling with a full tank will have a direct effect on fuel consumption. We carry enough water to use during our rest breaks and fill the tank once we reach the campground. If we are going to a dry camp, we will fill the tank at the last possible location before arriving at the campground.

• Refrigerator: Twenty-four hours before the trip, close the doors and turn on the refrigerator. It needs the time to cool down before you start packing it with food. We keep a temperature gauge in the refrigerator that can be purchased at any RV store. This insures that we keep the temperature at 40° or below for food safety.

• One last check: rig fully fueled, battery fluid level full, battery terminals clean, radiator fluid full, engine oil full, transmission fluid full, brake fluid full, tow mirrors in place.

Departure Day

The excitement and anticipation is running high. If something is to be forgotten this is where it will probably happen. We have discovered that having checklists for getting on the road is almost a must. We are not alone. Almost any RV book you pick up will emphasize having a checklist. We have two, an exterior checklist and an interior checklist. We use them every time we depart whether from our home or from the campground. Following is a small excerpt of what we use, but you will need to make your own list that pertains to your particular rig. The best place is to start with the owner's manual and add things you want to remember. We have revised our lists many times.

Exterior Checklist Before Departing

• Fresh-water tank filled to desired level and holding tanks emptied

- All shore connections unhooked, rolled up, and stored (cable TV, water, electrical, sewer hose)
- Propane turned off
- Awning rolled up and locked for travel
- All camping gear packed and stored for travel (bikes, firewood, chairs, outdoor carpet, children's toys)
- All outside compartment doors closed and locked
- Site cleaned for the next occupant
- Chocks and leveling devices removed and stored

Interior Before Departing

- Cupboards and drawers secured
- Hot water tank switch turned off
- Water pump switch turned off
- Furnace turned off
- Refrigerator turned off and door locked
- TV antenna lowered and TV secured
- All windows closed and blinds secured
- All roof vents closed
- Shower door closed and secured
- Doors locked on exiting
- Stair raised and locked for travel

Many horror stories happen because a checklist was not used. Imagine looking in the rearview mirror and seeing the awning half lowered, or pulling out of the site and hearing the electrical cord you forgot to disconnect ripping out of the RV.

By far, the worst of horror stories that we have heard is associated with hitching up to a fifth wheel. We have seen several fifth-wheels and trucks with body damage where the fifth-wheel became unhooked when the owner drove off, dropping the trailer down onto the bed of the truck. The best solution we know of is a detailed checklist for hitching that is followed to the letter every single time. When you start the hitching process do not stop until all steps are completed. Then review and recheck your checklist to verify the hitching process is completed. This is true whether it is a tow vehicle pulling the RV or the RV pulling the tow vehicle. Included in our checklists are:

- The hitching up steps
- Checking of the brakes
- Checking of the lights
- Rechecking of the safety and emergency mechanisms

We're On the Way

Driving an RV is not the same as driving an automobile. The added weight and length makes the handling more like a bus or semi-truck.

• The most important thing is awareness of the road and keeping your focus. When I get behind the wheel I concentrate on being aware of what is happening on the road. I keep both hands on the wheel more often than I do when I am not towing. I have learned that because of the added width of the trailer I have less leeway to be gawking at the scenery and still keep the rig in my lane. This is another reason why we take many breaks as we travel so that the driver can stay alert and focused when he or she is behind the wheel.

• Turning takes on a new meaning with a long RV. Navigating turns in cities often requires a long swing that blocks other lanes of traffic. You can't be taught how to do this navigation, you have to experience it. The best advice is practice, practice, practice. The best place to practice is in a large empty parking lot. Envision one of the parking spots as being the curb of a corner. Practice the turn without hitting the curb and observe how wide of a turn you had to make. How many lanes of traffic would you have blocked? While you are practicing your turns you might as well practice backing up. Sooner or later you will have to back that RV into a site or out of a jam. Don't be embarrassed. You may see other RVers in the parking lot practicing. We have.

• Overhead obstructions and dead end roads are some of the obstacles you will want to keep an eye out for. When driving a car, you probably zipped under these overhead obstacles and up unfamiliar roads without a second thought. Not so with an RV. Five miles from our home is a railroad overpass with a 10'10" clearance; our trailer is 11'2" not including the 8" vent cap. I never paid any attention to that overpass until we bought the trailer and then we noticed the overpass had quite a few dings in it. Somebody tried it without knowing the height of their vehicle. What is the height of your RV? Measure how tall your RV is to the top of the vent or air conditioner so you will know what you can pass under safely.

Friends of ours took their RV down a scenic drive with a loop at the end. Unfortunately, cars were parked all around the loop making it too narrow for them to navigate around the turnaround. There they sat blocking traffic while the police located owners and had all the cars moved. Not a fun way to spend the afternoon.

• Hills quickly become something you will try to avoid if they are long, steep or winding. Face it, you are not driving a sports car. You notice all those trucks going slow in the right lane? Get ready to join them. Relax and enjoy the ride. You will find that in an RV you are much safer and more comfortable driving at a reduced speed. Climbing hills can overheat the engine and the transmission. Know the speeds for each of your gears and manually gear down as you reach that speed range. Lower gears may cause you to go slower but it also reduces the heat build-up in your vehicle. Going slow and using the gears on the downhill side keeps you from having to use the brakes excessively. Braking for several minutes continuously can cause the brakes to overheat and fail.

• Another reason for reducing your speed is the stopping distance required by your RV. You see truck drivers leaving many car lengths between themselves and the vehicle in front of them. Follow their example; they do it from experience and training. They know the distance required to stop their rig, and you need to know the same—but not in an emergency braking situation. Like many other RVers, we drive slightly below the posted speed limit. At this speed, everyone else is passing us, leaving us and our lane with ample space to navigate our rig safely. The exception is when we are on a two-lane road and there is traffic behind us. We will drive the speed limit until there is a safe place to pull off the road and let the traffic pass—which we do every chance we get.

• Posted curve speeds will also take on new meaning. In a car you may have zipped around a curve 10 to 15 miles faster than the posted speed and done just fine. Try doing that with an RV and you may find yourself on two wheels hoping the tires return to the road. Be observant of the posted speeds, slowing down in advance of the curves so that you do not have to brake through the curve.

• Extreme dips or angles on roads can create their own hazard It's easy to forget that the rear of the RV has quite an overhang and that it doesn't take much of an angle to cause the tail to drag. We experienced it in a campground where the road came down a steep hill then immediately leveled off. Fortunately, we caught it quickly and used our leveling blocks to raise the back of the RV high enough to navigate from steep to level ground. Another time, we saw a fifth-wheel with bikes mounted on the back try to drive up a steep residential street. After bouncing and smashing the bike rims on the first ascent he quickly changed direction and stayed on the level road.

• Parking an RV has special considerations. You are driving down the road and decide you want to stop to eat or go shopping. Where do you park? Once you have parked will someone park in front of you blocking your exit? Just how much room do I need to turn this rig around? These are all questions you will need to answer. We heard of one RVer who pulled into a shopping area's parking lot and went down a parking lane that had no exit at the other end. There they sat blocking other shoppers from pulling out of their parking stalls as they learned how to back their RV up the lane from which they came. Try scheduling your stops at the non rush hours. When possible, park on the road itself. Park at the far end of a parking lot and walk. We often see RVers parked at the back of large parking lots for ease of exiting. Always park facing the direction of your exit.

• Check the systems regularly. During the trip we use each rest break as an opportunity to inspect the RV. We were able to see a tire going flat and change it at a rest stop instead of driving down the road and possibly experiencing a flat while in transit.

• We always try to travel with our refrigerator turned off and the propane turned off. Unless it is a hot day, the refrigerator will keep the contents cool until we reach that day's destination if we don't open the door. During our rest breaks, we will run the refrigerator and turn it off when we depart. On hot days, we have to make a choice of running the refrigerator for a portion of the trip or take a longer noon break letting the refrigerator cool to the normal operating temperature.

• Are the wheels heating up? At the rest breaks walk around the rig and place your hand on each wheel hub. Extreme heat is a warning of a potential mechanical failure, usually of the wheel bearings.

• Are any of the tires low? Any bulges or signs of tread separation? Check the air pressure with a gauge. It is better to catch a tire failure while stopped than while driving.

• Do as the truckers do; walk totally around the rig visually inspecting for abnormal conditions. As stated earlier, constant inspections will keep a horror story from happening to you.

• Inspect inside the rig for doors that may have come open or stored items that may have shifted.

We Made It

Once you have reached your destination a new checklist is needed. How do you set up your rig for a comfortable stay? Again, we use an exterior and interior checklist so each of us is participating in the setup cutting the time in half. Usually we can be setup in 15 minutes, faster in inclement weather. We keep a pair of work gloves in an outside compartment for the person performing the exterior checklist.

Exterior Checklist

- Position the RV in the site and check for level
- Chock the RV
- Unhitch the tow vehicle (a motor home pulling a tow vehicle would do this step first)
- Level the RV front to back
- Connect the shore connection
- Remove bikes, place outdoor carpet, lower awning, etc.

Interior Checklist

- Lower steps
- Unlock door
- Unpack stored items; clock, towels, books
- Place chemicals in black water tank
- Open vents and windows
- Raise TV antenna

While at the Campground

By reading, observing, and trial and error we have found some dos and don'ts to practice while camping.

• Since our electrical cord provides a path to the interior of our RV we have to block the opening to keep critters out. We use a round piece of plastic cut to fit around the cord and tape it flush to the electrical cord door. This blocks any holes exposed by the cord going through the door. We found the top of a margarine container works nicely for the plastic piece we need.

• To provide a slope for the sewer pipe we carry plastic rain gutter cut into 5-foot lengths. The sewer pipe sits inside the gutter and the slope is provided by gutter down spouts with varied lengths of down spout material. There are several products on the market that also serve this purpose.

• We leave the drain valves closed on both the gray and black water tanks. Invariably the gray water tank fills up first and we will empty it as needed. The black water tank is emptied only as it becomes full. This allows the chemicals to work longer. We plan for at least half a tank of gray water to flush the sewer hose after draining the black water tank.

• Awnings should never be left rolled out level. In a rain storm, water will gather in the center. Enough weight can be created to separate the awning material from the supports. Always tilt one side lower providing a slope for the water to run off. If you camp where wind occurs frequently, you may want to purchase additional tie downs along the sides. Recently we saw an awning rip on the edge from wind gusts.

• Water connections require more than just screwing in the water hose. First, always use a pressure regulator. Pressure over 40 pounds will weaken the interior tubing inside an RV. As stated earlier, we have seen RVs with water dripping out the sides ending what should have been an exciting vacation. Second, should you fill the tank and use the water pump or hook up the hose and just use the water pressure? We have done both. If we hook up to shore water we always turn the water off at the tap when we leave for the day. We just don't want to take the chance of a water pipe breaking while we are not there.

• Whenever I have to handle the sewer caps or hose I wear a pair of plastic disposable gloves. The package of 100 gloves is stored in a side compartment easily accessible. They can be peeled off and disposed of once this unsanitary task is completed.

• Our propane compartment holds two cylinders with a bar that can be locked in place to prevent theft. I have a padlock I use to lock the fifth-wheel bar in place while traveling and the propane cylinders' bar when parked. The propane level is checked once a week, more often when running the furnace.

• Everyone has to use something in the black water tank to control odor and break down the waste. When you are shopping remember to check if the chemicals contain poisons like formaldehyde. Be earth friendly and select a holding tank deodorizer that is environmentally safe.

Have a safe and relaxed RV trip!

Chapter 12

Chapter 12

Resource Lists

Oregon Coast Chambers of Commerce

Astoria-Warrenton Chamber of Commerce
111 W. Marine Dr., P.O. Box 176
Astoria, OR 97013
(503) 325-6311

Bandon Chamber of Commerce
300 S.E. Second, P.O. Box 1515
Bandon, OR 97411
(541) 347-9616

Brookings-Harbor Chamber of Commerce
16330 Lower Harbor Rd., P.O. Box 940
Brookings, OR 97415
(800) 535-9469 or (541) 535-9469

Cannon Beach Chamber of Commerce
P.O. Box 64
Cannon Beach, OR 97110
(503) 436-2623

Coos Bay-Bay Area Chamber of Commerce
50 E. Central, P.O. Box 210
Coos Bay, OR 97420
(800) 824-8486 or (541) 269-0215

Depoe Bay Chamber of Commerce
P.O. Box 21
Depoe Bay, OR 97341
(541) 765-2889

Florence Chamber of Commerce
270 Hwy. 101, P.O. Box 26000
Florence, OR 97349
(541) 997-3128

Garibaldi Chamber of Commerce
P.O. Box 5
Garibaldi, OR 97118
(503) 322-0301

Gold Beach Chamber of Commerce
29279 Ellensburg Ave., #3
Gold Beach, OR 97444
(800) 525-2334 or (541) 247-7526

Lakeside Chamber of Commerce
P.O. Box 333
Lakeside, OR 97449
(541) 759-3981

Lincoln City Chamber of Commerce
801 S.W. Hwy. 101 #3, P.O. Box 787
Lincoln City, OR 97367
(541) 994-3070

Lincoln City Visitors and Convention Bureau
801 S.W. Hwy. 101 #1, P.O. Box 787
Lincoln City, OR 97367
(800) 452-2151

Nehalem Bay Area Chamber of Commerce
P.O. Box 159
Nehalem, OR 97131
(503) 368-5100

Newport Chamber of Commerce
555 S.W. Coast Hwy.
Newport, OR 97365
(800) 262-7844 or (541) 265-8801

Pacific City Woods Chamber of Commerce
P.O. Box 331
Pacific City, OR 97135
(503) 965-6161

Port Orford Chamber of Commerce
P.O. Box 637
Port Orford, OR 97465
(541) 332-8055

Reedsport/Winchester Bay
Hwy. 101 & Hwy. 38
P.O. Box 11
Reedsport, OR 97467
(800) 247-2155 or (541) 271-3495

Rockaway Beach Chamber of Commerce
P.O. Box 198
Rockaway Beach, OR 97136
(503) 355-8108

Seaside Chamber of Commerce
P.O. Box 7
Seaside, OR 97138
(800) 444-6740 or (503) 738-6391

Tillamook Chamber of Commerce
3705 Hwy. 101 North
Tillamook, OR 97141
(503) 842-7526 or (503) 842-7525

Waldport Chamber of Commerce
P.O. Box 669
Waldport, OR 97394
(541) 563-2133

Yachats Chamber of Commerce
P.O. Box 728
Yachats, OR 97498
(541) 547-3530

Helpful Phone Numbers When Traveling

24-hour road conditions report
(541) 889-3999

Weather
(503) 243-7575

General Information

Oregon Tourism Division
595 Cottage St., NE
Salem, OR 96310
Inside Oregon, (800) 543-8838
Ouside Oregon, (800) 547-7842

Oregon State Parks & Recreation Division
525 Trade St.
Salem, OR 97310
(503) 378-6305

Oregon and Washington Campsite Reservations
(800) 452-5687
Provides campsite availability information
Weekdays 8 a.m.-5 p.m.
Reserve up to 11 months in advance
Pay your deposit with VISA or Mastercard

Oregon Parks Information Center
(800) 551-6949
For general information about Oregon State Parks

Oregon Dept. of Fish and Wildlife
P.O. Box 59
Portland, OR (503) 229-5403

General Resources

RV Rental Sources

Adventure On Wheels, (800) 601-7368

American Safari National RV Rental System, (800) 327-9668

Cruise America Motorhome Rental & Sales, (800) 327-7799

Worldwide Motorhome Rentals, Inc., (800) 350-8031

RV User's Guides

RV How-to Guide, Woodall Publishing Co., 28167 North Keith Dr., Lake Forest, IL, 60045 (847) 362-6700
Vol. 1: Illustrated introduction to RV basics
Vol 2: Illustrations on the operations of major RV systems
Vol 3: Emergency and money saving repairs and preventive mainentance

RVing Basics, Ragged Mountain Press/McGraw-Hill, Bill and Jan Moeller

Camping Clubs

Escapee Club, 100 Rainbow Dr., Livingston, TX 77351 (409) 327-8873

Family Motor Coach Assn., (motor home owners only), 8291 Clough Pike, Cincinnati, OH 45244 (513) 474-3622 or (800) 543-3622
Magazine: Family Motor Coaching

The Good Sam Club, P.O. Box 6060, Camarillo, CA 93011 (805) 389-0300
Magazine: Highways

Loners on Wheels, P.O. Box 1355, Poplar Bluff, MO 63902 (573) 785-2420

Family Campers and RVers, 4804 Transit Rd., Bldg 2, Depew, NY 14043 (716) 668-6242
Magazine: Camping Today

North American Family Campers Association, Inc., P.O. Box 2701, Springfield, MA 01101
Magazine: Campfire Chatter

RV Elderhostel, 75 Federal St., Boston, MA 02110-1941 (617) 426-7788

RVing Women, 21413 W. Lost Lake Rd., Snohomish, WA 98290 (800) 333-9992

SMART, Special Military Active Retire Travel Club, Inc., 600 University Office Blvd., #1A, Pensacola, FL 32504 (904) 478-1986

Publications for Campers and RV owners

Adventure West, P.O. Box 3210, Incline Village, NV 89450

Family Motor Coaching, 8291 Clough Pike, Cincinnati, OH 45244

Highways, TL Enterprises, 2575 Vista Del Mar Dr., Ventura, CA 93001

Northwest Travel, P.O. Box 18000, Florence, OR 97439

Oregon Coast Magazine, P.O. Box 18000, Florence, OR 97439

Oregon Outdoors, P.O. Box 1404, Bend, OR 97709

Oregon Outpost, P.O. Box 266, Canyon City, OR 97820

RV Times Magazine, 1100 Welborne Dr., Richmond, VA 23229

RV Today, 4005 20th Ave. W., #110, Seattle, WA 98199

RV West Magazine, Vernon Publications, Dept OU, 3000 Northrup Way, #200, Bellevue, WA 98009

Motorhome, TL Enterprises, 2575 Vista Del Mar Dr., Venture, CA 93001

Trailer Life, TL Enterprises, 2575 Vista Del Mar Dr., Venture, CA 93001

Travelin' Magazine, P.O. Box 23005, Eugene, OR 97402

Western RV News, 56405 Cascade View Lane, Warren, OR 987053

RV Lifestyle Publications Catalog, Recreation Vehicle Industry Association, Dept. POF, P.O. Box 2999, Reston, VA 22090

Workkamper News, 201 Hiram Rd., HCR 34, Box 125, Heber Springs, AR 72543 (501) 362-2637
For people who want to work while traveling

On The Road

Scenic Byways

Traveling off crowded highways and roads offers breathtaking views of mountains, forests, historical sites and waterways. For more information, write to: Scenic Byways, The American Recreation Coalition, 1331 Pennsylvania Ave., NW, Suite 726, Washington, DC 20004

Bibliography

Great books to guide you in your travels on the coast

Exploring the Wild Oregon Coast, Bonnie Henderson, The Mountaineers, 1994

Best Hikes with Children in Western & Central Oregon, Bonnie Henderson, The Mountaineers, 1992

Oregon State Parks, *A Complete Recreation Guide*, Jan Bannan, The Mountaineers, 1993

The Hiker's Guide to Oregon, Donna Ikenberry, Falcon Press, 1992

***100 Hikes/Oregon Coast & Coast* Range**, William L. Sullivan, Navillus Press, 1995

Mail-In Form

RVer's Best Guide to the Oregon Coast

I would like to see you include the following listing in your next update of this book.

Name:____

Address:____

City, Zip____

Phone:____

Type of service____

Why you think this listing should be included in the next revision:

Mail to:
Frank Amato Publications
P.O. Box 82112
Portland, Oregon 97282
Attn: RV Update

Your Name____

Address____

City, State, Zip____

Phone____